Performance Measurement of Computer Systems

INTERNATIONAL COMPUTER SCIENCE SERIES

Consulting editors	**A D McGettrick**	University of Strathclyde
	J van Leeuwen	University of Utrecht

OTHER TITLES IN THE SERIES

Programming in Ada (2nd Edn.) *J G P Barnes*
Software Engineering (2nd Edn.) *I Sommerville*
An Introduction to Numerical Methods with Pascal *L V Atkinson and P J Harley*
The UNIX System *S R Bourne*
Handbook of Algorithms and Data Structures *G H Gonnet*
UNIX for Super-Users *E Foxley*
Software Specification Techniques *N Gehani and A D McGettrick* (eds.)
The UNIX System V Environment *S R Bourne*
Data Communications for Programmers *M Purser*
Prolog Programming for Artificial Intelligence *I Bratko*
Modula-2: Discipline & Design *A H J Sale*
Introduction to Expert Systems *P Jackson*
Local Area Network Design *A Hopper, S Temple and R C Williamson*
Programming Language Translation: A Practical Approach *P D Terry*
Data Abstraction in Programming Languages *J M Bishop*
System Simulation: Programming Styles and Languages *W Kreutzer*
The Craft of Software Engineering *A Macro and J Buxton*
An Introduction to Programming with Modula-2 *P D Terry*
Pop-11 Programming for Artificial Intelligence *A M Burton and N R Shadbolt*
PROLOG *F Giannesini, H Kanoui, R Pasero and M van Caneghem*
UNIX System Programming *K F Haviland and B Salama*
The Specification of Computer Programs *W M Turski and T S E Maibaum*
Software Development with Ada *I Sommerville and R Morrison*
Text Processing and Typesetting with UNIX *D Barron and M Rees*
Syntax Analysis and Software Tools *K J Gough*

Performance Measurement of Computer Systems

Phillip McKerrow

University of Wollongong,
Australia

ADDISON-WESLEY
PUBLISHING
COMPANY

Sydney · Wokingham, England · Reading, Massachusetts
Menlo Park, California · New York · Don Mills, Ontario
Amsterdam · Bonn · Singapore · Tokyo · Madrid
Bogota · Santiago · San Juan

The programs presented in this book have been included for their instructional value. They have been tested with care but are not guaranteed for any particular purpose. The publisher does not offer any warranties or representations, nor does it accept any liabilities with respect to the programs.

Cover design by John Gibbs.
Cover graphic by Laurence M. Gartel.
Printed in Great Britain by T.J. Press (Padstow) Ltd, Cornwall.

First Printed in 1987.

British Library Cataloguing in Publication Data

McKerrow, Phillip
Performance measurement of computer systems.
—(International computer science series).
1. Electronic data processing—Evaluation
I. Title II. Series
004 QA76.9.E94

ISBN 0–201–17436–7

Library of Congress Cataloguing in Publication Data

McKerrow, Phillip, 1949–
Performance measurement of computer systems.

(International computer science series)
Bibliography; p.
Includes index.
1. Electronic digital computers—Evaluation
I. Title.
QA76.9.E94M39 1988 004.2′4 87-19363
ISBN 0–201–17436–7

In memory of Ian Paul and John Mark,
born 31 August 1981, died 1 September 1981

Preface

In this book, I have attempted to combine the results of the last three decades of research in measuring the performance of computer systems into a unified body of knowledge: theory and practice. Unification is based on a formulation of performance measurement.

We can model the code of a computer system with an abstract mathematical object. When this code is executed it becomes an executable object, which we can measure. To ascertain the extent of this executable object is the task of performance measurement. An object (computer system, task, program, procedure) is defined recursively in terms of lower level objects. In the theoretical section of this work, I have defined a set of measures for an executing object. These measures apply at every level of the object hierarchy, have been expressed in mathematical equations, and define a formulation of performance measurement. The measured data can be displayed in graphical form, making evaluation easier.

This formulation provides a general, overall context within which measurement and evaluation can take place. The purpose of measurement is not to collect numbers, but to gain insight into the actions of the object under study. By recording appropriate stimulus information, and by using graphical techniques to analyse the data, we can understand the actions of the object.

The formulation has been validated in a number of ways:

- measurement experiments have been conducted,
- measures proposed by the formulation have been compared to current measurement practice,
- other formulations have been compared to it, and
- corollaries have been hypothesized and tested.

From the results of these validation procedures, I have confirmed a high degree of correlation between the formulation and current practice. On the basis of the formulation, we have designed a hybrid performance analyser, which we have used in performance evaluation, in system optimization, in program execution monitoring, when debugging software, and for finding software related hardware faults. A number of future research areas, which flow out of the formulation, are proposed.

This book commences with an introduction to the field of performance measurement and an overview of various aspects of it. Then, the formulation of performance measurement is described in detail. Other formulations proposed by researchers in the performance evaluation field are discussed, and the underlying conceptual models of program execution are compared. Following this, measurement tools and techniques are reviewed. Next comes the design of a hybrid performance analyser, which is built around a logic state analyser, and is based on a philosophy of hybridization derived from the formulation of performance measurement. Finally, the design of computer systems for performance measurement is discussed. In the last two chapters, the formulation is extended to cover parallel processors, and measurement in a number of other applications.

Case studies are included to illustrate performance measurement methods and software debugging techniques. I have used these case studies to demonstrate the practicality and power of a performance measurement methodology based on the formulation of performance measurement.

Acknowledgements

I wish to thank the following for permission to reproduce material from published sources:

AFIPS Press and T.E. Bell, B.W. Boehm and R.A. Watson (1972) for Figures 3 and 4 from 'Framework and initial phases for computer performance improvement', *FJCC Proceedings,* No. 41, 1141-1154.

Domenico Ferrari for a figure from *Computer Systems Performance Evaluation* © 1978, p. 14. Reprinted by permission of Prentice-Hall, Inc., Englewood Cliffs, New Jersey.

Hewlett Packard for a photograph of the HP 1610A logic state analyser and a block diagram; also for photographs of the HP 1630 taken from their brochure no. 5953-9208.

The Institute of Electrical and Electronics Engineers, Inc. for various figures from the following: English, W.R., Engelbart, D.C. and Berman, M.L. (1967) 'Display-Selection Techniques for Text Manipulation', *IEEE Transactions on Human Factors in Electronics,* Vol. 8, No. 1, 5-20; Fromm, H., Hercksen, U., Herzog, U., John, K.H., Klar, R. and Kleinder, W. (1983) 'Experiences with Performance Measurement and Modeling of a Processor Array', *IEEE Transactions on Computers,* Vol. C32, No. 1, January, 15-31; Gehringer, E. F., Jones, A.K. and Segall, Z.Z. (1982) 'The CM* Testbed', *IEEE Computer,* Vol. 15, No. 10, October, 40-53; Segall, Z. *et al.* (1983) 'An Integrated Instrumentation Environment for Multiprocessors', *IEEE Transactions on Computers,* Vol. C32, No. 1, January, 4-14.

Northwest Instrument Systems, Inc. for a photograph of their μANALYST$_R$ connected to an Apple IIe.

Tektronix, Inc. for a photograph of a DAS 9129 logic analyser taken from their brochure no. 57W-5025.

K. Terplan for a table which appeared in 'Network Monitor Survey', *Computer Performance,* Vol. 2, No. 4, pp. 58-173 (Butterworth & Co. (Publishers) Ltd).

I also wish to thank Professor Juris Reinfelds, Professor Geoff Dromey, Richard Miller, Gary Stafford, and Michael Milway for their encouragement and direction during this research. Their comments forced me to clarify my ideas, prompting further avenues of thought and deeper insight.

The logic state analyser used in this research was bought with a grant from the Department of Science and Technology, Australian Research Grants Committee. The Apple microcomputer and other facilities were provided by the Department of Computing Science, University of Wollongong.

During the course of this research I have regularly prayed about problems and meditated upon insights. I have always found God to be one step ahead of me, and ready to give insight and understanding.

Finally I would like to thank my wife and family for the hours of my time they have given up so that I could write this tome. No acknowledgement is complete without heartfelt thanks to the typist, Mrs Lynn Maxwell, who can type faster than I can think, and to Mr John Murray from whose work the line illustrations have been prepared.

This book has been typeset on a Compugraphic phototypesetter using the troff word processor, at the University of Wollongong.

Contents

Chapter 1
Introduction

1.1 Performance measurement

Techniques used to evaluate the performance of computer systems can be grouped into four overlapping areas: measurement of system parameters, evaluation of collected data, modelling of system behaviour, and modifications to improve performance. In this work, I concentrate on the measurement of system parameters. Measurement is discussed in the context of the whole field when other areas of performance evaluation determine and constrain the parameters to be measured.

In the early days of computing, a programmer's main goal was to get a working program with little thought about its efficiency; however, there were some exceptions. Von Neumann (1946) compared the speed with which a number of early computers, including ENIAC, performed multiplications when computing ballistic trajectories. Herbst *et al.* (1955) measured the instruction mix of programs running on the Maniac computer.

In the early sixties, performance measurement was commenced in earnest. As computers became readily available, users sought ways to increase the productivity of both the computer and the programmer and hence to reduce the cost of computing. Computer throughput was increased by using operating systems to handle resource sharing: initially, simple batch systems; more recently, time sharing and multiprogramming. Program development time has been shortened through the use of high-level languages, structured programming, and other software engineering techniques.

Concurrent with these developments, and spurred on by the high cost of computing, has been a desire to evaluate how well systems are performing, and to find ways of improving that performance. During the sixties, performance measurement studies were carried out on many installations. By 1967, the field had grown to the point where Calingaert (1967) was able to publish a survey of the then common techniques, and a few years later Miller (1972) published a bibliography of over 250 papers. The early seventies saw a burst of measurement activity, which diminished to a mere trickle of papers by the mid-seventies as researchers turned to modelling techniques.

Measurement is a fundamental technique in any science (Curtis, 1980). The fact that little work has been reported on the measurement of computer systems in the last few years has been seen by some as an indication that all the work has been done. This is not true - computer performance measurement remains a collection of techniques with no unified body of knowledge. Research effort dwindled, not because all the problems were solved, but because of a number of other factors:

- Measurement ideas were several years ahead of the available technology. It is interesting to read papers from the heyday of measurement, and see the gradual transition from what we have done, to what we are doing, to what we think we might be able to do when we finish developing the tool. Consequently, most of the ideas are not new, but the technology of the early seventies was not cheap enough for the development of powerful, general-purpose tools.
- The complexity of computer systems increased rapidly, making measurement more difficult.
- Researchers were attracted by the mathematical tractability of modelling techniques, particularly analytical queuing models. Modelling provided a rich source of research ideas at a time when measurement was being frustrated by the increasing complexity of computer systems. The lack of tools powerful enough to handle this complexity made measurement too hard.
- The literature of the time consisted of descriptions of measurement techniques and their results. No unified body of knowledge had been established and no theoretical basis for measurement had been developed. Hence, there was no framework within which to tackle the measurement problems posed by the new, more complex systems.

During the last decade, advances in technology have made computing power so cheap that all new test instruments include microprocessors. One new instrument, the logic state analyser, is more powerful than any of the hardware measurement tools of a decade ago. As a result of these advances, technology is no longer a limitation in measurement. The growing use of microcomputers increases dramatically the need for effective performance measurement tools. However, the design of these tools must be grounded in a unified formulation of measurement if lasting results are to be achieved. Such a formulation is developed in the next chapter. In subsequent chapters, current measurement techniques are evaluated in the light of this formulation, and some of the implications of the formulation for future measurement techniques and tools are investigated. The result is a unified body of performance measurement knowledge.

1.2 Measurement categories

To develop a unified formulation of measurement we must gather all the independent measurement categories together under one umbrella. Then common principles can be extracted. The differences between measurement situations are differences in the application of theory and tools, not conceptual differences in either theory or tools. In the following paragraphs, the major applications of performance measurement are briefly discussed. As many of these areas overlap, the discussion is aimed at showing the breadth of performance measurement.

Human engineering is the design of computer systems for use by people. It includes measuring the interactions between the user and the system. Users influence the performance of a system by producing inputs: requests for program execution, data, system commands, new programs, etc. The response of the system to these inputs is important, particularly on an interactive system (Figure 1.1) where the user expects fast response to commands which are input at highly irregular intervals. If the response is too slow, the user gets frustrated and will use another system. If a terminal is poorly designed, people may refuse to use it. Ease of use can be partially evaluated by measuring human and system response times (Figure 1.2).

Lack of feedback to the user may result in the user executing additional commands to check if the previous command worked, significantly increasing the workload. The classic example of this occurred in 1963 when a major American airline was trying

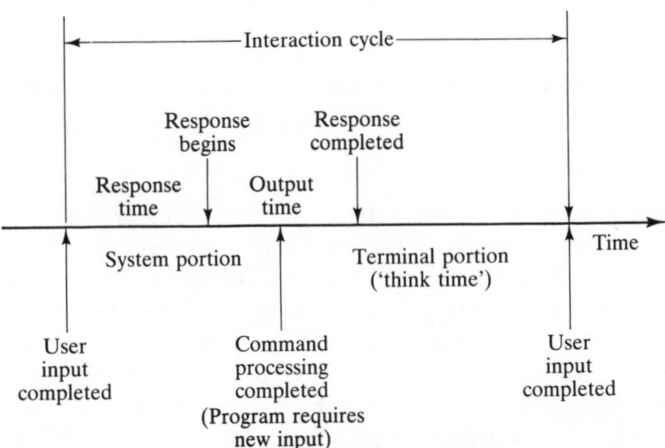

Figure 1.1 User-computer interaction cycle (Ferrari, 1978).

unsuccessfully to go on line nationwide with its new computerized reservation system (Warner, 1974). Everything went well until they tried to bring the last and busiest region, New York City, on line. The system crashed, hopelessly overloaded. When the system was measured, they found that before New York was brought on line the existing load was 90%, not 40% as predicted by simulation. Each operator, after keying in a reservation, would immediately enquire to see if the system had the data. The solution: the ball on the typewriter was wiggled to let the operator know the data was in.

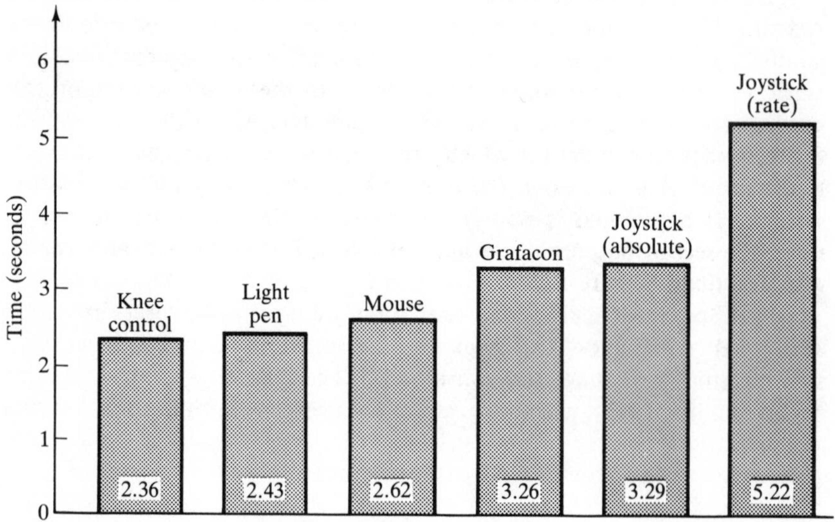

Figure 1.2 Comparison of average times taken by inexperienced users to locate a cursor at a character using a variety of graphics input devices (English *et al.*, 1967; copyright © 1967 IEEE).

Selecting new computing equipment for a company often involves the running of benchmarks on comparative systems in an effort to measure workload characteristics such as: capacity, throughput, batch turnround time, number of interactive users, response time of high usage programs, etc. Benchmarks range from the execution of typical application programs, for example a floating point number cruncher in a scientific application, to complex job control scripts, for example the reproduction of the workload from a typical day on an existing system.

Capacity planning includes measuring how the available resources are used by the system. With this data, management can schedule the workload and plan for growth. Workload can change unpredictably over short periods, so characterization of workload is done over long periods. Workload parameters (Svobodova, 1976a, Table 2.1) include: job CPU time, job I/O requests, CPU service time, I/O service time, job priority, job memory usage, and job paused time. Measured values for these parameters are used during system generation to establish the size of tables, and to determine the configuration of the system. They are also used during production to obtain the best system performance by controlling priority levels, and resource allocation strategies. An important part of the management of a system is billing the customer for resources used. System accounting involves the measurement of resources by individual jobs and the generation of accounts and statistics.

Operating system performance measurement is the examination of a running system to find bottlenecks or 'performance bugs'. Measurements of interest to performance analysts range from the interrupt handling time of an I/O device (Figure 1.3) to system overhead during the execution of a controlled workload. When analysts suspect a system is performing badly under certain conditions, these conditions are simulated and measurements made in an attempt to pinpoint the cause of the poor performance. Methods of improving performance, for example a different algorithm, can then be hypothesized, implemented, measured, and evaluated. System debugging, tuning, and optimization activities can greatly improve the performance of a system and as a consequence may delay an upgrade, saving the company money.

Developing new programs is one of the major tasks carried out on any computer system. Dynamic analysis of executing programs (program execution monitoring) is used to find faults, to pinpoint time consuming routines, and to compare the performance of algorithms.

System designers study the workload of existing systems and their performance, in order to design better systems (Bisiani *et al.*, 1983). For example, instruction mix studies are used in the design of new processor architectures, and in the development of new programming languages. One goal of performance measurement research is for the inclusion of performance instrumentation to be seen as a basic design requirement rather than as an afterthought. Some researchers (Boulaye *et al.*, 1977; Geck, 1979) have suggested that the ultimate goal of performance evaluation research is to be able to measure and adaptively control performance indices in real time, so that optimum performance can be maintained under varying system load conditions.

Models are often used to predict the performance of proposed systems. These models are built from data measured on existing systems, and validated and enhanced using data collected as the new system is implemented. Once a model has been validated, it can be used in capacity planning, and in operating system performance studies.

Another important area of measurement, particularly with microcomputer systems, is the determination of **software/hardware**

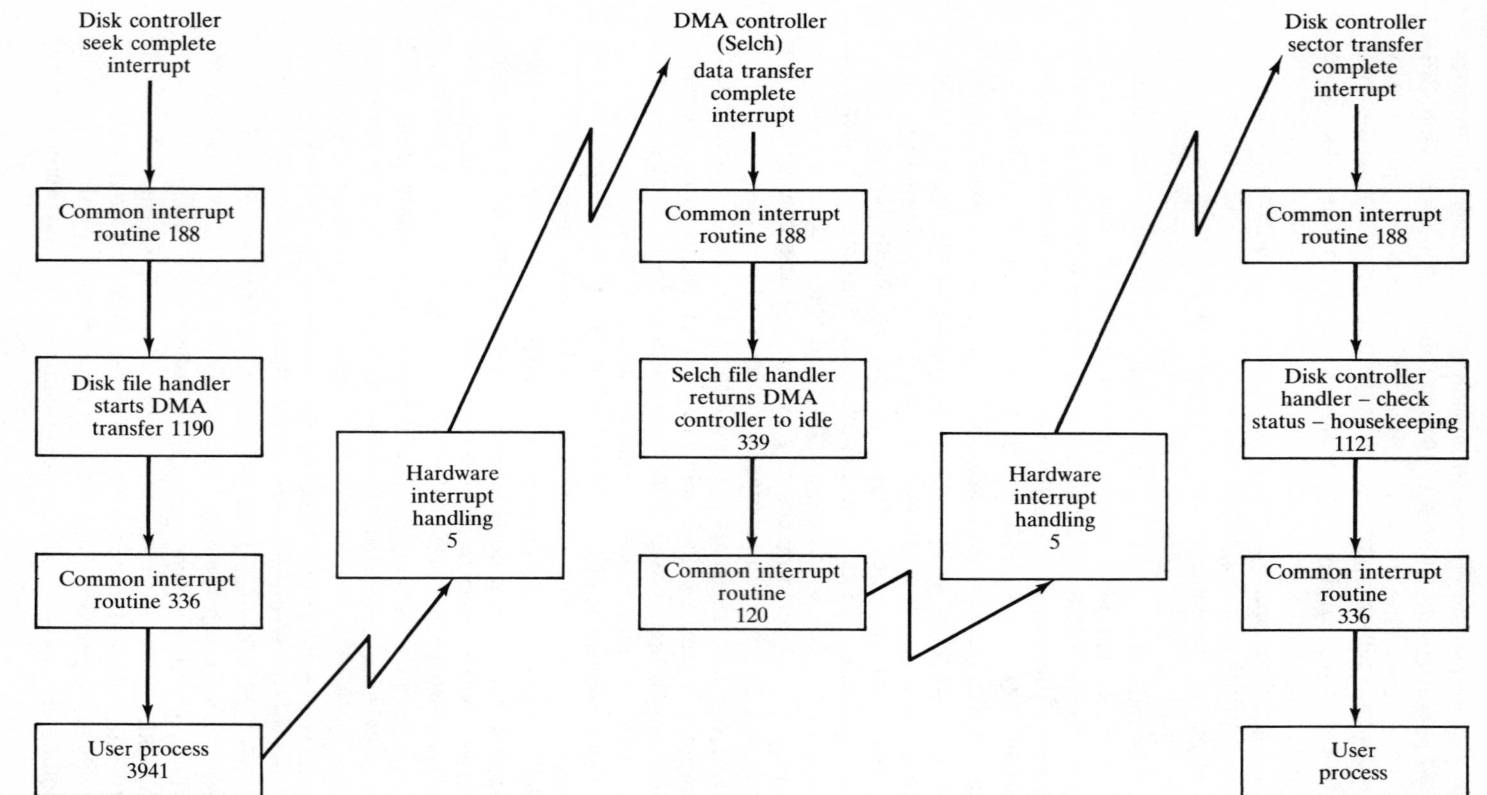

Figure 1.3 Interrupt handling sequence during data transfer from a disk under DMA control, measured on the UNIX operating system running on a Perkin-Elmer 7/32 (all times in microseconds).

compromises. Microcomputer development systems include monitoring tools, both hardware (logic state analysers) and software (in-circuit emulators).

Svobodova (1976b) has divided computer system measurement needs into three categories:

1. **diagnostic measurement**, necessary to secure correct operation while a computer system is in use and to restart correct operation in case of system failure;
2. **performance measurement**, necessary to ensure efficient operation and fast response of a computer system under dynamically changing demands; and
3. **analytic measurement**, necessary to develop understanding of the processing requirements and their impact on system behaviour and performance.

In all these categories performance is defined differently - usually in terms of the perceived goals of the measurement evaluation study. However, the question 'Where does the time go?' is common to all, as is the more fundamental question 'Why did it go that way?' Part of the verification of the formulation of performance measurement, developed in the next chapter, is study of measurements made in each of these categories, as reported by other researchers, to show that they fit into the framework defined by the formulation.

1.3 Measurement tools and techniques

One desirable outcome of a formulation of measurement is the development of measurement tools and techniques, based upon the formulation, which can be used in the applications described in the previous section. In this section, measurement tools, techniques, and problems are introduced. They are discussed in the light of the performance measurement formulation in Chapters 4 to 7.

The main sources of measurement data are existing accounting software, hardware monitors attached to the system, and software monitors. Normally, accounting data does not contain sufficient information, and a hardware or software monitor is thus required.

Conceptually, a measuring instrument consists of four parts (Figure 1.4). The task of the sensor is to sense the magnitude of the quantity to be measured, with software or hardware probes. In the transformer section, the measured data is manipulated and reduced to the desired form, e.g. a state analyser's ability to distinguish desired states in a continuous data stream. After data reduction, the measured information can be displayed directly or it can be analysed and the results of the analysis displayed.

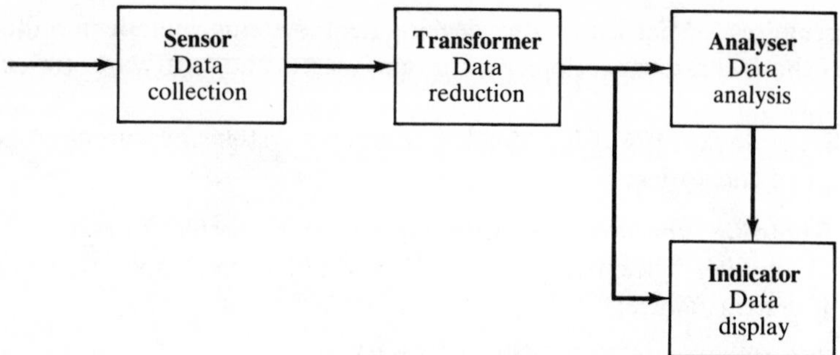

Figure 1.4 Four conceptual parts of a measuring instrument.

1.3.1 Hardware monitors

Hardware tools consist of additional hardware attached to the computer's backplane via test probes. Attaching the probes requires a detailed knowledge of the backplane and a clear specification of which signals are to be monitored. Consequently, hardware probes tend to make maintenance people nervous. Hardware monitors can detect events occurring at microscopic levels with high accuracy, e.g. individual instruction fetches. Potentially, their scope is broad since most of the interesting points in the system can usually be reached. The reduction in the number of accessible test points caused by the increasing scale of chip integration can be offset by including probe points at design time.

Hardware monitors are often used to check the accuracy of software monitors. Their main advantage compared to software monitors is that they do not interfere with the system being measured. Hardware monitors are inherently limited to measuring information that can be interpreted at the hardware level without knowledge of operating system activities. Consequently, information like CPU service time and file activity by process cannot be obtained easily. Distribution estimates (e.g. mean channel service time) can be obtained for the whole system, but not for specific workload classes. For these reasons, hardware monitors are often supplemented by software monitors or accounting data.

Logic state analysers used as hardware monitors (McKerrow, 1983) provide very accurate microscopic measurement, for example instruction execution path and execution time. They can also be used for certain types of macroscopic measurement (e.g. process execution time or path), but again they lack operating system specific information. Analysis of some processes is difficult (e.g. the scheduler) without intimate knowledge of the current system load.

1.3.2 Software monitors

In event-driven software monitors, significant events are defined (such as a process switch), and the operating system is modified to record information about these events. Monitoring detail is limited by the number of events recorded. Consequently, if after data analysis you find that a significant event has not been recorded, then at best the session has to be rerun, and at worst the operating system has to be modified to record the event.

Sample-driven software monitors record data at the end of predetermined sample periods. As the sample period is normally controlled by a timer, a time related sequence of states is recorded. Data collected during short measurement sessions can be recorded in memory, but normally disk file or tape storage is required.

An event-driven monitor has greater flexibility than a sample-driven monitor, but is likely to interfere with the system more. Depending on the particular system and monitor, a software monitor may consume 20% or more of system resources (particularly CPU and channel time) and thus produce very questionable results. If this overhead can be kept to 5%, by appropriate event definition and probe implementation, software monitor results are reasonably accurate (Sauer and Chandy, 1981).

In addition to interfering with system performance, software monitors have two other significant problems. First, the amount of data produced by an event trace may require excessive data reduction before meaningful results can be obtained. Second, software monitors must be specifically designed for the operating system. If not designed into the system they can be difficult to add.

However, software monitors can get at operating system specific information (such as system queues) which hardware monitors cannot. Also, they can readily associate physical activity with logical entities (e.g. disk access with file name). In many ways, software and hardware tools complement one another. Hybrid tools have been developed to try to utilize the advantages of both.

1.3.3 Hybrid monitors

Hybrid tools require the addition of hardware and software to the system we plan to measure. External hardware tools receive data collected by a software tool running in the system (Svobodova, 1973a; Sebastian, 1974). Consequently, hybrid tools are visible to the operating system. The hardware tool can be as simple as a hardware register, to which a software monitor writes data (Hughes and Cronshaw, 1973), or as complex as an 'intelligent peripheral device', which can interact with a software monitor (Nutt, 1975; Deutch and Grant, 1971). One type of hybrid monitor uses part of the existing hardware as the hardware tool, for example a channel processor (Stevens, 1968). Some allow sections of the hardware tool, e.g. event counters, to be allocated to users under the control of software (Nemeth and Rovner, 1971).

The interference of software tools can be minimized by implementing frequently used code in firmware – known as firmware tools. Burroughs have included a monitor micro instruction in the firmware of some of their computers (Wilner, 1972; Denny, 1977). This instruction writes a bit pattern, specified by the programmer, to pins accessible to the probes of a hardware tool.

A hybrid monitor (Figure 1.5) is connected to the system we want to measure with hardware probes and a data channel, which can be used for transferring information between the two. While the hardware probes are used to monitor an event, the data channel can be used to obtain information about the stimulus of the event, and thus to overcome the inherent limitation of hardware monitors. Alternatively, an event-driven software monitor can interrupt the external hardware monitor and instruct it to record the required event data, and thus reduce the overhead of the software monitor. The inclusion of computing power in the hardware monitor allows considerable real-time data reduction and analysis to be carried out, increasing the flexibility of the monitor.

Thus, hybrid monitors attempt to take advantage of the complementary nature of hardware and software tools. However, as Ferrari (1978a) comments:

> 'The simultaneous usage of co-operating tools of the same or different nature, their coordination, and the partitioning of their functions and jurisdictions create problems which are still open to research.'

One solution to these problems is discussed in Chapter 6.

1.4 Measurement methodology

Bell *et al.* (1972) have suggested that many performance improvement studies produce very few results, for a high cost, because their

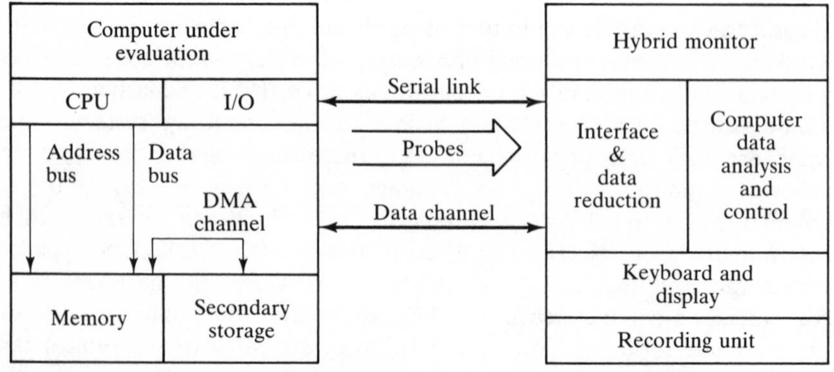

Figure 1.5 Basic components of a hybrid monitor.

measurement procedure resembles the flowchart of Figure 1.6. A number of researchers have suggested a formalized framework for performance evaluation studies based upon the scientific method. The most comprehensive of these, proposed by Bell *et al.* (1972) as a performance improvement procedure, is illustrated in Figure 1.7. Measurement is done to provide data to test hypotheses about the system, program, etc. under study.

Calingaert (1967) identified the crux of the measurement problem with his comment:

> 'The key to performance evaluation as well as to systems design is to understand what systems are and how they work.'

To enable understanding is the purpose of measurement. Measurement itself springs from an understanding of the problem at hand, and a knowledge of the basic principles of measurement. Nutt (1975) summarized it this way:

> 'The most important questions to be asked before attempting to monitor a machine are *what* to measure and *why* the measurement should be made.'

This throws us right back to the scientific method. We must base our methodology on a theory of measurement, which in turn must be developed from the presuppositions of science, if it is to be sound. To do this, we will find it helpful to look, briefly, at the philosophical basis of modern science, how that philosophy is viewed today, and its implications for computer science.

Modern science had its birth in the sixteenth and seventeenth centuries in the Christian civilization of Western Europe (Rhodes, 1965). The world view of Aristotle - which included the ideas that nature was divine and in a sense self-explanatory, and that no phenomenon can be studied until its final cause has been established - was rejected. In its place, the sixteenth and seventeenth century scientists accepted a Christian world view: because the universe was created by a God of order and purpose then nature must also be ordered, and therefore able to be studied and described in an ordered manner. From this world view, the basic presuppositions of science were developed. These are:

- a belief in an orderly, regular, rational universe,
- a belief that this orderliness of the natural world is intelligible to the scientist,
- a belief in the reliability of human reason,
- a belief in a broad principle of causality, and
- a belief in the personal integrity of the scientist.

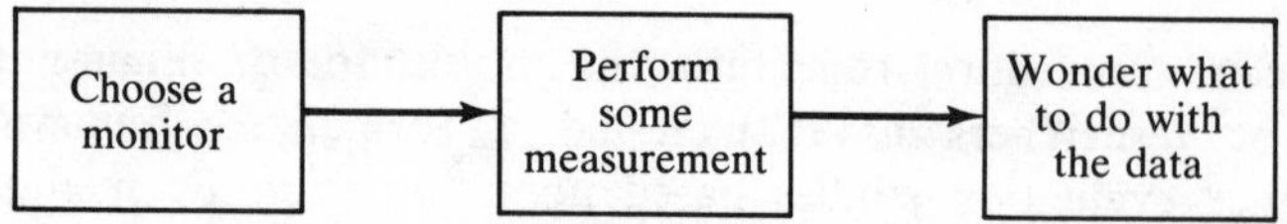

Figure 1.6 Common measurement methodology (Bell *et al.*, 1972).

The popularizers of science have created a vast gulf in the minds of many between science and Christianity. Some scientists claim that the empirical results of science have justified the validity of these basic assumptions, and hence no other foundation is needed. However, you cannot validate your axioms from within your axiomatic system. Others work within the framework provided by these presuppositions without thinking about their philosophical basis. A few, like the early scientists, justify their assumptions on the basis of their belief in the biblical doctrine of creation by a personal rational God.

In these presuppositions the method of inductive and empirical enquiry, the process of observation, experiment and hypothesis, has its foundation. Hypothesis formulation involves the abstraction of certain elements from the total range of human experience. Thus, the scientific method is only one of a set of methods of describing human experience.

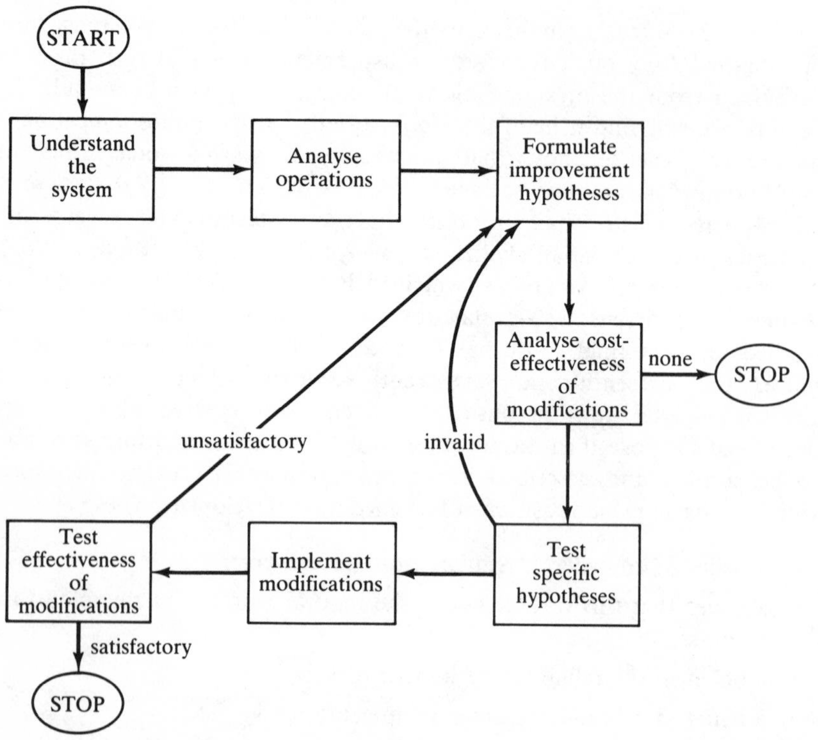

Figure 1.7 Proposed performance improvement procedure (Bell *et al.*, 1972).

These presuppositions are reflected in the following definition of computer science (Nygaard, 1982):

> 'Informatics (Computing Science) is the science which has as its subject of study the information aspects of processes and phenomena in nature and society:
>
> - their identification and properties,
> - their interaction with other aspects of reality,
> - how they may be understood and described,
> - and how they may be designed, implemented and modified.'

From these presuppositions, a number of measurement principles are developed. These form the basis of a formulation of performance measurement (Chapter 2). Using this formulation, I have derived a methodology for conducting performance measurement experiments (Chapter 6). The formulation defines the measures which can be made of a system, program, etc. during execution. Which of these measures are to be made during a performance evaluation experiment depends upon the hypothesis to be tested.

Chapter 2
A Formulation of Performance Measurement

'The purpose of measurement is insight not numbers'.
Hamming (Paraphrased by Cantrell & Ellison, 1968)

The measurement of computer systems is almost as old as computer programming. In 1967, Calingaert wrote the first survey article, and in 1972, Miller published the first bibliography of the field. Measurement techniques, and tools, are well documented in a number of books (Drummond, 1973; Svobodova, 1976a; Ferrari, 1978a). Yet the field remains a collection of ad hoc procedures with no unified body of knowledge. This lack of unity exists because:

> 'there is no general, overall context within which measurement and evaluation can take place'
>
> (Dumont, 1978).

Browne and Shaw (1981) claim that the whole field of software engineering, performance measurement included, lacks a scientific foundation. They recommend that future experimental work be based on the traditional principles of science, where the first considerations are principles which are invariant across all software, and across hierarchies of abstract models. One goal of this chapter is to develop a set of measures of performance which apply at all levels in a computer system hierarchy.

Curtis (1980) suggests that progress in a scientific basis for software engineering depends upon improved measurement of fundamental constructs. In his opinion, a model of relationships among constructs becomes a theory when at least some constructs can be operationally defined in terms of observable data. Measurement does not define a construct, rather it quantifies a property of a construct. A major goal in this chapter is to develop a formulation of performance measurement from a model of a software object during execution, by defining the model constructs in terms of measurable data. A formulation will help us concentrate on what we ought to measure, rather than on what is easy to measure.

In the last few years, the majority of theoretical work in performance evaluation has been in the context of analytical queuing models (Spragins, 1980). These models are mathematically tractable, have met with considerable success, and thus are attractive to theorists and practitioners alike. Also, they can be used during the design and development stages of a system, when measurement is not feasible (Sauer and Chandy, 1981).

During the same period, other areas of computer science theory have made considerable progress, starting with McCarthy's (1962) pioneering work on a mathematical science of computation. Hoare (1969) has given us an axiomatic basis for programming; Manna (1974) has given us a mathematical theory of computation; Dijkstra (1976) produced a discipline of programming; de Bakker (1980) has developed a theory of program correctness; etc. Wand (1980), in the introduction to his text, comments:

> 'If the past decade's work has one central thesis, it is that a program is a mathematical object.... We therefore study the mathematical properties of programs. We mathematically prove the correctness of programs. We also use mathematical techniques to help us write programs.'

The thesis of this book is: because we can model programs as mathematical objects, we can not only measure their performance, but we can describe those measures mathematically. This mathematical description constitutes a formulation of performance measurement. On the basis of this formulation, we have codified performance measurement into a unified body of knowledge. However, mathematical objects are abstract, and abstract objects cannot be measured. Any measurements that are associated with an abstract object are inherited from the real life entity that the abstract object models. Thus, we have to distinguish between an executable object (real life executing program) and a program object (an abstraction). Parameters measured with respect to the former can be assigned to the latter as abstract quantities.

2.1 Other formulations of measurement

By standing upon the shoulders of our forbears we can often see a little further than they, and sometimes a great deal further. In this formulation, the conceptual model of an executing program developed by Svobodova (1976a) and Ferrari (1978a) is expanded, and then generalized using Kolence's (1972) idea of a software unit.

Kolence's 'software physics' (Section 3.2) is relevant to developing a formulation of performance measurement because it is the world-view from which he developed software performance monitors. He proposed a software physics which corresponds to natural physics at the conceptual level. He defined a basic constitutive definition for the nature of software (that of a software unit), from which he developed conservation laws and definitions for software energy, work, force, and power. Kolence considered the computer performance measurement field to be best characterized as a set of numbers in a desperate search for unifying principles. He was concerned with the question: 'How is meaning derived from a set of observations?' Software physics was proposed as a way of finding that meaning.

Kolence published some experimental data to support his formulation, but others seem not to have been convinced, as they have not taken up his methodology. The idea of a software physics deeply related to natural physics has not been proven. In addition, software physics deals only with capacity management and thus is not a generalized formulation.

Ferrari (Section 3.3) and Svobodova (Section 3.4) have both developed formulations of program performance based upon similar models of program execution. The performance measurement formulation developed in this chapter is an expansion of both these formulations. Kolence's idea of a software unit (called an object here) has been used to generalize the formulation. Ferrari, Svobodova, and McKerrow use the same model of program execution, but look at it from different perspectives. In each case, the concepts of time sequence of events, state changes, and activity between events (modules) are present.

Ferrari emphasizes the time sequence of states and pays little attention to the activity between states, on the assumption that significant activity will be reflected by the occurrence of a new state. Svobodova emphasizes the occurrence of events, as these indicate the start and end of activities, on the assumption that we are interested in how often each activity occurs and for how long. I emphasize: the modules (activity between events); using the events to detect initiation, pausing, resumption, and termination of modules; and using the state (stimulus information) to give meaning to the actions of the modules. My perspective is that we want to know why execution has occurred the way it has, in addition to measuring the various indices.

2.2 World view

Although my definition of an object is similar to Kolence's software unit, the formulation developed in this chapter is based on a different perspective. Trying to express one branch of science with the terminology and principles of another branch can place a straitjacket upon one's thinking process. While the natural creation exhibits considerable order, the creator has shown great variety in the principles underlying his designs. The natural scientist studies the creation and seeks to develop mathematical descriptions (abstractions) of that reality. The computer scientist studies the information handling processes designed into creation, seeks to develop algorithms to describe that reality, and then seeks to code the algorithms into computer understandable form. Thus, algorithms are an abstract description of reality and programs are an implementation of that abstraction.

When we measure the performance of a program, we are measuring the performance of an implementation of an abstract description of a natural process. Ideally, we should be able to evaluate the performance of our implementation by comparing it to the natural reality. Unfortunately, this is not easy because often we cannot identify, and less often measure, a natural realization of the process in creation. This may be possible when we understand the human brain more fully. Hence the difficulty of selecting and quantifying performance indices for any measurement study. Performance indices tend either to be based on the performance of existing programs, or on a theoretical expectation of performance. For example, algorithms of order n are considered to be efficient and those of order n^2 are not, where n is the number of executions of a significant operation (presumably the operation which takes the most time).

The formulation developed in the next sections arose from thinking and praying about the practical problems involved in measurement with a hardware monitor (McKerrow, 1983), and the subsequent design of a hybrid monitor (McKerrow, 1984). In later chapters, the formulation is applied to a number of performance measurement issues, demonstrating its ability to codify the field into a unified body of knowledge.

The symbols used in the following sections are listed in Tables 2.1-2.3 at the end of this chapter.

2.3 Performance

Performance is what makes an object valuable to its user (Ferrari, 1978a). An object (O) is of value (V) to a user if it performs its functions correctly (C) and well (P).

$$V = f_1(C, P) \qquad (2.1)$$
$$= \textit{value}$$

How well an object performs is determined by evaluating its performance index: its measured performance (P_m) relative to a predetermined performance reference (P_r).

$$P = \frac{P_m}{P_r} \qquad (2.2)$$
$$= \textit{performance}$$

In Section 2.9, we expand this simple equation to include multiple performance indices. The extent to which an object performs its functions correctly can be described in a similar way (Equation 2.3). Measurement of relative correctness involves testing all functions implemented in the code. As this can be an impossibly large task, most programs do not perform all functions correctly. Such measurement is beyond the scope of this book.

$$C = \frac{C_m}{C_r} \tag{2.3}$$

$$= \textit{correctness}$$

Thus, performance evaluation seeks to ascertain the value of an object. Performance evaluation involves performance measurement which seeks to ascertain the extent (E) of the object. This is a dynamic measurement of the object during execution, not a static measurement derived by reading the text.

2.4 Object definition

An **object** (O) is the particular entity whose performance we wish to measure. Each object has a function and a context. The **function** (F) of an object is the set of transformations (T_d) the object performs on the set of input data (I_d) to produce the set of output data (R_d, results), i.e. the purpose of the object.

$$F = \mathrm{f}_2(O) = T_d \tag{2.4}$$

$$= \textit{set of transformations}$$

$$T_d : I_d \rightarrow R_d \tag{2.5}$$

$$= \textit{set of output data}$$

Context (K) is defined as the parts of the system, which execute before and during the execution of an object, that influence the meaning of the object, i.e. the environment in which the object exists. The parts of the system which execute directly after an object can help us determine the meaning of the object, but don't, with the possible exception of backtracking, influence the meaning of the object. Thus, context includes the input data (which are the results of the parts before) and external events (E_e) which occur during the execution of the object and have some influence on it.

$$E = E_e + E_i \tag{2.6}$$

$$= \textit{set of events}$$

$$E_i = f_3(I_d, T_d) \quad (2.7)$$
$$= \textit{set of internal events}$$

$$K = E_e \cup I_d \quad (2.8)$$
$$= \textit{context}$$

Meaning (M) is the reason for the actions of the object, and is related to the data the object is transforming.

$$M = f_4(K, T_d) \quad (2.9)$$

2.5 Object hierarchy

An object consists of a piece of executable code and its interactions with other pieces of code, with the computer, with peripheral devices, and with the user. An object can be as large as a complete system or as small as a single instruction. Normally, in the tradition of good programming practice, an object will have one entry point and one exit point. However, some systems are so unstructured that this may not be achievable.

An object at one level is defined as a set of objects at a lower level. For the sake of clarity, objects one level lower than the object we are measuring are called modules. The ordering of the modules in the object is not important, but is normally the order in which the modules occur in the source listing. A **module** (m) is a contiguous sequence of operations that occur in response to an event. An **event** is any action that initiates a significant change in the state of the object.

$$O_n = \{O_{n-1,1} \,..\, O_{n-1,m}\} \quad (2.10)$$

An object at level n = set of objects at level $n-1$.

$$O_n = \{m_1 \,..\, m_m\} \quad (2.11)$$

$$\textit{where } m_1 = O_{n-1,1} \textit{ etc.} \quad (2.12)$$

Thus, a computer system can be viewed as a hierarchy of objects where a higher-level object consists of a set of lower-level objects (modules). For a detailed theoretical treatment of the fundamental proposition that complex systems are often hierarchic, and that hierarchical systems are often nearly completely decomposable, see the monograph by Courtois (1977). There are situations where modules in an executable object do not map directly to modules in the program object. This can happen when code is rearranged by an optimizing compiler. However, these situations do not contradict the principle that an object consists of a sequence of modules, but they do make measurement indispensable. Practical problems caused by code optimization are discussed in Section 6.5.2.

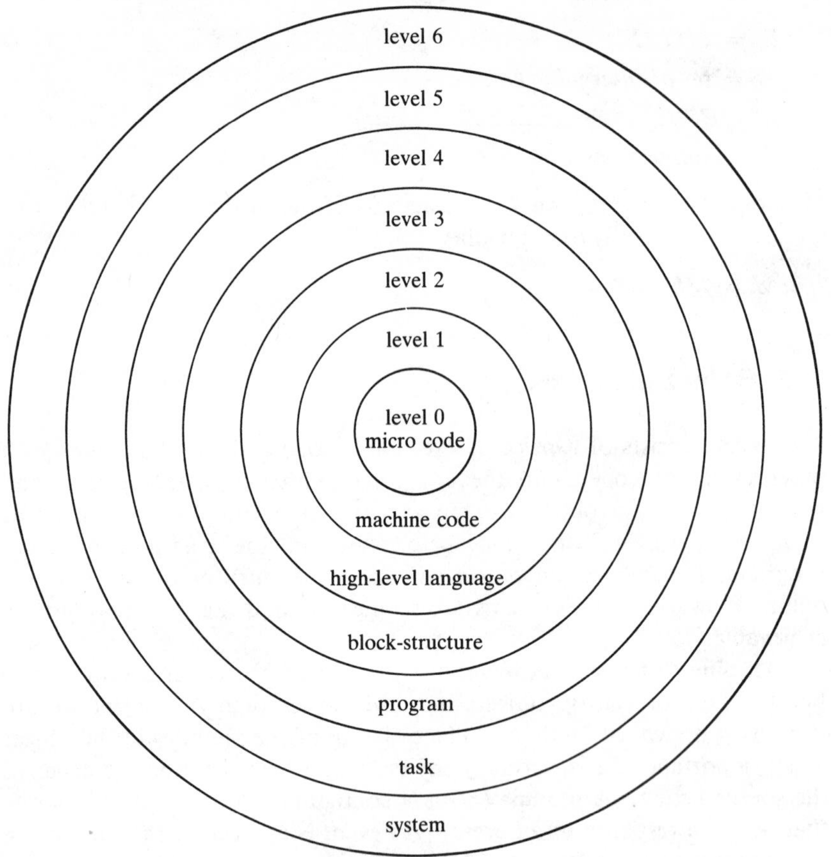

Figure 2.1 Object hierarchy.

The highest level object, or superset, is the complete computer system: hardware, software, and users (Figure 2.1). While the hardware of a system may be constant, the tasks executed by the system vary in response to user requests. To perform a task, the system executes a sequence of programs, or processes. Processes can be written in a high-level language or in assembler. In either case, they can be decomposed into blocks of code, which can be broken down into sequences of instructions. The result is a sequence of machine code operands.

As the machine code defines the architecture of a computer from the programmer's perspective, decomposition one level lower to microcode is uncommon. On most modern microprocessors, and minicomputers, machine code instructions are indivisible, but on some machines machine code instructions can be interrupted. In the latter case, you may have to measure the microcode.

Principle 2.1 Objects of interest in performance evaluation fit into the following hierarchy (Figure 2.1).

- System level - computer system and users
- Task level - a group of processes which execute to perform a request
- Program level - individual programs, processes, re-entrant routines, and supervisor calls.
- Block-structure level - sequential blocks of code, compound statements, procedures, and functions.
- High-level language level - individual instructions, interpreter calls.
- Machine-code level - assembler instructions, and memory bus cycles.
- Microcode level - microcode instructions and ALU cycles.

In some situations, some levels of the hierarchy may not exist. For example, a system programmed in assembler will not include the high-level language level, but will go from machine-code level to block-structure level.

Principle 2.2 An object at level zero is measurable.

$$\mathrm{M}(O_0) = \mathit{True} \tag{2.13}$$

where M is the predicate on the set of objects which is true if and only if that set is measurable. In theory, microcode instructions are measurable, because they are synchronized to hardware events. You can attach a probe to the microinstruction clock and measure the exact time for each instruction. In practice, the physical packaging of microprocessors precludes measurement of the microcode. On most computers, machine code can be measured by monitoring the instruction fetch clock, except in the case of on chip memory.

We can now hypothesize that, given a set of functions which map from one level of the hierarchy to the next higher level, then an object at any level is measurable.

Principle 2.3 An object that can be obtained recursively from measurable objects is itself measurable.

Note the similarity to the computability theorem:

'a function obtained recursively from computable functions is itself computable'.

(Cutland, 1980; Theorem 4.4)

We have already stated that the objects at level zero are measurable (Equation 2.13). If we assume that the objects at level n are measurable then we can prove by induction that the objects at level $n+1$ are also measurable. When we look at the set of measurements that can be made on an object we will see that they are:

a) defined in terms of measurements made at a lower level, and
b) composed of lower-level measurements in such a way that data reduction occurs (composition is usually by summation - Section 6.2).

Thus, a measurement at level $n+1$ is composed of measurements made at level n.

$$M(O_n) = \textit{True for all } n \tag{2.14}$$

Kolence expressed it this way:

> 'any truth we say about software units [objects] without a qualification as to size must be universally true from at least the level of the single instruction up to the set of all software ever produced'.

In this book, we claim that the recursive nature of an object leads to a generalized formulation of performance measurement which applies at all levels of the object hierarchy.

A significant problem in performance evaluation has always been the reduction of the enormous amounts of data available at level zero into a tractable set of meaningful data as we move up to higher levels. A second claim we make is: that the recursive nature of the object definition leads to natural methods of deducing high level quantities from low level data, and natural methods of data reduction.

Principle 2.4 Measurements of an object that has been obtained recursively from other objects can also be obtained recursively from the measurements of those objects.

Principle 2.5 Measurements made at one level in an object filter out lower level values, and hence lower level measurements cannot be obtained from higher level measurements.

Thus measurement tools selected for a particular level will automatically filter out lower level data.

2.6 Performance measurement

Program design is best tackled using the process of stepwise refinement (Wirth, 1971), where a problem is simplified by decomposing it into smaller problems. This process of decomposition is repeated until the problems are intellectually manageable, and detailed solutions can be studied. In a similar way, the hierarchical definition of an object is a means of decomposing one large measurement problem into a set of smaller measurement problems. This process of decomposition is repeated until the level in the hierarchy is reached where measurements can be made with the available tools.

At all levels of the hierarchy, performance measurement is ascertaining the extent of an object, often by measuring the extent of the set of modules contained in the object. Before we can define the extent of an object, we require a conceptual model of an executable object. An **executable object** is an ordered sequence of modules, where the order is the sequence in which execution occurs. This sequence is called an **execution path**. An object has one or more execution paths. Associated with each execution path is an **execution time**: the time taken to execute the object, which is the sum of the times taken to execute the modules in the path.

The termination of one module in the sequence and the start of the next is caused by an event. By detecting events with a measurement tool, we can decompose an object into modules. Associated with each event is a set of **stimulus information** (state, etc.). This stimulus information can be used by an analyst to determine why the object behaved the way it did, i.e. to give meaning to the actions of the object.

A monitoring tool should record an **event trace** of modules, and associated stimulus information. An event trace is a sequence of tuples containing a module identifier and the time at which the module commenced execution, relative to the start of the measurement period. Included in this trace are stimulus information triples, which contain stimulus information and a copy of the current event trace tuple (current module identifier, and the time at which the stimulus information is recorded relative to the start of the measurement period). From these records, an analyst can obtain the extent of the object.

To record an event trace, a monitoring tool must be able to detect the bounds of the modules in the object under study. These bounds include the start of execution of a module and the termination of execution of the same module. Termination of a module is often, but not always, indicated by the start of the next module in the sequence. In addition, external events can cause one module to pause, while another is executed, and then resume. So the tool must be able to detect the pausing and resumption of a module also.

From the recorded information, we can ascertain the values of the parameters which define the extent of the object (Figure 2.2). The values of some parameters - execution path, execution time, and stimulus information - are obtained from the event trace, while the values of other parameters - frequency of execution, throughput, relative execution times, utilization, memory usage, and data structure access - are calculated from trace data. These parameters are the measures which we can make of an executable object.

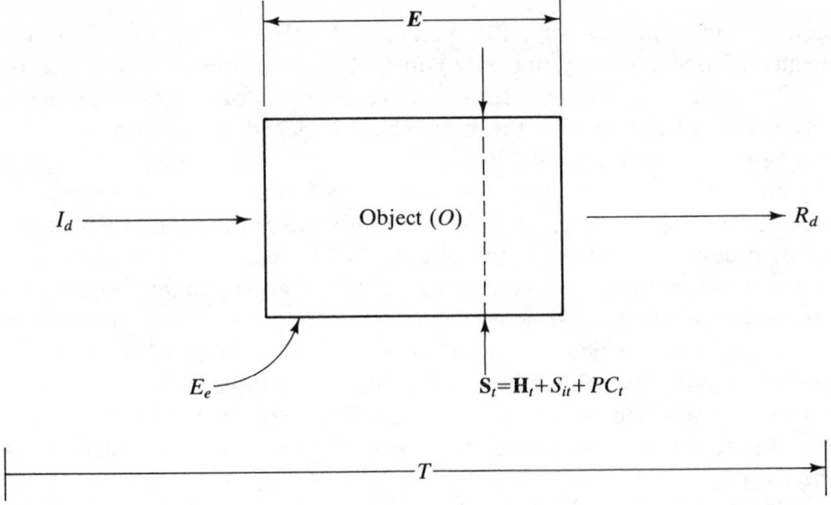

Object Bounds
start of execution
pause in execution
resumption of execution
termination of execution

Calculated Values
module-to-path execution time ratio
set of object execution frequencies
set of module execution frequencies
set of relative path execution times
set of relative module execution times
set of path utilizations
set of module utilizations
object state at time t
object throughput
module throughput

Measured Values
set of execution paths
measurement period
set of path execution times
set of execution path counts
total number of object executions
set of module execution counts
set of module execution times
set of module execution paths
total number of module executions
stimulus information
program counter at time t
execution history at time t
memory usage
quantity of data
job class

Figure 2.2 Graphical representation of an object. Symbols are defined in Tables 2.1 to 2.3 (pp.45-47).

2.6.1 Execution path

What path was taken through the object during its execution? At the machine-code level, an execution path is defined as one of the set of machine code instructions. Sequences of machine code instructions are measured at a higher level: either the high-level language level or at the block-structure level. An object at any level may have several execution paths, where each individual execution path (p_k) is an ordered set of modules.

$$p_k = \{m_1 .. m_2\} \tag{2.15}$$

and

$$p_k \subseteq O_n \tag{2.16}$$

The set of modules that make up an object is partially ordered, in that the order represents only one of the possible execution paths. The set of execution paths (P_{en}) for an object at level n includes all the possible execution paths through the object.

$$P_{en} = \{p_1 .. p_k\} \tag{2.17}$$

During a measurement period (T), each path is executed a number of times (c_k) giving a set of path execution counts (N_{cn}).

$$N_{cn} = \{c_1 .. c_k\} \tag{2.18}$$

We must remember that each module in an execution path is an object at the next lower level, with its own set of execution paths (P_m). At the lowest level there is only one member in the set, but as we move up the hierarchy the size of the set increases rapidly. This increase in complexity is a consequence of the recursive definition of an object, and methods of handling it will be discussed later. However, a significant reduction in the volume of data from that available at the machine-code level has already been achieved.

2.6.2 Execution time

How long does an object take to execute? Each execution path has a measurable execution time. Normally, an object will have as many execution times as it has paths: one for each path. Objects with a single execution path usually have a single execution time. There are two execution paths where this will occur: a sequence of non-branching instructions, and a loop with a fixed loop count. A few situations that cause a path to have a range of execution times are discussed in Section 6.1.2.

An object at level n has a set of execution times (T_{en}) which consist of an execution time (t_k) for each execution path (p_k). The execution time of a path (t_k) is the sum of the execution times (b_{mq}) of the modules in the path.

$$T_{en} = \{t_1 .. t_k\} \tag{2.19}$$

for the set of execution paths P_{en}.

The measured execution time (b_{mq}) of a module is one of the set of possible execution times for the module (T_m). As only one path is executed each time the module is executed, only one module execution time contributes to the path execution time for that module invocation.

$$T_m = \{b_{m1} .. b_{mq}\} \tag{2.20}$$

where there are q paths through module m.

If a module has only one execution path then the set T_m normally reduces to a single member. Exceptions to this are discussed in Section 6.1.2. The set of individual module execution times is a member of the superset of module execution times (T_{bn}).

$$T_{bn} = \{T_1 .. T_m\} \tag{2.21}$$

for the set of modules in O.

2.6.3 Frequency of execution

How often is each path through an object executed during the measurement period? How often is each module in the object executed during the measurement period? The measurement period (T) is specified in units of time, and normally corresponds to the time taken to complete a certain experiment rather than a fixed time interval. An object at level n has a set of execution frequencies (F_{en}) which consist of the number of executions (c_k) for each path (p_k) executed during the measurement period divided by the total number of executions (N_e) of the object.

$$f_k = \frac{c_k}{N_e} \times 100\ \% \tag{2.22}$$

= *frequency of execution of p_k as a percentage of the total number of executions.*

$$F_{en} = \{f_1 .. f_k\} \tag{2.23}$$

for the set of execution paths P_{en}.

$$N_e = \sum_{j=1}^{k} c_j \tag{2.24}$$

An object at level n is a set of m modules at level $n-1$ (Equations 2.11, 2.12). This object has a set of module execution frequencies (F_{mn}). The module execution frequency (e_m) for module m is the number of times module m was executed (a_m) during the measurement period divided by the total number of module executions (N_m).

$$N_m = \sum_{j=1}^{m} a_j \tag{2.25}$$

$$e_m = \frac{a_m}{N_m} \times 100\ \%,\ and \tag{2.26}$$

$$N_a = \{a_1 \,..\, a_m\} \tag{2.27}$$

$$F_{mn} = \{e_1 \,..\, e_m\} \tag{2.28}$$

for the set of modules in O.

2.6.4 Throughput

Is the object executed frequently? Object throughput (N_o) is the number of object executions per unit time, and is calculated by dividing the number of executions of the object (N_e) by the measurement period (T).

$$N_o = \frac{N_e}{T} \tag{2.29}$$

Module throughput (N_t) is the number of module executions per unit time.

$$N_t = \frac{N_m}{T} \tag{2.30}$$

2.6.5 Relative execution times

Does one path take considerably longer to execute than other paths do? Does one module take considerably longer to execute than other modules do? An object at level n has a set of relative path execution times (T_{rn}) which are derived by dividing the execution time for each path (t_k) by the maximum execution time for any path (t_p).

$$t_p = \max(T_{en}) \tag{2.31}$$

$$r_k = \frac{t_k}{t_p} \times 100\ \% \tag{2.32}$$

$$T_{rn} = \{r_1 \,..\, r_k\} \tag{2.33}$$

for the set of execution paths P_{en}.

An object at level n has a set of relative module execution times (T_{sn}) which are derived by dividing each member of the set of execution times for each module (b_{mq}) by the maximum execution time for any module (t_b).

$$t_b = \max(T_{bn}) \tag{2.34}$$

$$d_{mq} = \frac{b_{mq}}{t_b} \times 100\ \% \tag{2.35}$$

$$T_{sn} = \{d_{11} \,..\, d_{mq}\} \tag{2.36}$$

for the set of modules in O.

Each path through an object has a set of module to path execution time ratios (E_r) which are calculated by dividing the execution time of each module (b_{mq}) in the path (P_k) by the execution time for the path (t_k).

$$r_{zk} = \frac{b_{mq}}{t_k} \times 100\ \% \quad (2.37)$$

$$E_r = \{r_{1k} \,..\, r_{zk}\} \quad (2.38)$$

where there are z modules in the path.

2.6.6 Utilization

Does the object spend most of its time executing one path? Does the object spend most of its time executing one module? An object at level n has a set of path utilizations (U_{pn}) which are the product of the path execution time (t_k) and the number of times each path is executed (c_k) divided by the measurement period (T).

$$u_k = t_k \times \frac{c_k}{T} \times 100\ \% \quad (2.39)$$

$$U_{pn} = \{u_1 \,..\, u_k\} \quad (2.40)$$

for the set of paths P_{en}.

The number of times a module was executed (a_m) is the sum of the number of times each path (a_{mq}) in the module was executed, during the measurement period. An object has a set of module utilizations (U_{mn}), where the utilization of a module is the total execution time for the module divided by the measurement period.

$$v_m = \frac{\left\{\sum_{i=1}^{m} a_{mq} \times b_{mq}\right\}}{T} \times 100\ \% \quad (2.41)$$

In the case where there is only one path through a module, this equation reduces to

$$v_m = b_m \times \frac{a_m}{T} \times 100\ \% \quad (2.42)$$

$$U_{mn} = \{v_1 \,..\, v_m\} \quad (2.43)$$

for the set of modules in the object O.

2.6.7 Stimulus information

Which information gives meaning to the actions of the object? Which information can an analyst use to determine why an object behaves the way it does? Two overlapping sets of stimulus information exist in an object: the set of data used in decision making ($\boldsymbol{D}_d$), and the set of data being transformed by the object ($\boldsymbol{D}_t$).

$$S_{in} = \boldsymbol{D}_d \cup \boldsymbol{D}_t \qquad (2.44)$$

The set of stimulus information (S_{in}) for an object at level n is the union of the sets of stimulus information (s_k) for each path through the object, and also the union of the sets of stimulus information for each module (s_m) in the object.

$$S_{in} = s_1 \cup s_2 \cup \, .. \, s_k = s_1 \cup s_2 \cup \, .. \, s_m \qquad (2.45)$$

From Equations 2.8 and 2.9 we see that stimulus information includes: input data (I_d), output data (R_d), partially transformed data, and external events (E_e). Internal events are not included as they are a function of the input data and the transformations (Equation 2.7), and they cause a change in state which is indicated by the execution path. The first step in determining which stimulus data to record during a measurement session is to define the set of data used in decision making. This set is a subset of the union of the data being transformed and functions of that data (for example number of data elements).

One important use of stimulus information is workload characterization (Ferrari, 1972). To characterize the workload of a system, we want to know the type and size of that load during the measurement period. Type of workload is described by the class of the object (or job class J_c); for example batch, interactive editing, or Pascal compilation. Object class is a piece of stimulus information that both describes an object, and is used in decision making; for example: execute a Pascal program.

2.6.8 Memory usage

How much memory is used by the object during execution? Simplistically, the memory used (M_u) by an object during execution is the range of instruction accesses, i.e. the difference between the addresses of the lowest and highest locations from which instructions are fetched, plus the range of data accesses. In many situations, the above measure is too coarse. Instructions may be loaded into discontiguous segments, or data may be common to a set of objects, leaving large holes in the apparent memory usage.

We can refine our measure of memory usage (M_u) to be the sum of the set of instruction segments, where an instruction segment is defined by a contiguous range of instruction accesses, plus the sum of the set of data segments, where a data segment is a contiguous range of data accesses. This measure may not be the same as a static measure of memory usage (M_s) obtained from the object text, because parts of the object may not be executed, or the object may allocate memory dynamically. In the latter case, an accurate measure cannot be obtained from the text without knowledge of the stimulus information. The former case clearly indicates the possibility of a bug in the object.

At any time during execution, the object may be using only a portion of the total memory usage. For example, in a segmented system only some of the object may be in memory. It is in this context that analysts measure the working set of an object. The working set of an object is a list of the segments used by the object. Working set information can be obtained as stimulus information from the memory allocation process.

In the introduction to a special issue of *IEEE Computer* on program behaviour, Domenico Ferrari (1976) comments:

> 'Among the performance characteristics of programs, the patterns of memory references they generate have the unique property of being totally irrelevant in a non-virtual memory context, and perhaps the most important aspect of program behaviour in a virtual memory system.'

Understanding these patterns is vital to the rational design of virtual storage systems (Hellerman and Conroy, 1975). When monitoring a program, we often record the sequence of memory accesses of the program - known as a reference string or address trace (Section 3.8). From this string, we can determine the memory referencing behaviour of the program. This concept has been extended to a page reference string, from which the working set of a program can be determined, and to a database reference string, for the analysis of enquiries to a database (Rodriguez-Rosell, 1976).

These ideas fit closely with our conceptual model of an executing object: an ordered sequence of modules. At the machine code level, a reference string is the sequence of program instruction references interleaved with the sequence of variable access references. At a higher level, a reference string is the sequence of memory segments used by an object. Measuring reference strings is discussed in Section 6.3, where the event trace is extended to include address bus information.

2.6.9 Data structure access

What variables are accessed, and how often, during the execution of an object? During execution, an object will manipulate data. Data is stored in data structures, including: simple variables, arrays, records, stacks, queues, and trees. Some of these are static, and can be mapped directly onto object text; others are dynamic, and depend on the quantity of data (Q_d) being processed by the object.

While we can find the location of static data structures from the code object, we cannot do the same for dynamic data structures. We may be able to find the initial element of a dynamic structure, but not its size. Thus, when measuring dynamic data structures we must measure the size of the structure (i.e. the memory usage). We can do this either by measuring memory usage or by counting the data manipulations performed upon the structure (module execution counts).

Usually, we measure object access to static variables only during debugging. For example, linkage faults can be identified by monitoring a program's access to variables. One exception is the measurement of real-time systems, where communication between independent objects can occur through common data structures. Here, by monitoring accesses to common data, we can measure the sequence in which processes access variables, as well as which processes corrupt data.

2.7 Object extent and object state

Which parameters and stimulus variables we measure during the study of an object depends on the purpose of the measurement study, the function the object performs, the level of the object in the hierarchy, and the context in which the object is placed. However, we can determine the extent of an object during the measurement period by measuring the parameters defined in the previous section (Figure 2.2).

$$\begin{aligned} \boldsymbol{E} &= \{P_e, T_e, T_m, N_c, N_e, N_a, T_b, N_m, S_i, P_m, M_u, Q_d, J_c\} \\ &\cup \{F_e, F_m, T_r, T_s, U_p, U_m, N_o, N_t, E_r\} \\ &= \textit{measured values} \cup \textit{calculated values}. \end{aligned} \tag{2.46}$$

(These symbols are defined in Tables 2.1-3.)

The set of possible calculated parameters, involving all possible combinations and permutations of measured parameters, is very large. The subset in our definition of the extent of an object includes all those in common use. Some extensions to this subset move out of the field of performance measurement into the fields of performance comparison, for example the ratio of execution times of a program running on different processors, and performance evaluation, for example cost effectiveness - the ratio of throughput to system cost. System price, in dollars, is a value that is often ascertained, but it is not included in the measures because it only indirectly affects the extent of an executing object.

The state ($\boldsymbol{S}_t$) of an object at level n is the value of these parameters (measured and calculated) at any point in time (t) during the life of the object, the values currently assigned to all data variables ($\boldsymbol{D}_t$), and the program counter (PC_t). Thus, the state is the execution history ($\boldsymbol{H}_t$) up to this point in time, plus the current status of all variables. The values assigned to the variables reflect the execution history and the level of completeness of the transformations. The current execution path and the point at which execution is occurring at time t are defined precisely by the program counter.

$$S_t = H_t + S_{in_t} + PC_t \tag{2.47}$$

The history portion of the status is not explicitly carried along with the object and must be recorded as it executes. The data and program counter portions of the status are updated as the object executes. When an object is interrupted, it pauses, and the system saves these portions of the state, allowing the object to restart. Thus, to record the state of an object the measurement tool must also be able to detect the start, finish, pausing, and resumption of object execution.

When studying some objects, we want to measure pauses in their execution, and ignore any other objects which execute during these pauses. For example, when measuring a disk driver the time between a request to seek and a seek interrupt (the seek execution time) is important, but what the system does during the pause is irrelevant. In this situation, the pause can be classified as a hardware module with the execution path being the operation performed by the hardware. In other situations, a pause can be classified as a wait module with its execution path being the empty set. All our measurement parameters apply to these modules, providing a way of measuring interactions between software and hardware.

2.8 Data reduction and analysis

Due to the high execution speed of computers, enormous amounts of data are available for measurement. For example, an M68000 processor accesses memory 16.7 million times in 6 to 10 seconds (MacGregor and Rubinstein, 1985). For meaningful measurements to be made over longer periods of time, we must reduce the quantity of data we have to handle. Our formulation of performance measurement helps by decomposing a system into a hierarchy of objects, and by defining the set of information we must record. As we move up the hierarchy the rate at which data arrives reduces – roughly an order of magnitude for each level. Our measures reduce the amount of data available at machine code level to ordered sets of data for each parameter at the desired level. For objects at or near the level of the measurements, these sets are small and tractable. However, as we move up the hierarchy the volume of data grows, and consequently the difficulty of computing high level data from low level data increases. A number of data reduction and analysis methods are available to tackle this problem.

Traditionally the quantity of data has been reduced by selecting tools appropriate for the level of interest. These tools provide data at that level, but lower level data is lost. For example, a hardware tool for

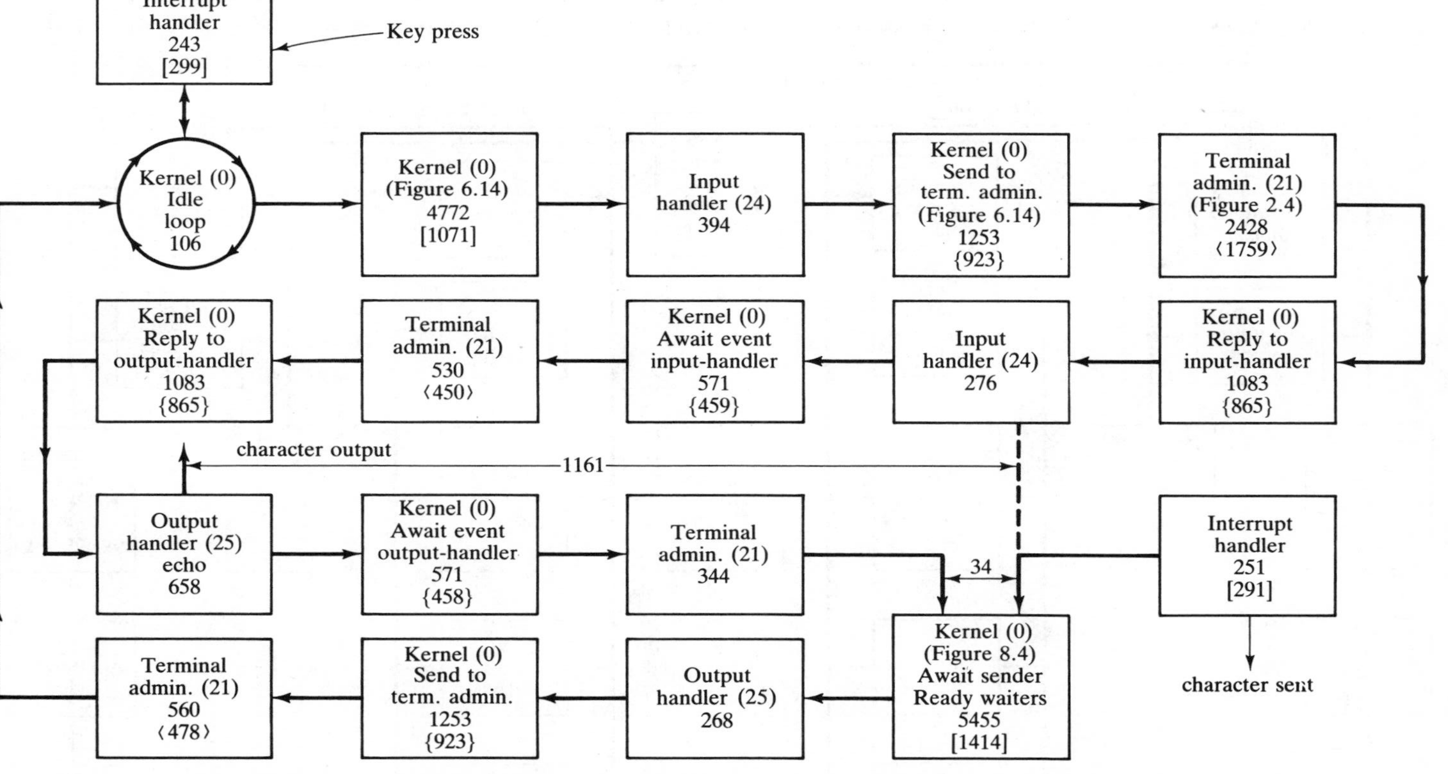

Figure 2.3 Event trace graph of a terminal administrator process showing the sequence of processes executed to handle the input of an alphabetic character from a keyboard (Section 8.4). All times in microseconds; numbers in round brackets are process numbers.

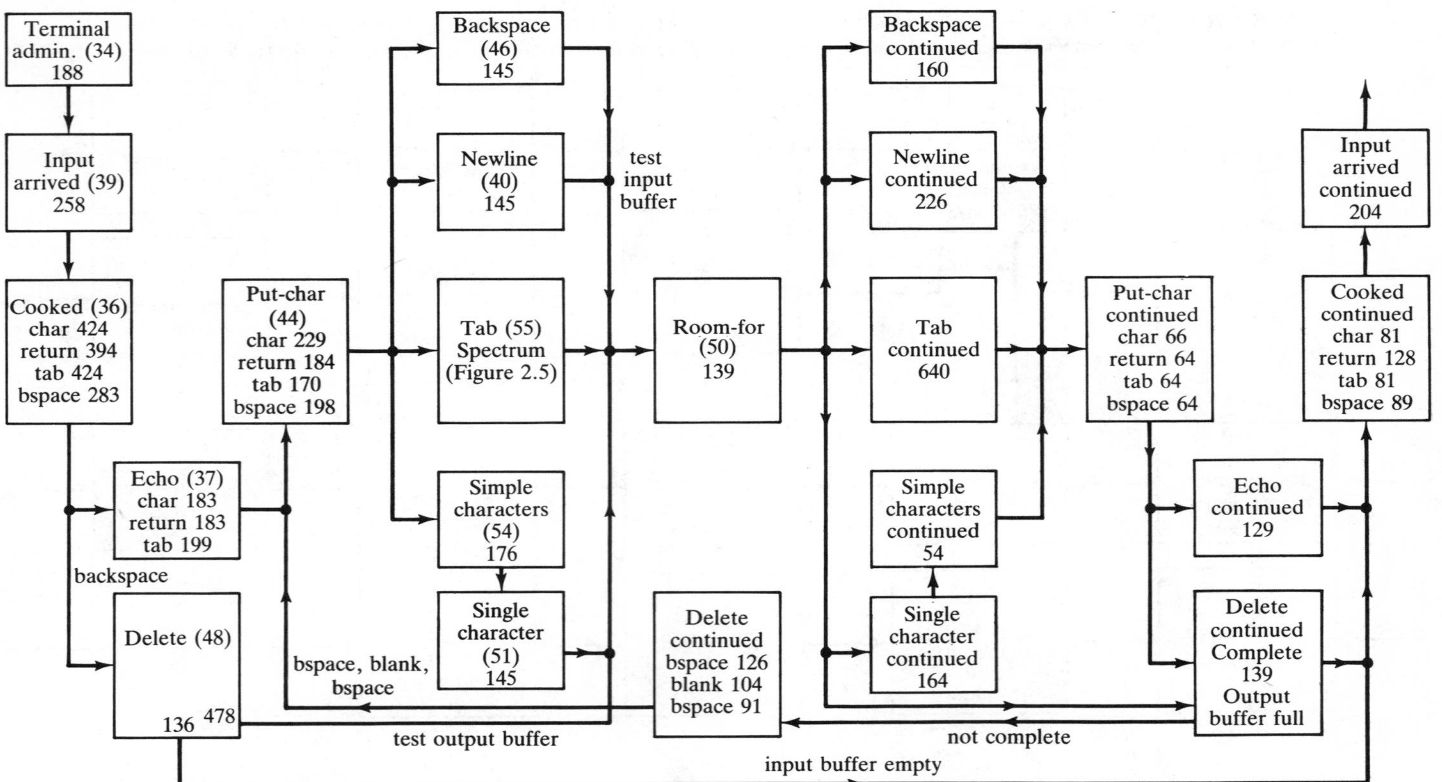

Figure 2.4 Execution path flow graph showing the set of execution paths through the terminal administrator process (Figure 2.3). All times in microseconds; numbers in brackets are module numbers.

measuring CPU utilization records the time the CPU is busy very accurately, but all other data is discarded. CPU utilization time is a measurement of the execution time of a system level object. Many software tools only record the number of times particular objects execute, once again reducing the data.

Graphical methods are often used in the display and analysis of performance data. Ferrari *et al.* (1983) illustrate a number of the commonly used data presentation methods. Graphs are easier for people to analyse than tables. We can use graphs to display the values of every parameter defined in the formulation. Some of these graphs are as follows:

- An **event trace graph** displays the event trace of an object, and stimulus information, with respect to time (Figure 2.3). This display allows the analyst to walk through the execution path of the object, and to study the conditions that caused that path to be taken.

- An **execution path flow graph** (Figure 2.4) shows one or more of the set of execution paths through an object. It is a directed graph of modules with execution times, or pointers to module spectrum, recorded in the nodes, and stimulus information recorded on the arrows. This graph gives a clear picture of the inter-relations between the modules in an object.

- An **object spectrum** (when referring to modules it is a module spectrum) is a plot of the number of executions of each path versus the execution time of the path, i.e. N_c versus T_e. A normalized object spectrum is the plot of the set of execution frequencies (F_e)

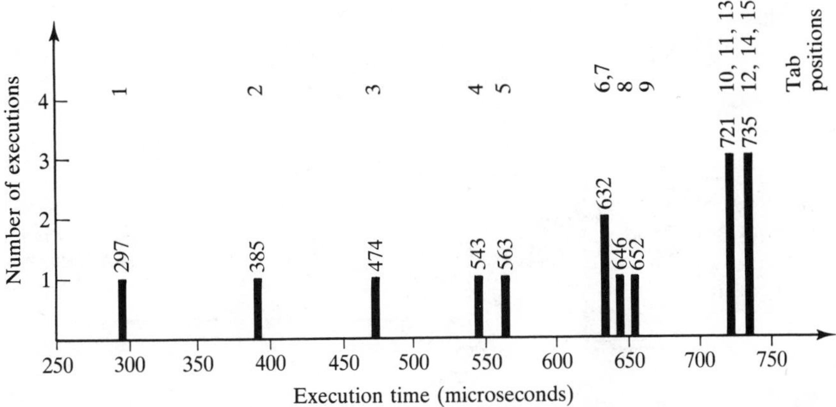

Figure 2.5 Object spectrum for the module Tab (Figure 2.4), showing the execution time for the first 15 tab positions across the screen. All times in microseconds.

versus the set of execution times (T_e) for each path in the set of execution paths (P_e). In both cases, the graph is a series of vertical spectral lines (Figure 2.5), one for each path. On the spectral lines, we record stimulus information. From the spectrum, we can read the most frequently executed paths, and the paths which take the longest time, enabling us to pinpoint areas of poor performance, and paths that should be optimized.

- An **execution path profile** (Figure 2.6) is a histogram of the set of execution frequencies (F_e), or the set of path execution counts (N_c), for the set of execution paths (P_e).
- A **module profile** (Figure 2.7) is a histogram of the set of module execution counts (N_m) for the set of modules (O). Again, a normalized version can be drawn by plotting the set of relative module execution frequencies (F_m). This graph highlights modules with very high usage and modules which are not used at all. Thus, we can use it to identify bottlenecks.
- A **path execution time profile** (Figure 2.8) is a histogram of the set of object execution times (T_e), or the set of relative path execution times (T_r), for the set of object execution paths (P_e).
- A **module execution time profile** is a spectrum of the set of relative module execution times for the set of modules (Figure 2.9).
- **Kiviat graphs** (Kolence and Kiviat, 1973), **Gantt charts**, and **utilization profiles** can be used to display utilization information (Figure 2.10).

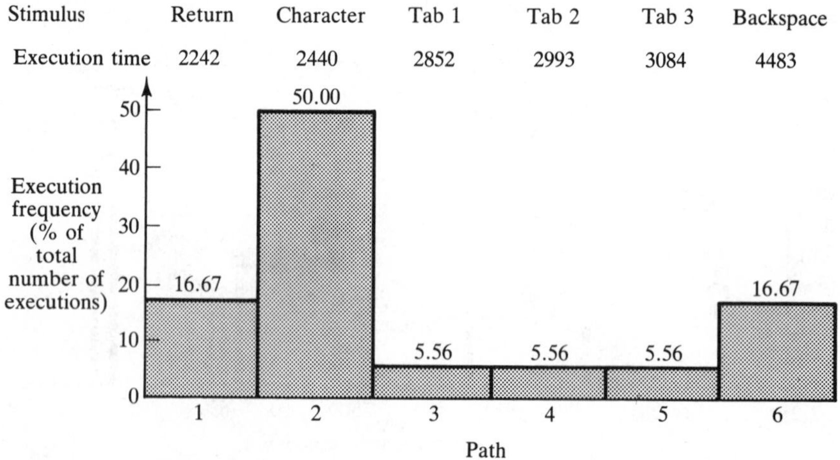

Figure 2.6 Execution path profile for the terminal administrator process (Figure 2.4) for a variety of input characters (18 characters). All times in microseconds.

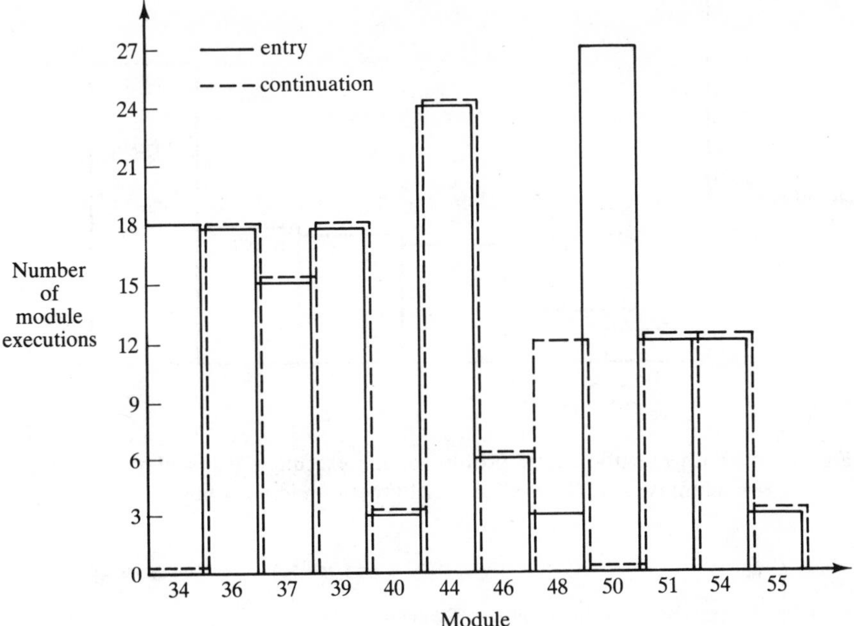

Figure 2.7 Module profile for the set of 18 execution paths shown in Figure 2.6. Module names are given in Figure 2.4.

The two sets of information that are displayed separately in the execution path profile and the execution time profile are combined in the object spectrum. In addition, some of the measurements can be profiled with respect to the value of a stimulus variable: for example workload, job class, data size, and disk track.

Also, we can use **statistical methods** to reduce and analyse the measured data (Section 4.8). For example, we can reduce the amount of data passed to higher levels by calculating the mean and standard deviation of module parameters, and passing them up. This is a useful way of collecting model data. Unfortunately, when we use statistical methods we lose data. To overcome this problem, some researchers are using **databases** to store the measured data, and database enquiries to analyse it. We can construct a database containing the extent of all objects at all levels in the system by extensive measurement of the system, once it is fully instrumented. Given such a database we can hypothesize three **recursive algorithms** for data reduction and analysis:

1. Given a set of stimulus data for an object we can predict the execution path and hence the extent of the other parameters. Thus, by combining the database with a recursive search algorithm we can produce a powerful simulation model with which we can predict the behaviour of the system under various conditions.

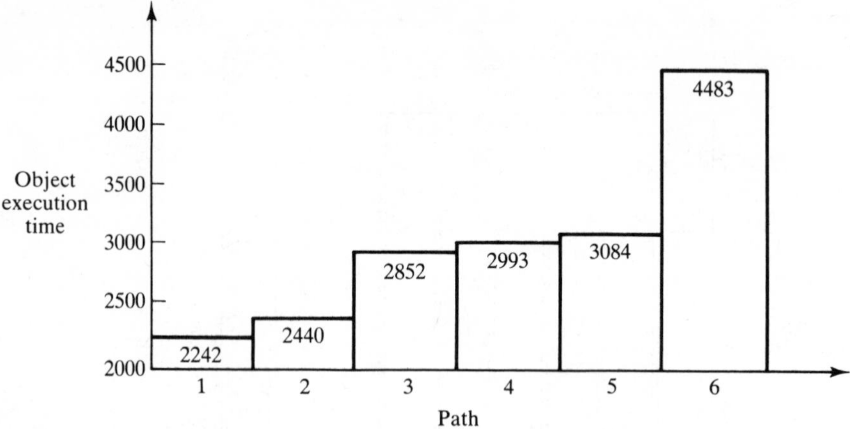

Figure 2.8 Path execution time profile for the execution paths of the terminal administrator (Figure 2.6). All times in microseconds.

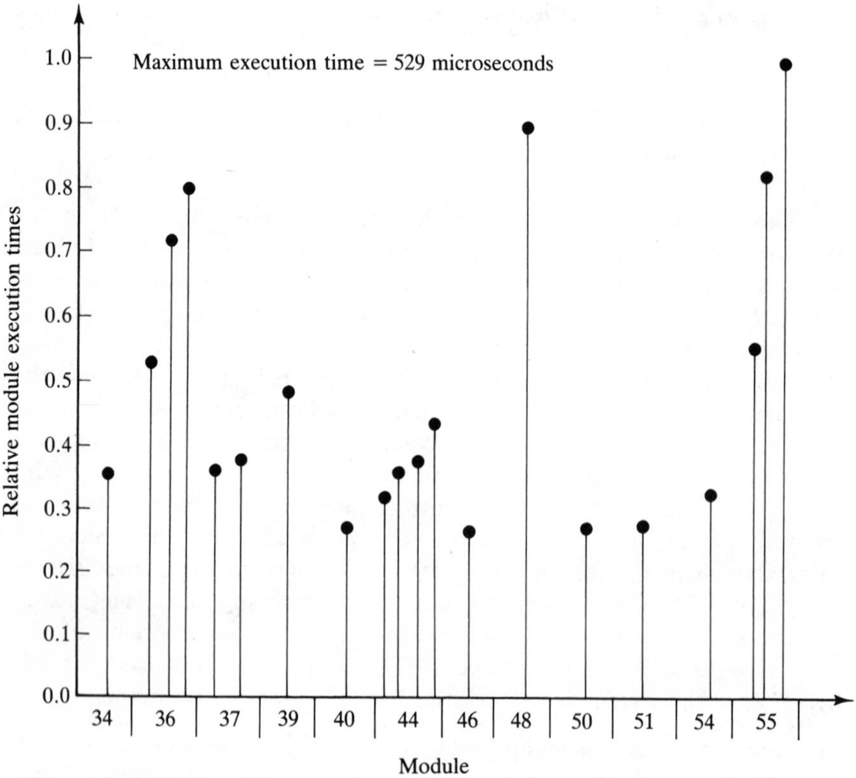

Maximum execution time = 529 microseconds

Relative module execution times

1.0
0.9
0.8
0.7
0.6
0.5
0.4
0.3
0.2
0.1
0.0

34 36 37 39 40 44 46 48 50 51 54 55

Module

Figure 2.9 Module execution time profile for the modules used by the terminal administrator (entry only – Figure 2.4) when executing the paths shown in Figure 2.6. Some modules have several execution times.

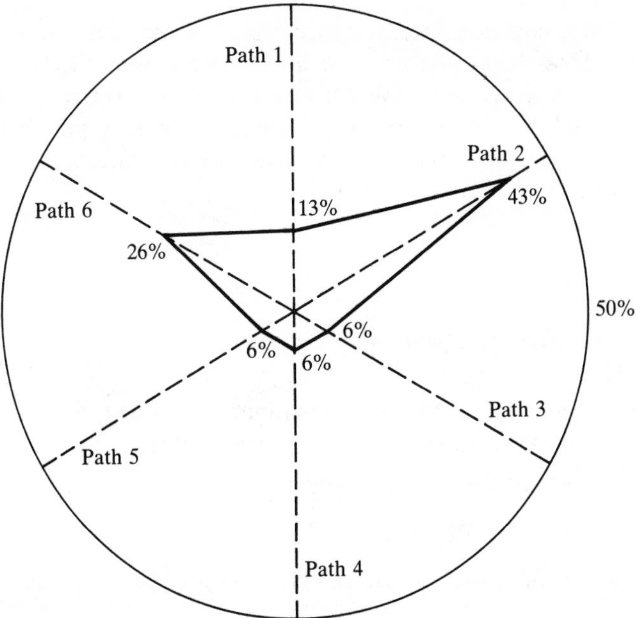

Figure 2.10 Kiviat graph of the utilizations of the execution paths in Figure 2.6.

2. Given a measurement of the extent of an object at level n, we can determine the extent of the object at lower levels, again using a recursive search, and evaluate what actually happened during the measurement period.
3. Given a graphical interface to the database, we can walk through an object by interactively selecting the execution path (for example) and seeing what conditions are required to produce different object states.

Validating these hypotheses is a subject for further research, as is the total instrumentation of a system and the construction of an object database.

2.9 Performance evaluation

Using the performance measurement formulation (Section 2.6), we can now extend our previous definitions of performance (Section 2.3).

$$P = \frac{P_m}{P_r} \tag{2.2}$$

In the above equation, performance has been reduced to a single index: the ratio of a single performance measurement to a single performance reference. However, we have defined a set of measurement parameters, each of which has a performance reference. For each parameter, we can define a performance index as the ratio of the measured value to the performance reference.

$$P_{i_n} = \frac{P_{m_n}}{P_{r_n}} \tag{2.48}$$

where n is the parameter number.

The set of these ratios for all the parameters defined in the extent of an object is a set of performance indices for the object.

$$P_i = \{P_{P_e}, P_{T_b}, P_{T_e}, P_{F_e}, P_{U_p}, P_{U_m}, P_{F_m}, P_{N_o}, P_{N_t}, P_{T_r}, P_{E_r}, P_{T_s}\} \tag{2.49}$$

where the subscripts are the symbols for the respective parameters.

When studying an object, the performance of the object is the subset of these indices of interest to the analyst. A number of functions are available for combining this set of indices into a single performance index. The most commonly used function is a weighted summation.

$$P = \sum_{1}^{n} \mathrm{w}_n \frac{P_{m_n}}{P_{r_n}} \tag{2.50}$$

where w_n *is a weighting function.*

In practice, assigning appropriate values to performance references can be more difficult than measuring the parameters. The aim of any modifications to improve performance is to get the performance index to approach 1.

$$P_i \rightarrow 1 \tag{2.51}$$

Similarly we can extend our definition of correctness (*C*).

$$C = \frac{C_m}{C_r} \tag{2.3}$$

$$C = \frac{T_{d_m}}{T_{s_i}} \tag{2.52}$$

$$C = 1 \tag{2.53}$$

for a correct object.

Correctness for a correct object is the set of ratios of measured transformations on the data (T_{d_m}) to required transformations on the data (T_{d_i}), and equals 1 for a correct object.

2.10 Validation of formulation

There are a number of ways of testing and validating a formulation:

- carrying out experiments to see if the results conform with those predicted by the formulation,
- investigating current practice to see if it fits the formulation (Sections 2.11 and 2.12), and
- applying the formulation to currently unanswered questions in the field, to see if it provides any insight into those problems (Section 2.13).

We have conducted a number of experiments to validate the formulation. These experiments are used as case studies in Chapters 7 and 8 to illustrate software debugging techniques and performance measurement methods. We built a hybrid performance analyser to measure the parameters defined in the formulation. A partial description of this tool is given in Section 6.6, and some measurements at the program execution level are given in Chapter 7. Also, we built a small computer system, a terminal multiplexer for a local-area network, with a full set of instrumentation based upon this formulation (Section 8.4). The measurements shown in the graphs, included in this chapter, were made on this system using the hybrid performance analyser.

2.11 Current measurement practice

For the formulation to provide a valid basis for unifying the field, it must encompass current measurement practice. Therefore, as part of the validation process, we must compare it to current measurement practice. One or two examples at each level are discussed briefly in this section, and current practice is discussed in detail in Chapter 4. The PRIME system (Ferrari, 1973) included two firmware tools for monitoring **microcode-level** activity (Section 9.4.1). One measured the utilization of the functional units (modules) of the processor (object), and the other measured the flow of control (execution path) of the microprograms.

Measurement at the **machine-code level** has changed little since the measurement of Maniac programs (Herbst *et al.*, 1955). Today, instruction mix measurements (Gibson, 1970) are used to optimize microcomputer instruction sets (Fairclough, 1982). If the set of instructions is an object then the instruction mix is the set of module execution frequencies.

Knuth (1971) used two different approaches to study the execution of FORTRAN programs at the **high-level language level**: the method of program profiles and the method of program status sampling (Section 4.4.2). A program profile was a module execution frequency table where the object was the program and the modules were FORTRAN statements. The second method produced a module utilization histogram which showed how much time was spent in each module rather than how often it executed. Knuth's suggestion that such measurements should impact compiler design has received an unusual twist in the design of the RISC microprocessor (Patterson and Sequin, 1982) where module execution frequencies, and utilizations, for high-level languages were used in the selection of hardware features to optimize instruction execution times.

Programs have been measured at the **block-structure level** with checkpoints (Ferrari, 1978a). A checkpoint is an instruction which is inserted into the code of a program, at the end of each structure. It either collects and stores data itself or calls a measurement routine. From this data, values can be assigned to all the parameters defined in the formulation. Ferrari demonstrates the use of checkpoints to measure execution time, module utilization, module execution frequency, and execution path (Example 9.3 in Ferrari, 1978a).

At the **program level**, benchmarks of programs (Patterson and Piepho, 1982) are a common measurement of execution time. In the design of a tool to analyse crashes of Ada programs, Holdsworth (1983) considered answers to the following questions to be a sufficient set of debugging aids:

- Where am I?
- Where have I come from?
- What are the values of the variables?
- How did I get here?

The above questions all pertain to the state of the program (Equation 2.47).

The **task level** is one of the more difficult levels at which to make measurements. Understanding individual processes in an operating system is relatively easy, but understanding the complex web of interaction between processes can be mind boggling. The instrumentation of Multics (Saltzer and Gintell, 1970; Section 8.1) included the following task level measurements:

- execution time and frequency of execution of supervisor modules,

- the utilization of memory segments (module utilization),
- the number of page misses per segment,
- the number of procedure calls,
- queue lengths (stimulus information), and
- the effect of the systems multiprogramming effort on individual users (execution time as a function of stimulus information).

At the **system level**, measurement of the working set helps the analyst to understand the inter-relation between the hardware and the operating systems. The object of interest is the set of memory pages, and the parameter of interest is module utilization - profiles of page usage and page misses. Other system level measurements include the measurement of CPU utilization, system response time, throughput rate, and capacity, all of which can be described in terms of appropriate objects.

One area where the formulation may need to be expanded, to take account of the complementary nature of computers and people, is in the measurement of behavioural issues (Miller and Thomas, 1977; Section 10.2). However, measurements that have been made of the use of graphics input devices (English *et al.*, 1967), and keyboards (Montgomery, 1982), have involved the measurement of response times, which can be considered to be the set of execution times of an object, where the object comprises the person plus input device.

The measures described in the formulation of performance measurement can also be used to obtain the extent of parallel objects. Utilization profiles give some clue as to the amount of parallelism. However, to measure the overlap of parallel modules, timing measurements have to be synchronized to an appropriate time base. Further research is needed in this area (Chapter 9).

2.12 Models

Kumar and Davidson (1980) have argued that a hierarchy of performance models, ranging from analytical models to detailed simulation models, is a very useful tool in the design of computer systems. The development and validation of models, both structural and functional, requires the measurement of actual system values. Application of the formulation to modelling is a subject for further research (Section 10.1); however, the following model information can be obtained by measuring parameters defined in the formulation:

- Service times, and visit ratios, for analytical queuing models (Rose, 1978) can be calculated by taking the mean of the execution times of appropriate modules, and the mean of their frequencies of execution.

Multiprogramming level, and job class, can be obtained as stimulus information.

- A simulation model represents the behaviour of a system in the time domain. As there is a conceptual similarity between simulation and measurement, the results obtained by measuring execution time, and execution path, can be used for the development, and validation, of simulation models.

2.13 Corollaries

Finally, we will hypothesize a number of outcomes of the application of the formulation to performance measurement. If the formulation is valid, it will provide a general, overall context within which measurement and evaluation can take place (Section 6.1). Within this context, we can design measurement experiments to study performance problems. Once we define the problem to be studied, the next step is to select an appropriate object, divide it into modules, and determine at what level in the hierarchy we wish to make measurements. Then we can define stimulus variables. And finally, we can choose a measurement tool suitable for that level in the hierarchy, and measure the required parameters.

Applying the formulation to actual measurement situations should produce the following results:

- A clear definition of what the parameters to be measured are, at each level in the hierarchy (Section 6.1).
- The design of a general purpose performance analyser (Section 6.4 – technology is no longer a serious limitation).
- A methodology for measuring the extent of objects at each level in the hierarchy (Section 6.1).
- A methodology for including performance instrumentation in a system at design time (Section 8.3).
- A set of criteria for the partitioning of the monitoring functions between hardware and software, and the cooperation and interaction of these functions, in a hybrid tool (Section 6.4).
- A specification detailing the signals needed on the pins of a microprocessor for performance measurement (Section 8.3).

In later chapters, we discuss each of these issues, apply the formulation, conduct experiments, and find that the results validate the formulation. Further work by other researchers will either validate the formulation of performance measurement or indicate the need for revision and expansion.

2.14 Conclusion

In this chapter, we have defined a program as an executable object. An object is defined recursively in terms of lower level objects. For this object, we have described a set of parameters which can be measured, a set of measures which apply to any object at any level in the object hierarchy. Parameter values and relationships between parameters can be displayed graphically. The formulation of the above measures into a set of equations is a formulation of performance measurement.

This formulation has been validated by:

- designing and executing experiments to test the formulation,
- comparing it to current practice, and
- hypothesizing and testing corollaries to the formulation.

So far, the results of these tests indicate a high degree of fit between the formulation and current practice. The measurements illustrated in this chapter were all made during experiments designed to test the formulation.

The formulation provides a general, overall context within which measurement and evaluation can take place. The purpose of measurement is not to collect numbers, but to gain insight into the actions of the objects under study. By appropriate selection of stimulus information, aided by graphical techniques of data analysis, we can gain this insight. Further research is needed to extend, validate and apply the formulation. A number of research areas, which flow out of the formulation, have been proposed.

Table 2.1 Symbols used and their meanings – roman and bold italic type.

Symbol	Meaning
f	mathematical function
w	weighting function
M	predicate
C	correctness of object
D	values assigned to variables
E	extent of object
F	function of object
H	execution history
K	context of object
M	meaning of object
P	performance of object
S	state of object
T	transformation
V	value of object

Table 2.2 Symbols used and their meanings – lower case italic type.

Symbol	Meaning
a_m	number of times module m was executed
a_{mq}	number of times path q of module m was executed
b_{mq}	individual module execution time
c_k	path execution count for path k
d_{mq}	execution time of path q in module m
e_m	execution frequency of module m
f_k	execution frequency of path k
m_m	module m
p_k	object execution path k
r_k	relative path execution time
r_{zk}	module to path execution time ratio
s_k	set of stimulus information for path k
s_m	set of stimulus information for module m
t_b	maximum module execution time
t_k	execution time of path k
t_p	maximum object execution time
u_k	path utilization
v_m	module utilization
Subscripts	
d	data
e	external event
i	internal event or performance index
k	object path number
m	module number, measured value
n	object level, parameter number
q	module path number
r	performance reference
t	time
z	position of module in object path

Table 2.3 Symbols used and their meanings – upper case italic type.

Symbol	Meaning
E	set of events
E_r	set of module to path execution time ratios
F_{en}	set of object execution frequencies
F_{mn}	set of module execution frequencies
I	input to object
J_c	job class
M	measurable predicate
M_s	static memory usage
M_u	dynamic memory usage
N_a	set of module execution counts
N_{cn}	set of path execution counts
N_e	total number of object executions
N_m	total number of module executions
N_o	object throughput
N_t	module throughput
O_n	object at level n
PC_t	program counter at time t
P_{en}	set of object execution paths
P_m	set of module execution paths
Q_d	quantity of data
R	results out of object
S_{in}	set of stimulus information
T	measurement period
T_{bn}	superset of module execution times
T_{en}	set of object execution times
T_m	set of module execution times
T_{sn}	set of normalized relative module execution times
T_{rn}	set of normalized relative path execution times
U_{mn}	set of module utilizations
U_{pn}	set of object path utilizations

Chapter 3
Other Formulations and Theories

'There is nothing new under the sun.'

Ecclesiastes 1:9

In the introduction to the previous chapter, we looked briefly at other formulations on which the formulation of performance measurement is based. Now we will consider several other formulations in more depth, particularly their conceptual model of an executing program, to see how they complement, predate, and are subsumed by our formulation of performance measurement. These formulations and theories show the capacity of the human mind for perceiving one object from many different perspectives.

3.1 Software science – Halstead (1977)

Maurice Halstead undertook an empirical study of algorithms to test his hypothesis that the count of operators and operands in a program is strongly correlated to the number of bugs. As a result of this study, he developed a set of laws to characterize algorithms. Like many others, he sought a way of analysing the complex problem of software production.

Halstead proposed an idealized software cycle, similar to the Carnot cycle in thermodynamics, which consisted of four processes: compilation from high-level language to assembly language, optimization of the assembly language, decompilation of the assembly language back into a higher level language, and finally expansion of the resultant high-level code back to the original code. As this cannot be done on an actual program without some loss of information, the cycle is considered to be ideal. To study the relationships between points on the cycle, Halstead defined two measurable properties: operators and operands, where operators are those parts which affect the value or ordering of operands, and operands are the variables or constants. Operands are used to split a program, written in any language, into tokens. All software science measures are functions of the counts of these tokens. The basic metrics are defined as:

$$n_1 = \textit{number of unique operators} \tag{3.1}$$

$$n_2 = \textit{number of unique operands} \tag{3.2}$$

$$N_1 = \textit{total occurrences of operators} \tag{3.3}$$

$$N_2 = \textit{total occurrences of operands} \tag{3.4}$$

$$f_{1,j} = \textit{occurrences of the jth most frequently used operator} \tag{3.5}$$

$$f_{1,i} = \textit{occurrences of the ith most frequently used operand} \tag{3.6}$$

$$\textit{where } j = 1 \,..\, n_1 \tag{3.7}$$

$$\textit{and } i = 1 \,..\, n_2 \tag{3.8}$$

Generally, any symbol or keyword in a program that specifies an algorithmic action is considered to be an operator, while a symbol used to represent data is considered to be an operand. Most punctuation marks are categorized as operators.

The vocabulary of a program n is:

$$n = n_1 + n_2 \tag{3.9}$$

and the length of the program N is:

$$N = N_1 + N_2 \tag{3.10}$$

and

$$N_1 = \sum_{j=1}^{n_1} f_{1,j} \tag{3.11}$$

$$N_2 = \sum_{i=1}^{n_2} f_{1,i} \tag{3.12}$$

The length N is obtained by observation in contrast to a second length measure N which is calculated:

$$N = n_1 \log_2 n_1 + n_2 \log_2 n_2 \tag{3.13}$$

An analysis of the first dozen algorithms published in the 'Algorithms Section' of the *Communications of the Association for Computing Machinery* showed a very close correlation between measured and calculated length. However, this result is based on programs written by experts. Can the same be said of programs written by average programmers?

Additional metrics are defined using these basic terms. The volume V of a program is the actual size of a program in a computer in bits, if a uniform binary encoding for vocabulary is used.

$$\begin{aligned} V &= N * \log_2 n \\ &= \textit{length} * \textit{vocabulary} \end{aligned} \tag{3.14}$$

The potential volume V of a program is the volume not of the optimum solution for the problem but of the smallest piece of code required to invoke a solution to the problem, for example a procedure call with operands as parameters. This makes LOGO one of the highest level programming languages, because of its ability to define procedures as new words in the language. Thus, volume becomes a measure of program level L rather than a measure of algorithm quality (optimality).

$$L = \frac{V}{V} \tag{3.15}$$

The value of L ranges from zero to one, with $L = 1$ representing a program written at the highest possible level (i.e. minimum volume). As the volume of a program increases the program level decreases and the difficulty D increases.

$$D = \frac{1}{L} \tag{3.16}$$

Thus, the use of high-level language constructs should reduce the difficulty of programming. The effort E required to implement a computer program increases as the size of the program increases.

$$E = \frac{V}{L} = D * V \tag{3.17}$$

The time taken to implement a program T is a function of the programming effort and the time required by the human brain to perform the most elementary discrimination.

$$T = \frac{E}{S} \tag{3.18}$$

where $5 \leq S \leq 20$ *discriminations per second.*

In his book, Halstead (1977) also looks at the ratio of operators to operands, program intelligence content, and program purity. A large amount of empirical evidence suggests that software science is the best measure of programming effort we now have. Some researchers have raised serious questions about the underlying theory of software science (Shen *et al.*, 1983), while others have produced experimental evidence supporting some of the metrics (Christensen *et al.*, 1981; Fitzsimmons and Love, 1978). Researchers agree that the simple measure of counting the number of lines of code is inadequate for predicting programming effort. They also agree that we need either a model of the programming process, based upon a manageable number of major factors, or a scientific theory of algorithm development.

Halstead's intuitive model appears to be: programs are produced by programmers working through a process of mental manipulation of the unique operators and operands. Thus, volume can also be interpreted as the number of mental comparisons needed to write a program and programming effort is measured in terms of elementary mental discriminations. Coulter (1983) has questioned the validity of this model on psychological grounds. Short term memory properties have been incorporated into models involving other memory stages. Studies of human memory searches do not support a fundamental software science conjecture: that humans use binary search, implying that we store things in ordered lists. Results concerning psychological time appear to be misused in software science; consequently, those theories were applied to the wrong stages of memory. Two theoretical problems with software science are raised by Shen *et al.* (1983): firstly, no method of classifying operators and operands in high-level language programs is provided; and secondly, some of the assumptions are weak.

Software science metrics (Equations 3.1-3.8) are obtained from a static analysis of the program text in contrast to our performance measurement formulation, which is based on the dynamics of execution. Hence, at most, we can expect the two hypotheses to be complementary, but, as they are based upon different axioms, they can neither prove nor disprove each other. Software science seeks to answer a different set of questions.

3.2 Software physics – Kolence (1972)

While many researchers have taken up Halstead's work, few have done independent tests of Kolence's formulation (Morris, 1976; Prichard, 1976; Febish, 1981), yet it bears greater relevance to performance measurement. Software physics deals with computer sizing and workloads, and has been used as a basis for the development of software performance monitors. Kenneth Kolence postulated a software physics based upon the same fundamental concepts as natural physics. Then he developed performance measures based on these concepts and sought to verify them empirically. Kolence saw that without a unified formulation the computer performance measurement field would continue to be an aggregation of measurement methods characterized by a state of confusion about how to interpret the data.

The basic constitutive definition of a science tells us what the objects of our investigation are made of. This definition determines the direction our research will take. Kolence proposed a basic constitutive definition for software physics: a software unit. A **software unit** is a set of transformations and other relationships (e.g. positional, etc.) over data, container and symbol structures. Our definition of an object (Section 2.5) is essentially identical to a software unit. It has the same hierarchical nature and consequently the same claim to a set of relationships which hold across the hierarchy.

Kolence defines the terms data, symbol structure, and container by example and does not give precise definitions. This is partly because the definition of a software unit is essentially hierarchic, and hence examples at levels in the hierarchy are easier to understand than a general definition. **Data** is the information being processed. **Symbol structure** is the set of labels by which the data is referenced and changed (i.e. the code). A **container** is the thing which holds the data, for example a register at the machine-code level, or a stack at a higher level.

The transformations and other relationships mentioned in the definition of a software unit have a domain - those containers from which the contents are transferred - and a range: those containers which receive the domain contents. The domain is effectively the set of inputs to the object and the range is the set of outputs. Those properties of a software unit which are dependent on both structure and relationship in the hierarchy are considered to be **level dependent**, and those properties which are independent of relationships in a hierarchy, and will therefore add up to the total value of the system, are considered to be **level invariant**. Kolence hypothesized the existence of conservation laws for all level invariant properties of software units.

The basic concepts of software physics are the software force, work, and energy of a software unit. **Software energy** is the capacity to cause a change in the state of a software unit. **Software work** is the actual change in energy state of a software unit effected by some transformation. One unit of software work is performed on a storage medium when one byte of that medium is altered. **Software power** is the software work performed per unit of time.

Software force F is defined by analogy with quantum physics as:

$$F = \frac{1}{c} * \frac{\Delta E}{\Delta t} \qquad (3.19)$$

where ΔE *is the change in energy in ergs*

Δt *is the time taken*

and c *is the velocity of light*

The direction of the force is from the domain of the transformation to the range. This definition raises the question: Is Kolence stretching the idea of a correspondence between natural physics and software physics a bit too far? After all, what does the speed of light have to do with the execution of a program?

Although these concepts are necessary to demonstrate the linkage between natural physics and software physics, the direct measurement of work and force is rather difficult. Also, the software energy available in a system is quite complicated to calculate. Operational definitions expressed in more measurable terms were developed to form a usable formulation for performance measurement (Kolence, 1985).

Units of work are defined directly in terms of changes in the contents of known containers. For example, we can measure the work (W_o) done by an I/O device, which transfers data in n byte blocks, by simply determining the number of containers (blocks) transferred.

$$W_o = \sum \textit{blocks transferred by each I/O operation} \tag{3.20}$$

Also, the work (W_c) done by a central processing unit is the number of memory accesses used by the central processing element, and thus is a function of the instruction mix (k) for a given program workload. Information theoretic work (W) done by a workload is:

$$W = kW_c + W_o \tag{3.21}$$

where $k = 1$ *for most uses within an installation.*

The work (W) performed by a machine is related to the work (W_{P_i}) performed by some software unit (P_i). This relationship (Equation 3.22) holds at all levels of the machine and software hierarchies. Thus, software work is conserved, and is level invariant with respect to both job mix and equipment hierarchies.

$$\begin{aligned} W &= \sum W_{P_i} = k \sum W_{cP_i} + \sum W_{P_i} \\ &= kW_c + W_o \end{aligned} \tag{3.22}$$

Software power (P), or rate of software work, is the work done per unit time, i.e. the number of memory accesses per unit time. Thus, power usage is proportional to CPU utilization - one of the standard performance measures. On the other hand, I/O power usage is not proportional to I/O device busy time, due to the variable rate of data transmission. Also, transmission time includes setup times (e.g. seek time) when no transmission can occur. Consequently, I/O power is seen to be level dependent.

$$P = \frac{W}{\Delta t} = \frac{kW_c}{\Delta t} + \frac{W_o}{\Delta t} = kP_c + P_o \tag{3.23}$$

Software energy is the product of the power used during a period of time and the length of the time period. It can be measured by counting the memory accesses. Maximum energy is consumed when the CPU is fully utilized and the input/output devices are transferring data at full speed. Thus, the software energy available for use by software units is partially dependent upon the machine configuration, the characteristics of the workload, and the operation of I/O devices.

Kolence claimed that measuring these properties will provide us with sufficient data to determine the effectiveness with which different computer systems will process various classes of workload. Thus, he proposed a scientific method for selecting computer systems. Kolence gave experimental data to support this claim, but others don't seem to be convinced as they have not taken up this methodology.

Kolence (1975) replaced a number of traditional measures with measures of work and work vectors, measures like the number of lines printed, CPU seconds used, and the number of I/O operations. Having got the numbers, what do they mean? While no one questions the importance of the concept of work in physics, we still measure the work done by a tip truck in cubic metres of earth moved, not in ergs. If the CPU is a module in an object, then Kolence's measure of the CPU power used by an object is proportional to our measure of module utilization. In the case of the power and the utilization of an I/O device the situation is more complex. The question 'Which measure, power or utilization, is more meaningful?' requires careful consideration.

Kolence started with a definition of a software unit very similar to the definition of an object we used in Chapter 2, but his world view led him in a different direction. Software physics deals only with capacity management: how to keep the computing equipment matched to the changing workload of a system. The idea of a software physics deeply related to natural physics has not been proven. However, the measures produced (work, energy, force, and power) provide a conceptual framework for thinking about performance.

3.3 Program performance indices – Ferrari (1978a)

Knuth (1968) has defined a program as:

> 'An expression of a computational method in a computer language.'

From the performance viewpoint, a program can be considered to be a black box which takes input data and transforms it to output data. The time taken for a correct program to execute is a measure of the degree of difficulty of the transformation. When comparing two programs which effect the same transformation, execution time becomes a performance measure. A second, related index, is the price we have to pay for the resources used by the program.

The basic question of program performance analysis is: 'How does a program spend its execution time?' If a program is considered to be a set (S) of disjointed states ($S_1 .. S_n$) then the behaviour of a program can be described as the sequence of states visited during execution and by the time spent in each state.

$$S = (S_1 .. S_n) \qquad (3.24)$$

$$Sequence = \{i_j(t_j)\}\ [j = 1,2..,;\ i_j \in (1 .. n)] \qquad (3.25)$$

where t_j is the duration of the jth interval of execution which is spent in state S_{ij}, and i is the state number. If, for all j and for $k = 1..n$, we define:

$$t_j(k) = t_j \text{ when } k = i_j \text{, and} \qquad (3.26)$$

$$t_j(k) = 0 \text{ when } k \neq i_j \qquad (3.27)$$

then the total time spent in state S_i during the execution of the program is:

$$t(i) = \sum_{j=1}^{r} t_j(i) \tag{3.28}$$

where r is the number of intervals into which the execution time has been subdivided. The execution time (t) is

$$t = \sum_{i=1}^{n} t(i) \tag{3.29}$$

This is clearly a subset of the formulation developed in Chapter 2, in which object execution time and module execution time are defined, if a state is considered to be a module. The representation is more complex, but the concepts are the same. If modules correspond to various hardware resources, then we can characterize program performance in terms of resource demand patterns, by decomposing the object execution time into module execution times, and associated module execution paths (the sequence of states visited during execution). This characterization is very close to that normally used for calculating charges for program execution.

Other types of decompositions, leading to different performance indices, are also possible. For example, a program may be divided into blocks. At any instant during the measurement period, the program will be accessing one of these blocks. Referencing a block, or a distinct subset of blocks, may be viewed as a state of the program, and the execution time may be decomposed into the intervals spent in each state. The sequence of states (execution path) defined by the blocks is a description of the referencing pattern produced by the program when processing a specific set of input data.

Ferrari raises the possibility of other decompositions, for example a program trace, and suggests that practically all the questions regarding the behaviour of a program during execution can be answered if the trace and listing of a program are known. He then illustrates this technique (Example 9.1, Ferrari 1978a) by decomposing a FORTRAN program into blocks, first at the subprogram level, and then at the instruction level. In each instance, execution paths and execution times for the blocks are measured and discussed. If the frequency counts for each statement are known then a program profile can be drawn. Ferrari then goes on to discuss the use of the address trace (or reference string) of a program in studying the page allocation strategy of a virtual memory system.

Our performance measurement formulation is a generalization and expansion of Ferrari's program performance indices, and embodies much of it. Kolence's idea of a software unit was used in the generalization, and extension was achieved by defining a full set of decompositions. Ferrari's viewpoint is slightly different to ours: he considers a sequence of states where we consider a sequence of modules which are initiated by state changes; but the result is the same. Thus, Ferrari's chapter (1978a, Chapter 9) on 'The Evaluation of Program Performance' is a rich source of ideas for applying our formulation to measurement and for evaluating the results of those measurements.

3.4 Measurement concepts – Svobodova (1976a)

Liba Svobodova's book on performance measurement includes a small section (Chapter 6.1) on measurement concepts. She says the measurement problem is to determine:

- what information is pertinent to a specific measurement objective,
- where such information can be found, and
- how it can be extracted and recorded.

Svobodova's model of a system is a sequence of changes of system state, where information about system state is contained in the system's memories. A change in system state marks either the beginning or the end of a period of activity (or inactivity) of a system component (hardware, software or process). Since several components (processes) can be active simultaneously, a change in the system state is a change in the level of system activity. A change in system state is called an event. Events can be both hardware and software related.

System state can be described by a vector composed of binary elements representing the states (O or I) of individual memory elements. An activity a_k can then be represented by a logical function that has the value of 1 on a subset x_k of the set of all possible states x, $x_k \subset x$. An initiation event e_k occurs when an activity a_k begins, causing the system to change from state $x_{old} \neg\in x_k$ to state $x_{new} \in x_k$. A termination event $\neg e_k$ occurs when an activity a_k terminates, causing the system to change from state $x_{old} \in x_k$ to state $x_{new} \neg\in x_k$.

Using this model of system behaviour, Svobodova divides measurements into four categories according to the type of information recorded about an activity. For a measurement period $t_o .. t$ the categories are:

- An event trace, which is a sequential record of all initiation and termination events during the measurement period. An activity can be completely described by a sequence of pairs (t_{ki}, T_{ki}), where t_{ki} is the time of the ith occurrence of this activity and T_{ki} is the corresponding duration of this activity. The result of obtaining this information from the event trace is a time stamped record of all the invocations of the activity, indicating when the activity started and its duration on each occasion. She appears to make no allowance for the pausing and resumption of an activity, unless the resumed activity is considered to be a separate activity. The problem with the latter is that the pause can be caused by an external agent, for example an interrupt, which has no relevance to the current activity, and hence the place where the activity pauses is arbitrary. Interaction between activities has not been considered by Svobodova, but it could be studied by drawing the event trace as an activity flow graph.

- Relative activity r_k, which is the ratio of the total time of the activity a_k and the total elapsed time.

$$r_k = \frac{1}{t - t_o} \int_{t_o}^{t} a_k(\tau) d\tau \qquad (3.30)$$

where $t - t_o > 0$,

$a_k = 1$ if $x(\tau) \in x_k$,

and $a_k = 0$ *otherwise.*

- Event frequency (c_k), which is the number of times an activity is initiated during the measurement period i.e. the same idea as module execution frequencies.

$$c_k = \frac{1}{t - t_o} \sum_{t_n} e_k(\tau) \qquad (3.31)$$

where $t \geq t_n \geq t_o$,

$e_k = 1$ for $\tau = t_n$,

$e_k = 0$ *otherwise*,

and t_n *is the number of occurrences of* e_k.

- The distribution of activity intervals ($f_{kn}(T)$), which is the distribution of the duration times (T) of an activity (a_k) at the time of the nth termination of the activity, i.e. the same idea as an execution time histogram.

$$f_{kn}(T) = \frac{1}{n}\sum_{i=1}^{n} g(T, T_{ki}) \tag{3.32}$$

$$\textit{where } g(T,d) = 1 \text{ for } T = d$$

$$\text{and } g(T,d) = 0 \textit{ otherwise.}$$

The measurement categories presented by Svobodova all have equivalents in our formulation, and are a subset of the latter, although her mathematical description reflects a slightly different perspective on program execution.

Ferrari, Svobodova, and McKerrow are using the same model of program execution but are looking at it from different perspectives. In each case, the concepts of time sequence of events, state change (event), and activity between state changes (modules) are present. Ferrari emphasizes the time sequence of states and pays little attention to the activity between states, on the assumption that significant activity will be reflected by the occurrence of a new state. Svobodova emphasizes the occurrence of events (state changes) as these indicate the start and end of activities (modules), on the assumption that we are interested in how often each activity occurs and for how long. I emphasize the activities (modules); using the events to detect initiation, pausing, resumption, and termination of modules; and using the state (stimulus information) to give meaning to the action of the object. My perspective is that we want to know why execution has occurred the way it has, as well as what execution has occurred, how long the execution took, and the order in which the modules were executed. Thus I have attempted to produce a more comprehensive measure of system activity.

3.5 Monitoring program execution – Plattner and Nievergelt (1981)

Bernhard Plattner and Jurg Nievergelt were interested in dynamic program analysis, particularly as a debugging tool for use during software development. They developed a set of basic concepts of program execution which they used as the basis of a series of execution monitoring experiments. The program under test was compiled using a modified compiler, and run on a target computer. The modified compiler produced an extensive description of the target process, and they added a hardware breakpoint device to the target processor. During the execution of the target process, the hardware breakpoint device sent state information through a first in first out queue to a monitoring processor. The monitoring processor used this state information together with the extensive description of the target process to model precisely the execution of the target process. This monitor worked in real time, did not impact the target process, and used the queue to solve synchronization problems. However, the monitor appears to be suitable only for the study of programs in isolation.

Plattner and Nievergelt thought of a process as the trajectory of a point moving through space. They defined the monitoring activities of interest as: requesting notification when the trajectory enters some prespecified region; halting the motion of the point; and restarting a new trajectory at some other point in space. The structure of this state space $S(P)$ is completely defined by the program P in execution, where P is written in a programming language PL, and the semantics of the programming language. A point s in $S(P)$ is a potential state of some execution of P: it corresponds to an assignment of values to all variables of P and a specification of a point of control PC. By executing P, starting in an initial state so, a process denoted by $p(P,so) = so \;..\; sn$, will be created. In this context, the PC is not simply the hardware program counter, but includes all procedure calling chains of the target process. A process state consists of a control component (the PC) and a data component (input data and internal variables). Thus the trajectory is defined as the sequence of states through which the program moves as it executes.

The monitoring process requires that the entire state space be accessible, i.e. the monitoring process should have a complete record of all the states of the process as well as the states through which the trajectory passes. Monitoring is achieved by means of predicates that assign a truth value to a target process, and actions that modify the target process (they wanted the ability to stop the target process and restart it under different conditions - a useful facility when debugging programs). Predicates fall into two classes: process predicates, which answer questions relating to the process - for example: 'How often are two statements executed in sequence?'; and state predicates - for example: 'Let me know when the trajectory crosses the boundary from one region into another.'

Plattner and Nievergelt also discuss the complexity of the structure of the state space with respect to programming language data structures, and to dynamic memory allocation. The state space of a recursive tree traversal program is discussed to illustrate some of the details involved in defining the notions of process state and state space.

These concepts are based on a description of program execution very similar to Ferrari's, but the underlying conceptual model is different. This model is useful for studying processes in isolation, but is restrictive when studying interaction between processes and processors. Is each process a separate trajectory with a separate point, or does one point traverse all trajectories, or do we have several spaces each with their own points and trajectories? In each of these cases, how do you describe the jump from one trajectory to another? Thus, their formulation is not as general as ours, but it does provide an interesting perspective on a principle underlying our formulation: that debugging programs and performance evaluation are differences of application of formulation and tools, not conceptual differences in either formulation or tools.

3.6 A sequential program model – Franta *et al.* (1982)

Franta *et al.* (1982) worked on the development of a distributed system testbed at the Honeywell Corporate Computer Sciences Center. They believed that instrumentation of computer systems is concerned with the observation and control of events, specifically those events that constitute or precipitate changes of computer system state. They formalized the notion of an event using the following model of a centralized system. Their extension of this model to cover distributed systems is discussed in Section 9.2.2.

A variable or data object x is an entity with a name 'x' that can take on any value $V(x)$ of a certain defined set of values, and upon which any of a defined set of operations can be performed. The set of values together with the group of operations is called the data type of x. The state of x is its value $V(x)$. Given a set X of n objects $[x_1 \,..\, x_n]$ where x_i is of type T_i, the current state q of X is given by a vector of values of the objects.

$$q(x) = \langle V(x_1) \,..\, V(x_n)\rangle \qquad (3.33)$$

The state space $S(X)$ is the set of all possible such vectors.

A single terminating sequential program B defined over a set of objects X effects a state transition on X in that it is invoked with the objects in one state $q(X)$, and terminates with the objects in another state $q^1(X)$. Such a program may be modelled as a binary relation M on $S(X)$; M is a collection of ordered pairs of states. The interpretation of this relation is that the pair $\langle q(X), q^1(X)\rangle$ is an element of M when B is guaranteed to halt when invoked from state $q(X)$, and when $q^1(X)$ is one of the states in which B can halt when invoked from $q(X)$. From this interpretation it follows that the domain of M (i.e. the set of states that can be first components of pairs of M) is exactly the set of initial states from which termination of B is guaranteed.

A particular execution of the program B over X defines a state sequence.

$$s(X,B) = q_o(X) \,..\, q_n(X) \qquad (3.34)$$

where $q_o(X)$ is the state at invocation of B. If $q_o(X)$ is an element of the domain of M, then $s(X,B)$ is finite; and if $q_n(X)$ is the last state in $s(X,B)$, then $\langle q_o(X), q_n(X)\rangle$ is an element of M.

There is a state transition sequence

$$h(X,B) = t_1(X) \mathinner{..} t_m(X) \tag{3.35}$$

associated with the state sequence $s(X,B)$, where the transition $t_i(X)$ is the ordered pair of states $<q_{i-1}(X), q_i(X)>$. These transitions are referred to as events, and the event sequence is termed the history of the program. The set $H(X,B)$ of all possible history sequences constitutes the set of possible histories of program B. For a deterministic sequential program B, there is a unique history $h(X,B)$ for each pair of initial and final states $<q_o(X), q_n(X)>$.

This is a perfectly valid conceptual model, albeit rather complex, of program execution based upon the data flow concept, i.e. events are defined in terms of what happens to the data. Once again, an event trace is produced, but the event trace lacks timing information. Also the concept of execution path is missing. As it is, this model is inadequate for performance measurement.

3.7 A measure of computational work – Hellerman (1972)

Hellerman (1972), Constantine (1968), and Rozwadowski (1973) have attempted to define a work unit based on information theory. Hellerman claims that the work done by a process is a universal measure of performance. To establish a consistent method for measuring work, a canonical formalism must be found, a formalism with which all processes can be implemented. The quantitative attribute of this formalism which measures work is the universal measure of performance.

A number of canonical forms have been suggested: logic based on NAND gates, Turing machines, and formal descriptions in terms of inputs and outputs; but in each case examples can be found where the proposed quantitative attribute fails as a measure of work. Hellerman (1972) proposed a measure that is a function of the number of inputs to the process and of how these inputs are distributed among the outputs. The canonical form of a process is its table lookup implementation, and the quantitative attribute is the quantity of information stored in memory.

Let $f: X \rightarrow Y$ be a process defined on a finite number $|X|$ of inputs. The domain X may be partitioned into n domain classes X_i, each comprising all points in the inverse image of some point in the range Y. The work of f is then

$$w(f) = \sum_{i=1}^{n} |X_i| \log_2 \left\{ \frac{|X|}{|X_i|} \right\} \tag{3.36}$$

where $|X|$ = *number of possible inputs*
$|X_i|$ = *number of inputs which can produce output* Y_i
n = *number of possible outputs.*

Since computational work is measured in terms of information, the unit of work (a wit) is the same as the unit of information (a bit). Computational power (a wat) is measured in terms of wits per second.

This contrasts with Kolence's measure of work, where a unit of work is a change in the state of a bit rather than the fact that information is stored in the bit. Thus, this definition of work does not appear to take into account the number of actions performed on the input to produce an output.

3.8 Program behaviour: models and measurements – Spirn (1977)

The development of virtual memory systems gave impetus to the modelling of programs, as a separate, but parallel, endeavour to the modelling of systems. Jeffrey Spirn (1977) attempted to draw together the concepts of program behaviour in a survey of the field. He argued that programs must also be modelled for performance studies of systems. A program does many things which might be of interest to model: it references memory, issues input/output requests, generates various kinds of interrupts, acquires and releases resources, communicates with other programs, and interacts with the user. In his book, Spirn concentrates on memory reference behaviour, primarily because little is known about other aspects of program behaviour.

Central to his models of program behaviour is the phenomenon of locality. The principal of **extrinsic locality** is: a good predictor of a program's future behaviour is its immediate past behaviour. In contrast, the principle of **intrinsic locality** is: expected future behaviour will only agree with past behaviour while the program is in a given state. Thus, an intrinsic locality model consists of a state transition mechanism, and a characterization of the behaviour within each state. In contrast, extrinsic locality models are ignorant of internal state transitions. Thus, extrinsic locality is specified by an external measurement, whereas intrinsic locality is specified by a state. In the study of memory reference behaviour, extrinsic locality denotes the set of addresses (or pages, at a higher level) referenced recently by a task. Intrinsic locality denotes the set of addresses likely to be referenced while the task remains in its current state.

A program is a sequence of instructions written by a programmer. When discussing program behaviour, we mean the behaviour of programs *in execution* on a processor. Interruptions to the program are ignored by postulating a **virtual time** clock, which runs only while the given program is executing. A program in execution in virtual time is called a **task**.

The memory references of a task are the set $r(1) .. r(k)$, where $r(t) \in N$ is the page referenced at virtual time t and $N = 0 .. n-1$ is the set of pages belonging to the task. A sequence of references $r(t) .. r(t+k)$ in some virtual time interval is called a **reference string**. $S(t)$ is the set of pages in main memory just after the reference at time t. For all t we have $S(t) \subseteq N$, and $|S(t)| \leq m(t)$, where $m(t)$ is the memory allocation of the task at time t, and $M(t) = 0 .. m(t)-1$ is the set of page frames in main memory allocated to the task. The set of pages currently 'in use' by the task is the locality set $L(t)$, where $L(t) \subseteq N$ and $|L(t)| \leq n$.

The working set at time t, $W(t,T)$, consists of the set of distinct pages in $r(r-T+1)..r(t)$. The working set size (number of pages) of $W(t,T)$ is $w(t,T)$, and $w(T)$ is the virtual time average value of $w(t,T)$ over a specified time interval. The **working set curve** is a plot of $w(T)$ against T for a given task, where T is the time taken for a task to complete one reference to memory (average of memory references with and without page faults).

In his book, Spirn develops several models of program behaviour: a working set model, intrinsic locality models, stack models, an independent reference model, etc. These models are used to study paging and paging algorithms. Measurement for, and validation of, these models is also discussed.

3.9 Workload models – Hellerman and Conroy (1975)

All measures of performance are based on a model of the system being monitored. One popular class of models are workload models, or job processing models (Hellerman and Conroy, 1975; and other books). A workload model is an analytical model which yields equations that relate parameters of workload, system resources, and scheduling to performance. Seen from this perspective, a system is an interconnected configuration of resources supplied with a workload of jobs.

A workload model consists of:

- A workload description – a statement of how jobs are characterized, for example by arrival time, required execution time, or resource usage. This description becomes important when classifying jobs for measurement experiments; for example, benchmarks using a synthetic workload, which should be representative of the expected workload.

- System structure – the individual resources, resource queues, and input/output paths.
- Scheduling – the way jobs are selected for execution, and resources are allocated to jobs.
- Performance indices – measures of the 'goodness' of the system. Measures are categorized into two classes: user oriented measures, such as response time and throughput, called job stream performance; and system oriented measures, such as resource utilization and overlap, called resource performance.

Complex systems are difficult to manage intellectually, so we develop models to help us deal with that complexity. These models are an abstraction of a portion of the system, and reflect the goals of our performance study. Consequently, there is no single workload model for all systems, but rather a methodology for developing workload models. This methodology is based on queuing theory, a mathematical theory of how limited resources are shared among comparatively unlimited users. The relationship between the measurement parameters defined in our formulation of performance measurement and the parameters of a queuing model are discussed in Chapter 10.

3.10 Conclusion

In conclusion, all measures of performance are based on models, theories, or formulations. The measures you make are determined by the model you use. As a model is an abstraction of a highly complex system from one perspective, a variety of models exists for performance evaluation. Some models are specific to the system under study, others are more general. From the descriptions of the models, theories, and formulations proposed for performance measurement that we have described in this chapter, we see that the model on which our formulation of performance measurement is based is general enough to include their key elements. Hence, we have been able to use it to bring together a wide range of seemingly disparate measures, tools, techniques, and models.

Chapter 4
Measurement Tools and Techniques

Two approaches to performance measurement are found in practice: the stimulus approach and the analytical approach (Svobodova, 1976a). In the stimulus approach, a system is treated as a black box, with a limited number of known functions. Stimuli (simulated inputs) are supplied to the black box and its response (output) is measured. This record is a benchmark. In the analytical approach, a system is separated into parts, and the internal behaviour of each part is measured in detail. At times, these approaches are combined. Both involve measurement, and both can be used at any level in the object hierarchy.

To conduct an experiment, the target process is executed under the control of a monitoring process, which supplies the stimulus and records the response. Data can be transferred between these processes over three distinct paths (Figure 4.1):

1. Information obtained with software tools is either passed to an internal monitoring process or to an external hardware tool. The latter combination of tools forms a hybrid tool.

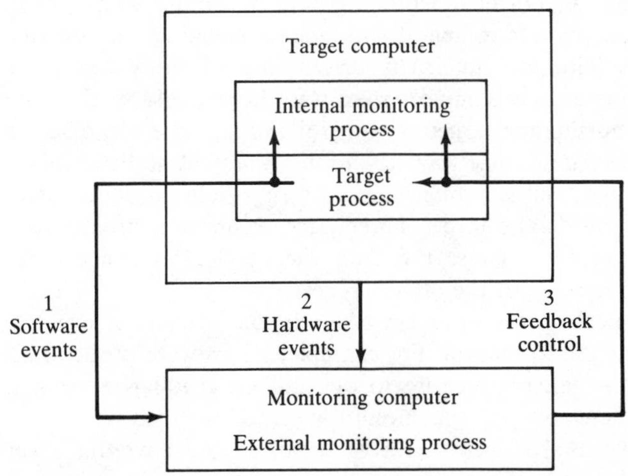

Figure 4.1 Information paths between a target process and a monitoring process.

2. Hardware event information is collected with hardware probes. This information can be recorded, or transformed using counters and comparators (a hardware tool).
3. Stimuli are supplied to the target process from the monitoring process. Over the same path, information can be fed back to a target process, for use in the adaptive control of the operating system.

The data paths used by a monitoring tool to collect information, and the location of the monitoring process - either internal to the target computer or in a separate monitoring computer - classify the tool into one of the three major categories: software, hardware or hybrid. Firmware tools are often considered to be a separate classification, but they generally form part of a tool in one of the other categories.

4.1 Measurement tool modules

A measurement tool can be divided into four conceptual sections: sensor, transformer, analyser, and indicator (Figure 1.4). The **sensor** section is the interface between the target process and the measurement tool, that is the front end of the measurement tool. The sensor detects events of interest and measures the magnitude of the quantities being monitored. Sensors are often referred to as probes. A software probe is usually a sub-program, inserted into the target process, and a hardware probe is usually a set of connectors, attached to the back plane or to special test points. Data collected by probes is either in the form of single bits (flags) or in functional groups of parallel signals (words).

Sensors operate in one of two modes depending on how the action of sensing is initiated: internally driven, or externally driven. Externally driven tools usually sample system state in response to the occurrence of an event outside the target system, for example the end of a time period. Data collected in this way has to be analysed statistically to produce meaningful results. Internally driven tools usually detect events occurring inside the target system, for example a procedure call or an interrupt vector. Thus, the data they collect is synchronized to the internal operation of the target process.

A typical sensor produces a continuous stream of event descriptors and stimulus information. For example, a hardware probe attached to an address bus can produce up to one million readings a second. At this rate, the memory of the monitoring tool is filled in a few seconds, leaving the analyst with a lot of detailed data covering a very limited period. As we move up the object hierarchy, the rate of event generation drops rapidly, from microseconds at the machine code level to milliseconds at the process level - roughly an order of magnitude per level. Only a subset of this observable information is of interest in any one measurement experiment.

The volume of data available from the probes is reduced to this subset in the **transformer** section. If the volume of data is reduced prior to storage, the monitor may be able to store several minutes of recording, enabling the analyst to observe a more realistic set of system operations. Usually, the transformer selects, and often massages, the subset of measured data to produce the set of measurements relevant to the experiment. Events of interest are selected from the event stream with comparators. These events are either recorded or used to trigger the recording of other information, often by mapping the event descriptor to a structure of data pointers. Another way to reduce the volume of data is to count events. Counter outputs are recorded, and can trigger the recording of other information. Finally the transformer adds time stamps to event and stimulus records. In summary, operations performed by the transformer section are:

- Data is stored without change.
- Data is masked to remove unwanted bits before storage.
- Data is compared to reference values, and then flags are stored, which represent: equal to, less than, greater than, within range, and outside range.
- Data is logically manipulated by a function generator before storage - for example, two signals ANDed.
- Sequences of data patterns are detected and stored.
- Sequences of data patterns are detected and used to initiate storage of selected data sets, which occur either before, during, or after the sequence.
- Successive data inputs are compared and the results stored.
- The results of the above filters can be counted, i.e. counting the occurrence of specific data patterns.
- The time period between the occurrence of specific data patterns can be measured.
- Some of the above filters can be combined to produce more complex reduction schemas.

The resultant set of information (event trace and stimulus information) is stored in a database, for example the object record described in Chapter 6. Small quantities of data are held in the tools memory and larger quantities are held on back-up store. The creation of this database is an important function of the transformer.

In the **analyser** section, the data stored in the database is processed to produce the final output of the experiment, for example tables and graphs (Section 2.8). These outputs plus the database information are displayed by the **indicator** section. The analysis to be performed upon the data is determined by the hypothesis the experiment was designed to test. Analysis may take place at a later time using recordings of several experiments. However, there are significant advantages in being able to analyse the data, on-line, as the experiment progresses (Fuller *et al.*, 1973):

- Analysis may indicate a flaw in the measurement specification, or inadequacies in the filtering done by the transformer. On-line analysis enables these to be modified during the experiment, thus curtailing useless measurements.
- Analysis may indicate an error in the hypothesis, confirm the hypothesis, or indicate the need for further experiments. On the basis of this analysis, the experiment can be modified and re-run, speeding up the evaluation process.
- On-line tools can be used to test and debug programs interactively.
- The results of real-time analysis can be used to tune the operating system dynamically.
- On-line analysis gives the analyst greater control over the experiment, and reduces evaluation time (Aschenbrenner *et al.*, 1971).

4.2 Measurement tool characteristics

Any measurement instrument can be described in terms of a set of characteristics typical of that class of tool. The characteristics used to describe performance monitors are: interference, accuracy, precision, resolution, scope, pre-reduction capabilities, ease of use, compatibility, and cost (Ferrari, 1978a). **Interference** occurs when a monitoring tool impacts the operation of the system. It can occur in a number of ways:

- Incorrect connection of hardware probes can degrade signals causing apparent hardware faults.
- Software tools use memory space, reducing the space available to the target process.
- The execution of a software tool uses system resources, causing a degradation in the actual performance and introducing inaccuracies into the measurements.
- Improperly designed software probes can change the operation of the target process, by introducing logical errors into the target process.

The **accuracy** of a measurement tool is defined by the characteristics of precision and resolution. **Precision** is the number of digits available to represent data. **Resolution** is the maximum frequency at which events can be detected and correctly recorded.

The **scope** of a tool is the range of event classes which the tool can detect. A time counter used to count the length of time a CPU is busy has a scope of one event. On the other hand, a logic state analyser has a wide scope because it can be used in a variety of situations.

The **pre-reduction capabilities** of a tool determine the type and size of experiments for which it can be used. Measurement experiments can be limited by the number of comparators, the number of counters, the size of the plugboard, the available logic functions in the transformer, the number of signal connections, the size of the data storage memory, and the availability of signals for event detection. Lack of suitable event detection, event selection, and signal recording facilities can result in information loss.

Ease of use has a big impact on the acceptance of a tool by analysts. Important considerations when selecting a tool include: quality of the documentation, interactive setup of the transformer, ability to define events of interest, degree of difficulty of probe insertion (ease of installation), ability to activate and deactivate the recording of events, methods of accessing the database, and the power of the analysis tools.

Compatibility is the ability to match signal levels etc. at the interface between the target system and the monitoring system. Electrical voltage levels must be the same and hardware probes must not load signals. Software probes must not violate system protection mechanisms, or interfere with the operation of the system.

As with other measurement tools, you get the features you are willing to pay for. The **cost** of purchase, installation, usage, expansion, and maintenance of a tool should be compared to the expected cost savings due to performance improvement.

When installing a tool, three general problems have to be addressed:

1. What impact will the tool have on the system?
2. Is a suitable clock available, or does an external clock have to be added?
3. What can be measured with the tool?

Having discussed the properties of measurement tools and techniques in general terms, in the next sections we will look at specific tools and how they have been used.

4.3 Hardware tools and techniques

Hardware tools are external monitoring tools, which interface to a target system with probes (Figure 4.2). These probes connect electrical signals to the monitor, and do not interfere with the software on the target system. Transformation, analysis, and display functions are performed in the external tool.

Hardware tools are classified according to their flexibility, and the power of their transformation logic. Their flexibility is a consequence of whether the logic in their transformer section is hard wired, hardware programmable, or software programmable. **Fixed hardware tools** are completely hard wired. They are designed to measure specific parameters, and are often incorporated in the initial design of a machine. In the latter case they are called **internal tools**, in contrast to external tools, which are added as needed. Timing meters (Figure 4.3) and counting meters are typical fixed hardware tools (Svobodova, 1976a). A **timing meter** measures the duration of an activity, for example channel busy, by sampling the state of a signal associated with that activity. Timing meters can be used to measure execution time and utilization. **Counting meters** count the occurrences of events, for example the references to a memory bank. Counting meters can be used to measure execution frequencies and throughput. Sometimes, the event to be counted is detected by an **event trap**, which then generates a pulse to the counter - for example, on detection of subroutine calls. The information accumulated by a meter can usually be read by an operator from a display, and in some cases it can be read by a program. The simplest fixed hardware tool is the CPU wait light.

The transformer section of a **wired program hardware tool** includes a logic plug board, which is used to implement a variety of boolean, counting, and filtering functions. Logic gates are used to combine and sequence signals. Counters are used to implement timing meters and counting meters. Comparators and sequence detectors are used to trigger recording devices. The output of these event filters is displayed, or saved

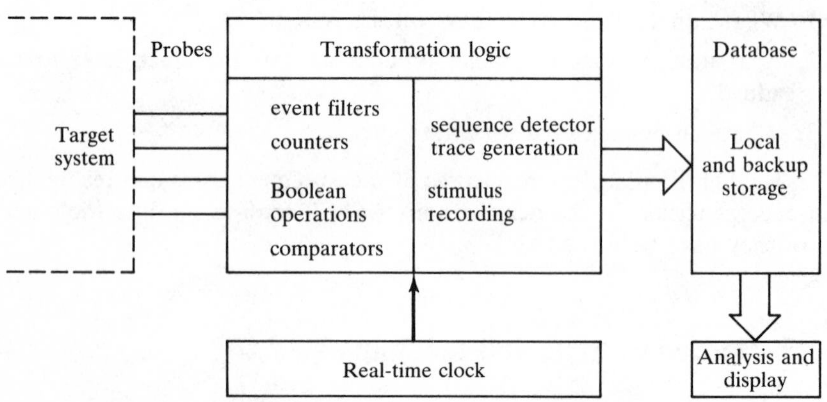

Figure 4.2 Block diagram of a hardware monitor.

in a database for later analysis. Event filtering is changed by rewiring the plug board. In some advanced systems (Murphy, 1969), associative memory is also used to detect events. Wired program tools are normally **external tools**: free-standing devices that sense electronic signals in the circuitry of the measured system, and record them externally.

In a **stored program hardware tool** the logic plug board is replaced by a computer controlled event filter. Filtering functions are set up with electronic switches under software control. The logic state analyser (Chapter 5) is the latest development in stored program tools (McKerrow, 1983). Their ability to control filtering with software makes stored program tools more flexible and easier to use than wired tools, particularly if an interactive user interface is provided. Some early tools, however, did not have the resolution of wired tools.

4.3.1 Characteristics of hardware tools

Many parameters of interest to performance evaluators can be measured with both hardware and software techniques. Hardware tools have some advantages relative to software tools, and some disadvantages:

- Hardware tools cause little, or no, interference to the system being measured, and thus they can be used for long periods.
- They have high resolution - often greater than the clock frequency of the system under study.
- Simultaneous measurement of overlapped activities is possible.
- Some hardware related activities are accessible to hardware tools but not to software tools - for example data transfer in a buffered peripheral.
- Hardware monitors can be used on any system, provided the relevant signals are accessible.
- Software related events can be sensed only when they are accompanied by an instruction at a known address.

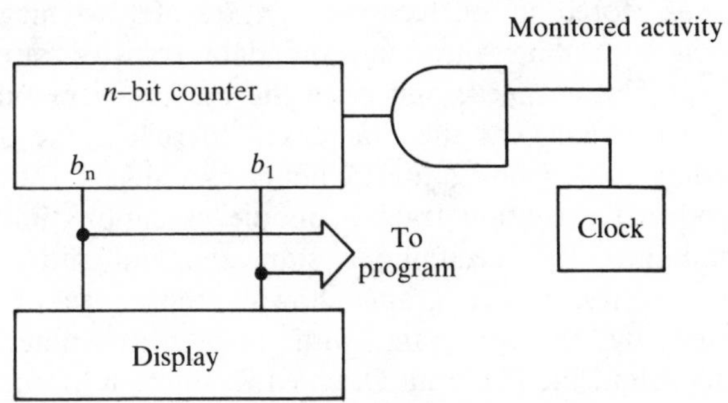

Figure 4.3 Timing meter.

- The state of a memory location can be monitored only during read or write operations to that location.
- Due to their high resolution and low interference, hardware tools provide very precise readings.
- Attaching hardware probes to a computer makes maintenance men nervous. Poorly installed probes can load signals, and impact performance.
- Probe attachment takes time and skill. Improperly attached probes produce misleading information. A means of verifying that the readings are correct is essential.
- Hardware tools can be used to monitor system crashes, and subsequent recovery.

4.3.2 Some actual hardware tools

The first hardware monitor was built by IBM in 1961 to measure how much system time was spent doing I/O operations, and how much CPU time was spent waiting for I/O operations to finish (Warner, 1974). This monitor included a set of six digital counters, some wired logic, and a few electromechanical counters which stored and displayed the results. It was physically large, and required an interface built into the 7090 computer. The digital counters were used to count events, such as instruction executions, and to measure the elapsed time of functions, such as time spent using a channel. The outputs of these digital counters were accumulated in electromechanical counters. At the start of an experiment, the electromechanical counters were reset by hand, and at the end of the experiment, the information in these counters was copied down by hand. Within a year, a streamlined version, known as the 7090 Channel Analyser, went into production. About two dozen were built.

In 1962, the Program Execution Monitor (Apple, 1965) was built to find where and when loops occurred, by tracing program execution. Trace data was stored in buffers pending transfer to magnetic tape. However, even with data encoding, the data transfer rate was slow compared to processor speed, and once the buffers were full data was lost. A second problem was the time taken to reduce the data: a 5.5 minute recording took from 2 to 7.5 hours to reduce. Data reduction programs produced execution traces, module execution times (where a module was defined by specifying a start and end address), module execution frequencies, and a graph showing the range of instruction addresses used by the program with respect to time. A more sophisticated version, the Program Oriented Evaluation Monitor (POEM) reduced the quantity of data by event filtering, but it required too much system knowledge for general use.

The Program Event Counter (PEC), built in 1964, was an enhanced version of the channel analyser and included an important new feature: a removable logic plug board that could be programmed by wiring. Signals coming into the plug board could be routed through AND/OR logic to perform various functions, the results of which were summarized in counters. Events could be timed, or counted, simply by appropriate wiring of the plug board. In addition to channel operations, overlap with other channels and the processor could be measured. Another feature introduced in the PEC was the ability to test for an address equal to a specified address or within an address range. This was achieved with three pairs of address comparators, which compared the contents of the memory address and data registers to preset values. With this tool, module execution time and module execution frequency could be found for code at known memory locations. Data reduction was still a problem.

The Systems Analysis Measuring Instrument (SAMI), built in 1967, was a bigger and better PEC. It had 50% more electronics than the IBM 360/50 and weighed 4 tons. It introduced the idea of the sensor or probe which could measure virtually any available signal on the system, not just those provided by the hardware interface. A smaller version of SAMI, the Basic Counting Unit built in 1968, used a probe as the only interface to the system. In 1969 the System Utilization Monitor (SUM), a portable version (TV size) of SAMI with 20 probes, plug board, magnetic tape, and analysis programs, was released as a product to the general public by Computer Synectics of California. Arndt and Oliver (1971) discuss the use of the SUM monitor in the evaluation of a real-time system used in satellite command and control.

Another interesting experimental device, developed at IBM in 1965, was the Execution Plotter. A cathode ray tube (CRT) was used to display a real-time graph of program execution: memory address versus elapsed time. It provided a good overview of program execution but it was limited by the CRT technology of the time.

Another monitor, the Time Sharing System Performance Activity Recorder (TS/SPAR), was built to study the IBM System 360/67 time sharing system (Schulman, 1967). It was able to monitor up to 256 simultaneous signals, reduce them to a maximum of 48 measurable events, record periodic summaries of these events on tape, count events and measure their duration, interrupt the CPU when a specified state occurred, and respond to CPU-generated control signals. These signals could be used as flags or, more importantly, to control the measurement activity of the monitor. This ability of the target processor to control the measurement tool was a new idea. Data reduction facilities included counters for accumulating event parameters and comparators for dynamic monitoring of data paths. Schulman (1967) discussed a number of the significant computing developments where measurement was needed - multi-tasking, multi-processing, virtual memory allocation, dynamic address translation, re-entrant code, I/O handling - but he did not report whether measurements were ever made in these areas with TS/SPAR.

The System Logic and Usage Recorder (Murphy, 1969) used associative memory in the event filter, to detect if the incoming data was new. For example, when measuring the time a program spent in various areas of memory, the program counter was connected to the associative memory, where the current program address was compared to the address ranges already recorded. If the address was in one of those ranges, the appropriate counter was incremented; if not, a new counter was automatically assigned to the new address range and incremented. At the end of the experiment, a set of memory block execution counts was read from the memory, and the time spent in each memory block was calculated. Murphy (1969) discusses a number of applications of this very powerful tool.

Researchers outside IBM have also developed hardware tools. Roek and Emerson (1969) built a hardware monitor for the specific purpose of monitoring program flow by recording and profiling the execution of jump instructions. Restricting the measurements to jump instructions significantly reduced the amount of data. Further reduction was done on the fly by detecting simple loops and recording the location of the first loop jump, the number of loop jumps, and the duration of one pass through the loop. These techniques illustrate the wisdom of understanding the operation of the object you are trying to measure. Further data reduction produced graphical (address versus time) and statistical information (module utilization).

The Neurotron monitor system (Aschenbrenner *et al.*, 1971) is considered by many to be the penultimate hardware monitor. This monitor combined the best features found in previous monitors; overcame the stated deficiencies in many previous hardware monitors; and let the operator interactively control the data accumulation, analysis, and display processes. The monitor used a minicomputer with a multi-tasking, priority scheduling, operating system. Data reduction and event filtering logic was configured under program control. A small plug board was included to aid in I/O selection. Programmable registers controlled the selection of input signals, logic functions, sequence detectors, counters, signal paths, and control functions for a particular experiment. Sequence detectors were used to record event sequences, and to detect variation from defined event sequences. Counters, or groups of counters, were enabled and disabled under program control, and sampling intervals were completely at the discretion of the programmer.

A key element in the acquisition of data was a random access memory with an associated arithmetic unit. When gathering statistics, this memory was used as a set of accumulators (timing and counting meters). Since the memory could be loaded from both the monitoring processor and the target system, it could be used as a set of comparators. The output of this sophisticated set of event filters was passed to the analysis and display processes through buffers. By using rotating buffers, double buffering, and other techniques, statistics with a resolution of a few milliseconds, involving significant filtering and data compression, could be recorded and displayed. Amiot *et al.* (1972) discuss the use of this monitor to evaluate a remote batch processing system.

The ADAM hardware monitor (Shemer and Robertson, 1972) was a specialized minicomputer built to monitor the Xerox Sigma computer. Measurement programs were developed on the Sigma system and, together with preset data, were loaded into the monitor. The Sigma system controlled the measurement program running on the ADAM monitor, and periodically the acquired data was transferred from ADAM to Sigma for analysis. Use of a solid state associative memory and parallel instruction execution gave ADAM the capacity to monitor the Sigma system at the instruction execution rate. Collins (1976) reports on the use of the ADAM monitor to localize and identify performance problems in an overlay loader.

Fryer (1973) describes a memory-bus monitor which he designed to assist in program development on dedicated real-time computers. This monitor was a piece of hardware attached to the bus which connected the central processing unit to memory. In many ways it was the forerunner of the modern logic state analyser. A simple memory-bus monitor could detect accesses to a specified memory location, and display its contents. A more sophisticated version included an address stack. As each address appeared on the bus, it was pushed onto the stack. When a selected address appeared, the stack was frozen and its contents displayed, effectively providing a 'come from' trace.

The power of the monitor was increased by replacing the address stack with a content addressable memory, which could be used as a stack or as a set of comparators. Also, a data stack and a timer were added, and the number of address comparators increased. The resultant monitor could be used to:

- look at bus traffic when the computer was operating in single step mode,
- detect and stack accesses to specific memory locations,
- stack bus activity, and halt stacking when an activity of interest occurred, so the stack contained a trace of bus activity immediately prior to the activity of interest,
- time blocks of code, such as loops, and
- count the number of times a branch was taken, an opcode was executed, or a memory location was referenced.

Deese (1974) sought a solution to some of the operational problems with hardware monitors. These include: the difficulty of locating test points, signals not available at test points, signals not synchronized, the adverse consequences of poorly attached probes, the problems involved in changing probes, and the increasingly large number of probes required. To overcome these problems, he introduced a new concept: the monitor register. All signals of interest are multiplexed through this register to an external hardware monitor. Once the multiplexer is installed, probe connection is simple. In his monitor for the fire control system on the Trident submarine, he wired signals to eight input registers. A microprogram multiplexed the contents of one of these input registers to the output register, for transfer to an external hardware monitor, where this data was recorded together with the number of the input register. By designing performance monitoring features into the machine, he reduced the operational difficulties of using a hardware monitor.

Hempy (1977) discusses the use of a Channel Utilization Monitor, to evaluate the performance of the IBM 3850 mass storage system. The monitor was attached to the channel interface to collect data about each interaction between the channel and the devices attached to it. The data was recorded as an event trace of channel interactions (channel command or device response to a command). Each interaction record included: a command identifier, the number of bytes transferred, the time taken by the channel to execute the command, channel status bits, the device addressed, and a time stamp. He found that evaluating this data to detect bottlenecks was an enormous task, so he expanded the trace to record the type of activity the device was carrying out (for example seek or read), and used this information to filter out data for a specific activity.

Clark (1983) used a Dynaprobe hardware monitor to measure the performance of the cache on a VAX 11/780. Most of the signals were available on the backplane, but logic had to be added to the processor cards to sense some signals. He made measurements with the cache enabled, half the cache disabled, and the entire cache disabled. Using this tool, he measured the hit ratios of data and instruction references, the rate of cache invalidation by I/O, and the amount of waiting time caused by cache misses. One set of measurements was made with the system running an interactive workload of up to 30 users, and a second set with a simulated workload. The performance he measured was lower than cache simulations suggest, with an average data hit ratio of 91.4%, and an instruction hit ratio of 83.8%. With half the cache disabled the hit ratios dropped to 84.3% and 76.9% respectively, with a resultant decrease in throughput of 10% (measured in MIPS).

4.4 Software tools and techniques

Software tools consist of instructions which are added to the target process to gather performance data; these instructions are called probes. Generally, no additional hardware is required. Software probes collect data, reduce it, and store it in internal buffers. At regular intervals, a monitoring process transfers the contents of these buffers to backup store. Analysis of this data and display of results are usually carried out at a later stage.

Most systems use software tools to collect data for the generation of system accounting logs. System managers use these logs for capacity planning and customer billing. The simplest log is a sequence of messages that record information about the start and termination of activities, information such as the time of day and the name of the job which caused the activity. More sophisticated logs record the CPU time, the I/O time per device, and the memory usage for each job. From this job related information, an accounting program generates customer accounts.

From logged data, analysis programs generate a record of system activity, and calculate system statistics, statistics like resource utilization and system throughput for different job classes. Information stored in these logs can be used to calculate parameter values for use in performance evaluation. However, as these logs are normally designed for accounting purposes, they may not include some desirable measures. In addition, at the termination of each job, some systems report to the user the real time and CPU time used by his job.

A useful debugging tool is a set of programs which measure and display a profile of program execution. Two profiles are commonly measured: a profile of the number of times each line of code is executed, and a profile of the number of times each variable is accessed. Prior to compilation, a preprocessor inserts checkpoints into the program to detect variable accesses and flow of control branching. During execution, these checkpoints increment counters. After execution, counter data is displayed as a profile.

All software tools are event driven. **Sampling tools** execute in response to events external to the system, events which define the end of the sampling period. When an event occurs, the state of the target process or system is read and recorded. In many systems, the state is the contents of the operating system tables. Data collected in this way is analysed using statistical methods. Sampling techniques reduce the amount of data needed to estimate some quantities. In a sense, sampling is equivalent to taking the pulse of a system. The essence of sampling is that the measures are synchronized to the termination of a sampling period, not to changes in the internal state of the system.

Samples can be taken at periodic or random intervals. In time sampling, a timer initiates the sampling process at the end of a specified time interval. In count sampling, a counting meter initiates the sampling process when a specified count is reached, for example *n* disk accesses. A counting meter can be a hardware device, such as those discussed in Section 4.3, or a software device: a memory location that is incremented every time a procedure executes. In some systems, the sampling program detects the event by periodically checking the value in the meter. When the meter reaches the desired value, the program resets the meter and records the desired state information. In others, the meter routine detects the event, and calls the sampling program. In this case we have an internally driven tool.

Internally driven tools execute in direct response to events within the system, events such as the termination of a process. Thus, they are synchronized to changes in the internal state of the system. An internal event is detected by the execution of a software probe, a routine inserted into the target process. For example, in an interrupt driven operating system, processes are scheduled to handle hardware and software interrupts, making interrupt routines a logical place to insert probes. This is a neat way of decomposing the system object. Monitors based on software probes in interrupt routines are called **interrupt intercept monitors.**

Software probes can be inserted at points of interest in the target process, not only to detect the execution of an instruction but also to detect a data structure being updated or a variable being assigned a certain value. Thus, they can be used to gauge software specific information; information like user name, disk file name, variable contents, and job class. When using system resources, and when reading system tables, software probes may have to use supervisor calls to get around system security. A software probe can either collect data itself, or call a measurement program for the same purpose. Once the required data is recorded, the software probe returns to the calling process. This data is usually stored in a set of in memory registers, which are transferred to backup store when they are full, or when the experiment is complete.

A **fixed software tool** is a software probe which is permanently installed in a program to collect data every time that program executes. Fixed tools are used to implement software meters, and to collect accounting data. When enabled, a software timing meter increments a memory location every time the clock routine executes; for example, user time is incremented whenever a user process is executing. The overhead associated with software meters can be minimized by implementing the counting routines in firmware (Blake, 1980).

Tools which can be enabled and disabled, or inserted and removed, at will are **non-fixed tools**. Some non-fixed tools are installed permanently, and can be enabled when desired by the monitoring process; others are inserted and removed with special probe insertion software. In some non-fixed tools, the event to be detected can be modified, or the data variable to be recorded can be changed. With these tools, the user can tailor the measurements to the experiment at hand, which reduces interference by eliminating the execution of unwanted software probes.

Some systems (Deutch and Grant, 1971) allow the insertion of user supplied software probes. These must be verified before installation to ensure that they do not introduce logical errors into the target process. To facilitate automatic verification, routines must conform to a standard structure and loops must have fixed indexes. The criteria which must be checked for and eliminated include: branches into the target program, use of illegal or privileged instructions, indeterminate execution time, excessive execution time, storage of data outside the defined data collection area, self modifying code, re-entry problems, and violation of security and/or privacy.

Other systems provide a macro facility (Ferrari and Liu, 1975) that enables the combination of standard checkpoints into measurement macros, for example a macro to trace the flow of control in a program. Standard checkpoints supported by these measurement systems include: counting meters, timing meters, enable/disable checkpoints, set/clear flags, record time, record event trace tuples, transfer statistics to backup store, and clear monitor registers.

4.4.1 Characteristics of software tools

Software tools have some advantages relative to hardware tools, and some disadvantages:

- Software tools interfere with the system (Bourret and Cros, 1980). Software probes take time to execute and use up memory. If the software tool uses less than 5% of system resources, then measurement accuracy is generally adequate. If a writable control store is available, interference can be reduced by implementing checkpoints in firmware routines, which are callable as assembler instructions.
- Resolution is lower than for hardware tools. They are most suited to recording infrequent macroscopic events.
- They can record events only in a sequential manner, and they stop the execution of the target process while they are recording data.
- Hardware related events can only be detected if they are accompanied by the execution of a program instruction or the updating of a known memory location. Also, peripheral devices can

only be monitored through their communications with the central processing unit.

- Software monitors can only be used on the system they were designed for.
- Software related information can easily be sensed by software probes; information such as program name, variable contents, and dynamic data structure access.
- Software tools can read the contents of memory locations at any time.
- Software tools can only provide rough timing measurements, depending upon the precision of the system clock.
- Insertion of faulty software probes into a system can cause program faults, and may even cause the system to crash.
- Software tools are usually easier to install than hardware tools, particularly for programmers, and may be more flexible. Also, they generally cost less.
- Changes to an operating system can drastically affect the accuracy of software tools, requiring compensating modification to these tools.
- Software tools can handle the dynamic environments which create problems for hardware tools: relocation of code modules, virtual memory, recursion, dynamic data structures, and interpretation of programs.
- For a software tool to provide accurate data, it must detect pauses in the execution of processes, pauses caused by external interrupts, which are easy to detect with hardware tools, but may be difficult to detect with software tools.
- A major headache with software tools is verifying their accuracy. Analysts often use hardware monitors to verify the accuracy of software tools (Carlson, 1977).

4.4.2 Some actual software tools

Who did what first with software tools is not altogether clear, because many people wrote simple tools to help with their work and never reported them. As a result, they became part of the folklore of computing. Herbst *et al.* (1955) used software tools to measure the instruction mix of Maniac programs. Estrin *et al.* (1967) proposed the use of **checkpoints** to produce program execution profiles, by incrementing counting meters. These checkpoints were to be added by a preprocessor, prior to compilation of FORTRAN programs.

Knuth (1971) popularized the ideas of **program profiles** and **instruction mix measures** for high-level languages. He used two approaches to dynamic program analysis. In the first, he produced a program profile by inserting **meters** into the program. Using this profile, in conjunction with a knowledge of the instructions used in the program, he produced instruction mix tables. His second approach was to **sample the program counter** at regular intervals, and count the number of times addresses within specified address ranges were accessed. At the end of a program run, Knuth plotted the number of samples per address range with a histogram. By combining the recorded addresses with the address map of the FORTRAN program, he was able to plot a course profile of instruction utilization.

Snuper Computer (Estrin *et al.*, 1967) was a system proposed at UCLA. How much of the proposal was realized is not reported. The proposal included the production of a number of graphical displays for data reduction and analysis. Three development phases were proposed. In phase 0, the self measurement phase, source programs were to be instrumented with a procedure which would build an execution profile. In phase 1, the output of the instrument procedure would no longer be written into an array, but would be written to an external tool, introducing the concept of a hybrid tool. In phase 2, sufficient data about the program would be produced by the compiler and transferred to the external tool to enable a hardware monitor to examine the operation.

The idea of passing information about the program to the external tool prior to execution is one contribution made by this project. This idea was taken up and extended by Plattner and Nievergelt (1981) during the development of a program execution monitor. Estrin *et al.* (1967) were the first to propose the concept of a hybrid monitor, a name invented later, where both hardware and software tools combine to measure a system. Thus, they contributed some valuable ideas to the field.

Bussell and Koster (1970) discuss two self measurement tools that were implemented as part of the UCLA computer instrumentation project: a self simulator that closely duplicated the operation of the machine it was running on, and a program for making precise measurements (2 microsecond accuracy) of the time duration of events. In the first tool, a data gathering routine collected instruction mix statistics, while the target program was executing on the simulator. Using a simulator enabled complete instrumentation of the target process by instrumenting the simulator. In the second tool, a time subroutine started and read a precision hardware clock, every time it was called by a user process.

Cantrell and Ellison (1968) measured the performance of General Electric's GECOS II multiprogramming operating system, which consisted of 64 system and user programs. The GECOS system kept a running total by program of all processor, channel, and device times for accounting purposes. These totals were updated at the end of each period of processor use, and after each I/O transaction. When a user program terminated, all of its accounting times were written to an accounting file, and the time counters reset. The accounting file did not include data on operating system programs, but system data could be dumped to a separate file on request.

Analysis of user program data did not give a clear picture of where execution time went. Analysis of system data indicated that overhead processing was small, and idle time was high. To obtain more precise information, they added a trace mode to the instrumentation, and recorded trace entries on magnetic tape. In trace mode, information was added to a circular list for every major operating system event, such as handling an interrupt or dispatching a process. Unfortunately, during five minutes execution, 350,000 trace entries were recorded, producing a significant data reduction problem. They tried a succession of data reduction and analysis techniques, and finally settled on two methods: one to process accounting data, and one to process trace data.

To reduce accounting data, a program sampled the timing counters, calculated the changes since the previous measurement, calculated the percentage of processor and channel time used by each process, and recorded these percentages, every two seconds. In addition, at program initiation or termination, run averages and the name and core map of the current program were recorded. To reduce trace data, the same program, in an alternative mode, recorded the complete event trace, produced an event report from this recording, and calculated the distribution of computer time within each program.

Cantrell and Ellison used these tools to study the execution of individual programs, and to look at the interaction between programs within the operating system. During this study, fourteen performance bugs were found and fixed, an average throughput improvement of 30% was achieved, and their understanding of how the operating system really worked was increased.

In this system, we have a combination of software techniques: timing meters, event detectors, event trace, and sampling. In the early days of measurement, while people were learning what to measure and how to measure it, researchers installed as much instrumentation as possible in an attempt to ensure that all the data they might need was recorded. The result was that too much information was available with no way of reducing it to meaningful data. In Cantrell and Ellison's work a key measurement principle can be seen: a large quantity of data is of little use if you have no method of reducing it to meaningful values. As researchers understood more about operating systems, they experimented with a variety of measurement and reduction techniques, with the goal of determining what measurements are useful in which situations.

Campbell and Heffner (1968) discuss additional techniques used when measuring a later version of the operating system, GECOS III. They found that it is important to be able to measure the length and wait time of system queues, and suggest that these measures should be included in the design of the system. An idea they introduced to help find system bugs was **system auditing**. To 'audit' means to check and verify. Audit programs were written to check operations on system queues, to calculate the checksum of critical tables every time they were referenced, and to calculate the checksum of all system files as they were loaded into the system. With these audits they quickly pinpointed the occurrence and cause of data corruption in system critical areas.

While analysing these audits, Campbell and Heffner had difficulty inferring what had happened prior to a system failure. When they studied the system, they found that all communication between modules passed through a common routine. They modified this routine to record information about each intermodule transfer in a circular list, so that, at any time, a trace of the latest transfers could be obtained, and the operation of the system summarized.

This trace facility eased the task of analysing system failures, but the interference was high and important information was lacking. To eliminate these shortcomings, they implemented an event trace to record the occurrence of system events (over fifty). Events were traced by inserting probes into system modules, probes which could be turned on or off at system start up time.

The System Internal Performance Evaluation program (SIPE) was used to record data about significant events as they occurred in the IBM System/360 Time Sharing System (Deniston, 1969). Events were detected by **hooks** inserted at strategic locations in the supervisor. When flow of control reached a hook, an interrupt was generated, and flow of control was transferred to the SIPE monitor, which collected the desired data. A simple mechanism existed for enabling and disabling hooks, such that they were either all on or all off.

Balzer (1969) developed the EXDAMS system: an extendible debugging tool for high-level language programs. In this debugger, a dynamic display of program execution was generated by combining an execution history with a static model of the program. This model was obtained by analysing the source code, and the execution history was measured by inserting probes into the object code. The execution history contained all the dynamic information needed to update execution time either forward or backward. To study the execution of a program and to debug it, the operator could replay the execution of the program, in slow motion, both forward and backward, using a motion picture display.

The Informer (Deutch and Grant, 1971) was designed to attack three problems that arise in large programming systems: debugging, performance analysis, and environment analysis. With the informer, users could name an arbitrary checkpoint in a process, and specify a measurement routine which was to be executed each time flow of control reached that checkpoint. To ensure that no bugs were introduced when user supplied measurement routines were inserted into a process, measurement programs were tested to check that they did not modify the environment, or take an excessive time to execute. Tools were provided to minimize the time and effort involved in composing, debugging, and executing measurement programs. Attaching a measurement routine to a checkpoint was not as easy as it may appear. The user had to have a way of specifying the checkpoint location, the loader had to have a map of spare memory into which it could load the measurement routine, the system had to maintain the integrity of register contents, and the target process had to be patched.

Two commercial software monitors were developed by Boole and Babbage Inc (Holtwick, 1971). One, called the Configuration Utilization Evaluator (CUE), was oriented towards the systems programmer; the other, called the Problem Program Evaluator (PPE), was designed principally with the applications programmer in mind. Kolence (1972) developed his software physics during the design of these tools. Both tools consisted of two parts: an extractor which sampled for user specified data, and an analyser which transformed the extracted data into reports.

The PPE extractor ran as a normal OS/360 job, and collected performance data on a program as it executed. The program under study was sampled at a rate specified by the user in multiples of 1/60 of a second. At each sample, the absolute program address, the program status (waiting, executing, etc.), the program name, and the overlay segment number were recorded. PPE reports were used to pinpoint areas of a program which were executed often or used an excessive amount of time.

The CUE monitor ran as the highest priority task in the system, and sampled the system as it operated, with a sampling period specified in multiples of 1/60 of a second. It collected detailed data concerning utilization of equipment, length of queues, mechanical access movements on direct access storage devices, how often the loader was in memory, distributions of I/O requests, and the distributions of transient areas in use. CUE could be used to investigate the cause of bottlenecks, job scheduling strategies, multiprogramming contention, and the effect of file placement on access time.

The OASIS system was developed at Stanford to support both batch and interactive modes of operation on an IBM 370, but it was slow. A software monitor (OEM) (Svobodova, 1973a) was built to measure the scheduler and the OASIS resource routines: routines which allocated tables of blocks to on line tasks. Software probes were inserted into the executive to count the resources in use, for each of the four OASIS resource types. Also, a probe counted the number requests for an OASIS resource which could not be granted because the resource pool was empty. These counters were sampled every 60 seconds, and their values recorded in a buffer. After 20 records were accumulated, they were transferred to disk together with an array containing scheduler information. At the end of each scheduler pass, a counter SQ_{ij} was incremented, where i is the scheduler-queue length, and j is the number of tasks on the queue the scheduler interrogated before it found one which could be dispatched.

Svobodova combined measurements made over a period of weeks to produce scheduler statistics, and she used counter information to detect the exhaustion of resources. These measurements confirmed that deadlocks were occurring because task requests could not be completed due to a lack of resources. From measurements made when no on-line tasks were executing, Svobodova calculated the system overhead was 11 to 12%. A complementary hybrid tool will be discussed in Section 4.5.

The Mesa Spy (McDaniel, 1982) is an interactive sampling tool that gathers real-time performance data on Mesa programs, by using an extension of the program counter sampling technique. Ingalls (1972) and Rafii (1981) have also used this technique, a technique first reported by Knuth (1971). The Spy is an independently compiled Mesa module which is loaded into the system with the target program. It does not contain built-in information about the target program, but exploits knowledge of the Mesa language and run-time environment. Information in the run-time call stack is used to determine what code is responsible for the resources being consumed. Optimizing compilers modify the mapping between the program counter and the source language, and hence interfere with the ability of the Spy to record analysed data in terms of source-level statements. The Spy provides an interactive, symbolic, user interface which lets the user describe the target program by module name, or procedure name, and it provides symbolic output at the module level, or at source level.

The Spy has two modes of operation: coarse grain data collection and fine grain data collection. In the coarse mode, the Spy collects information about program execution on a module basis. Every module (compilation unit) in the system has a module number (an index into a special table that belongs to the Mesa run-time system). The Spy maintains an array of data collection buckets as its basic data structure, and this array is indexed by module number. Each bucket contains a counter, a pointer, and a charge the caller flag. When the Spy samples the state of the system, it increments the counter for the currently executing module, if the charge the caller flag is reset.

If the charge the caller flag is set, the Spy follows module nesting back up the call path until a bucket is found where the flag isn't set. The counter in this bucket is incremented to charge the resources used by the currently executing module to the calling module. With this facility, the execution of system library modules, and other common procedures, can be charged to the module which uses them, giving a truer picture of resource utilization. By switching this flag on and off for successive runs of the same experiment, excessively used routines can be pinpointed and analysed.

The pointer in the data collection bucket points to a data structure used for fine grain collection, or is nil if fine grain collection is turned off. The fine grain data structure is a set of tuples, one for each non-overlapping program counter interval in the code space of the module, with each tuple containing a counter and a charge the caller flag. Fine grain data collection operates in the same way as coarse grain data collection, but collects data at the block-structure level, not at the process level.

Some important software tools have not been mentioned in this section as they are covered in later chapters. Systems that have been designed for measurement are discussed in Chapter 8, and multiprocessor instrumentation is discussed in Chapter 9.

4.5 Hybrid tools and techniques

Hybrid monitors (Figure 1.5) attempt to take advantage of the complementary nature of hardware and software tools. In a typical hybrid monitor, software tools detect events within the system and write information relative to those events to a hardware interface. Data arriving at the hardware interface is recorded, together with other hardware signals, by an external hardware tool, where it is analysed and displayed. Not all hybrid tools fit this pattern, and a wide range of variations is possible. Hybrid monitors have the potential of being able to measure all the information about a system, with the precision of a hardware tool, but with less interference than a software tool. In a sense, a hybrid monitor is an intelligent peripheral or, at minimum, an intelligent alternative to a backup store.

The major decision to be made when designing a hybrid monitor is: 'Which section should measure what?' If you do not have a well thought out philosophy of hybridization, you may end up with an ad hoc collection of dissimilar components rather than an integrated measurement system. This question of hybridization is analysed in the context of the performance measurement formulation in Section 6.4.1. Designing an integrated measurement system involves selecting a combination of hardware and software tools, determining the power of each tool, dividing data reduction functions between these tools, specifying the communications protocols between these tools, and deciding what data analysis and display techniques are to be used.

Some hybrid tools are simply a combination of components from existing hardware tools and software tools; others are designed with a specific hybridization goal in mind. Hybrid tools can be loosely classified according to how measurement functions are partitioned between hardware and software. All hybrid tools aim to minimize the interference of the software tool. However, some do this only during the execution of an instrumented process and use considerable target system resources to set up the target process. These tools use a modified compiler to produce an extensive model of the target process, which, together with a load map, is passed to the monitoring computer before the target process is executed. During execution, the monitoring computer traces the execution path of the target process, and records variable assignments, using hardware techniques. Note the assumption that the hardware section of a hybrid tool includes a computer; this is generally true but not always. These hardware measurements are combined with the process model to produce a detailed execution history. In this style of hybrid tool, the two computers act as communicating processors and measurement is usually controlled by the monitoring tool. For the monitoring tool to have total control over the measurement experiment it must be able to request the execution of processes on the target processor.

A second approach, which also produces zero interference during the execution of the target process, is for the loader to pass a load map of the target process to the hardware tool. During execution the hardware tool collects the specified data. When execution terminates, the recorded data is passed back to the target processor for analysis. In this case, the hardware tool is an intelligent data reduction and capture device under control of the target processor - an intelligent peripheral. This tool is usually more restricted in the range of measurements that it can make than the previous tool.

If some interference is acceptable, other approaches are possible. One approach is to pass the target process through a pre-processor which adds software probes before compilation. During execution, these probes pass information to the hardware tool. A hybrid tool can often be used to measure the interference, allowing the analyst to compensate for measurement errors. The above tools are all suitable for analysing the execution of individual programs, but are unsuitable for instrumenting a complete system.

When instrumenting a system, it is best to add fixed probes at design time, probes which present a continuous stream of information to the transformer section of the hardware tool. Where they are placed in the code of the system is determined by the designer's formulation of measurement, and his planned use of the data. A record of the location of each probe and the parameter it measures must be available to the analyst. These probes produce some interference, but using fixed probes minimizes the use of system resources to set up the instrumentation. In some systems, analysts have attempted to reduce the interference by including probe enable/disable flags, but testing these flags can often cause more interference than the probes themselves. Fully instrumented systems often include a combination of tools to enable measurements at all levels in the object hierarchy.

A major consideration in the design of hybrid tools is the selection of sensors. Some of the criteria you must consider when selecting sensors are:

- Your formulation of measurement and your philosophy of hybridization.
- The number and type of quantities to be measured.
- The sensors which can be used to measure each quantity.
- Of the available sensors, which one has the most advantages and the least disadvantages?
- Is data reduction to be done at the sensor or in the external tool?
- Can the sensors be installed easily?

Hybrid tools add a new element to our basic measurement tool configuration: the interface between the software tool and the hardware tool. This interface can be as simple as a parallel output port, or as complex as a direct memory access channel. Some interfaces are passive: the hardware tool simply reads the information the software tool writes to it; others are dynamic: the hardware tool can request information from the software tool. Some interfaces allow the hardware tool to pass information to the software tool, or to interrupt the target process. These features are useful for feedback control of operating systems, and for debugging, where the analyst may want to control the execution of the target process.

Data flow through this interface is controlled by the hardware tool. It may sample the data at regular intervals, it may look for specific bit patterns, or it may respond to interrupts generated by the interface when data arrives from the software tool. The hardware section of a hybrid tool usually includes a computer. Data analysis, display, and as much reduction as required are done by programs running on this computer.

4.5.1 Some actual hybrid tools

The concept of a hybrid tool seems to have originated with the Snuper Computer proposal (Estrin *et al.*, 1967). In phase 1, hybridization was proposed as a way to reduce the interference of the software tool used in phase 0 (Section 4.4.2). Software probes were still to be added to the target process, but instead of summing event data, they would write it to a hardware interface. This interface would calculate a memory address from the emitted event descriptor, and increment that location in the memory of the monitoring computer. Incrementation of memory-location counters could be disabled with a software settable flag. At the end of the experiment, a table of event counts (module execution counts) would exist in the monitoring computer, rather than in the target computer. During the measurement experiment, the monitoring computer would produce a dynamic display of event activity.

Another proposed feature was to interrupt either the target computer or the monitoring computer when a particular event occurred, instead of incrementing a counter. Thus, in this tool all sensing was to be done by software; but data reduction was to be done by a combination of probe placement and hardware techniques; and data recording, analysis, and display were all to be done by the external tool. The techniques proposed for this tool can be used at any level in the hierarchy by inserting probes to detect the start of objects.

Phase 2 of the Snuper proposal sought to eliminate interference during the execution of the target process. To do this, software probes were discarded, and instead the compiler and loader were to be modified to provide sufficient information about the target process for the monitoring system to define and detect significant events. To detect these events, the hardware tool would have to monitor memory bus activity. All data appearing at the hardware probes was to be clocked into a first in first out queue. As the data left the queue, it was to be used to address a bit in an event-table memory. If the bit was set, the data related to an event of interest, and was to be recorded; otherwise it was to be discarded. For each bit in the event table that was set, there would be a pointer to an element in an array. When an event was detected, this element would be incremented. Several pointers could point to the same array element, allowing events belonging to the same class to be counted. Also, a second event filter could be used in conjunction with the first to treat pairs of events as one event.

The SPY monitor (Sedgewick *et al.*, 1970) was developed at Western Electric to evaluate the operation of OS/360 MVT executing on an IBM system 360/50. A parallel data path connected the target processor to the monitoring processor, and a hardware probe monitored the state of the wait light on the target computer. By using the monitoring computer in place of the backup store normally associated with a software monitor, real-time analysis and display of the dynamic action of the target system was possible. Information was displayed in four windows on a cathode ray tube display: one window containing specific information on the jobs being processed, one showing the utilization of the direct access devices, one containing running averages of selected summary information, and one containing a continually recycling graph of CPU utilization.

A software tool, running on the target processor, sampled selected information, accumulated statistics, and transferred the collected data to the monitoring processor at selected intervals. This tool had three defined sampling intervals: one for sampling internal information, one for gathering statistics, and one for data transmission. Information about individual tasks was obtained from the tables in the task queue. Information about direct access devices was also obtained from operating system tables. All this data was collected by sampling programs running under the operating system, without having to modify it. This approach requires an intimate knowledge of the operating system, and can only produce coarse measures.

Nemeth and Rovner (1971) took a completely different approach in the instrumentation of the TX-2 computer at MIT Lincoln Laboratory. The TX-2 was a time shared system with extensive facilities for supporting interactive graphics. Each user had a virtual computer to himself, a virtual computer which appeared to have all the facilities of the actual system. Their aim was to monitor the user's virtual computer, and to interrupt this virtual computer when an event of interest occurred. Events of interest included: the execution of n instructions, supervisor calls, subroutine calls, and references to particular variables. In response to the interrupt, a routine collected information about the state of the virtual computer.

The TX-2 was equipped with extensive hardware maintenance facilities. About 160 of the internal signals were wired, in functional groups, to a maintenance probe. The values represented by these functional groups could be compared to values stored in switch registers. The outputs of these comparators could be ANDed with up to 39 other signals to detect an event of interest. When an event of interest was detected, the processor was interrupted, or the event was counted and the processor interrupted when the event counter overflowed.

Thus, the hardware device was used to detect events of interest, and to call an internal measurement routine to record the state of the target process. A user of this measurement system initialized the comparators manually, and armed the interrupts and initialized the event counters with software. Again, a whole host of system parameters could be measured without having to modify the code of the target process. However, a detailed memory map of the target process was required, which became a problem with dynamic memory allocation schemes. Also, the addition of a hardware tool of this nature to an existing system can prove to be a difficult exercise.

The CPM-X monitor (Ruud, 1972) was a commercially available tool which expanded the power of standard hardware techniques by gaining access to software related information through a channel interface. The memory of the monitoring processor had three ports: one connected to the monitoring processor, one connected to the target processor, and one connected to the output of a programmable event filter. Some of the event filtering was implemented in microcode stored in a writable control store.

The target processor could write information directly into the memory of the monitoring processor over the DMA channel. To transfer information in the other direction, the monitoring processor interrupted the target processor, which then read the monitoring processor's memory to determine the cause of the interrupt. This facility could be used to request the transfer of operating system tables or event counter contents from the target system to the monitoring system.

The Burroughs B1700 Computer (Wilner, 1972) included microinstructions which could be used to write bit patterns to test points accessible to hardware probes. These instructions were used to indicate the occurrence of events and to pass data to an external tool. A monitoring system built with these instructions included programs to measure and plot module execution frequencies and execution time profiles.

In a previous section, we described the monitoring of the OASIS system with a software tool. This tool worked well at the system level, but Svobodova (1973a) feared that the interference would be too high, if she used it at the task level. So she developed a hybrid tool for task level measurement, the OASIS task monitor (OTM).

An additional byte was allocated to the system table for each task, in which the scheduler stored the current state of the task. An interactive task can have a number of states: executing, I/O busy, not logged on, waiting on terminal input, etc. Whenever the state of a task changed, a probe routine wrote this status byte together with a task identifier to a fixed memory location. An address match circuit detected writes to this location. This circuit was part of a hardware debugging aid integrated into the computer. Every time this memory location was written to, the address match circuit sent a sync pulse to the external hardware monitor (Computer Synectics SUM monitor), which recorded the data on the memory bus.

As the state bits were in the same location in the state word for each task, changes in the bits could be counted to obtain event counts of various system activities, for example I/O requests. Also the time between events could be measured, for example the time a task waited for I/O. Thus, by appropriate event mapping into status flags, information about the behaviour of individual tasks and about tasks in general could be obtained. The insight here is that a common piece of code is executed every time the state of any task changes - in this case the scheduler. Thus, by detecting this one event the system object can be decomposed neatly into task objects, and the task objects into modules. The software probe was ten instructions long; eight were used to update task state, and two to write it to the monitor.

HEMI (Hybrid Events Monitoring Instrument) was an experimental tool developed for use on CYBER computers, during an experiment to ascertain the economic and technical viability of integrating performance measurement and evaluation instrumentation into computer systems (Sebastian, 1974). One of the peripheral processors on the CYBER was used as the monitoring processor. Peripheral processors had direct access to central memory and could manipulate data in central memory. As peripheral processors were usually used to control I/O channels, the hardware data acquisition front end was attached to a channel.

This front end included probes, timers, counters, and sequencers. The monitoring computer read the output from the front end with the I/O channel, and read the contents of the registers and memory in the central processor with machine code instructions. Because HEMI could access both hardware and software data simultaneously, software events could trigger hardware data collection, and vice versa. Data was recorded on a storage device attached to the host system. Measurement experiments were set up and controlled from the host processor.

DIAMOND (Hughes, 1980) was developed at Digital Equipment Corporation for use in developing software for their family of computers. DIAMOND includes two processors: a minicomputer for experiment management and event filter control, and a stored-program micro-machine for data analysis and event filtering. The micro-machine is used to implement a 250-nsec resolution programmable event filter and data recorder. In the design of the micro-machine, Hughes classified and analysed 750 measurement algorithms. From these, he selected a small set of fundamental algorithms, and defined an architecture capable of executing these algorithms efficiently. To achieve efficiency, each algorithm was realized in a single micro-instruction loop. That is, in response to each input stimulus from the target system, the micro-machine performs all data processing in a single instruction step. This mandated a highly parallel architecture.

The selected algorithms traced system state, monitored address space activity, and measured the elapsed time between events. Address space activity and elapsed time are displayed with histograms. The program counter histogram algorithm captures and displays two distributions in parallel: the intensity of program activity in a given address space by frequency count, and by execution time. In terms of our formulation of measurement, this is the set of module execution counts and utilizations for machine-code modules. The event time histogram algorithm is used to capture a frequency distribution of the elapsed time between occurrences of two events. If the first event is the the start of an object and the second event is the end of that object, then the elapsed time can be used to identify paths through the object, and the frequency distribution is the set of path execution counts.

In case the histogram arrays were not large enough, automatic checks were included in some measures to detect values outside the array range. In these situations, an out of range counter is incremented, and the value which violated the range is saved. This information is used to detect unexpected program operations, and to modify experiment specifications. Also, these algorithms are used by some other measures, for example histograms of data accesses.

Before, during, or after an event, successive states of the target system can be recorded with a trace absolute algorithm. Events include the start of a task, the termination of a task, access to specified memory locations, and the expiry of a period of time since a task commenced. The following state variables are recorded: task identifier, CPU mode, program counter, and a time stamp. Also, data accesses can be traced.

For each target processor (PDP 11, VAX), a plug in card was built to collect, buffer, and multiplex signals. This card simplifies probe attachment. From these signals, the control microprocessor selects the subset required by the measurement experiment. This subset is masked and compared to range values in four double comparators. The output from these comparators is combined to produce a code, which modifies the opcode of the currently executing microinstruction to select the measurement algorithm required by the experiment.

Software specific information is passed to the monitor through two registers: one register contains the current task identifier, and the other the output of any software probes that the analyst has inserted into his program. Considerable emphasis was placed on the design of a clean, forgiving, friendly user interface, in an attempt to gain acceptance by programmers. Areas of concern in the design of the user interface included: minimal set up time, natural language interface, semi-automatic replication of experiments, maintenance of a measurement audit trail, and automatic adjustment to the user's level of competence.

Ferrari and Minetti (1981b) designed a low cost monitor (HPM) to measure a microcomputer destined to be a basic component in Olivetti's local area networks. HPM includes a programmable event filter which transfers recorded data directly into the memory of the controlling minicomputer, over a DMA channel. The controlling minicomputer programs these event filters to collect the data required by user defined measurement scenarios. The event filters monitor the address bus, data bus, and clock signals of the target processor, and up to 12 other signals from the target processor. HPM event filters are very similar in power and function to the event filters found in a logic state analyser. In addition, software probes write information to a fixed memory location. This write is detected with an event filter, and the monitor records the information from the data bus of the target computer.

4.6 Virtual machine emulation

Modern mainframe operating systems support multiple virtual machines on a single physical system. Each virtual machine can support an operating system, and hence, a complete user environment, which may be different from that supported by other virtual machines in the system. As a virtual machine is a functional prototype of a complete hardware system, it can be used to test software functionally - a technique known as virtual prototyping. It can also be used to evaluate the performance of that software.

Until recently, virtual machines have not been used for performance evaluation because of the difficulty of simulating time. Because several virtual machines share one set of hardware, the timing environment of a virtual machine is unpredictable, and consequently the performance of a system running on a virtual machine differs greatly from that of the same system running on a real machine. In virtual machines, a higher level of pausing complexity is introduced: the pausing and resumption of the machine itself.

Cannon *et al.* (1980) developed a virtual machine emulator to evaluate the performance of proposed systems, by extending the virtual machine environment of an IBM VM/370 system to include timing simulation. To do this, they extended the virtual machine environment to:

- establish a consistent virtual time base, independent of real time, and to
- derive all virtual clock values, and the timing of all asynchronous events, from this virtual time base.

With their virtual machine emulator, they could observe the behaviour and performance of prototype systems running real workloads without having to construct the target hardware. Changes to hardware timing and configuration were easy to make, and the impact of these changes could be evaluated by executing a workload. Because an actual workload is run, the results are more accurate than the results of analytic and simulation modelling; and, because a virtual machine is used, the cost is much lower than the cost of hardware prototyping.

The emulator supports virtual machines in which only virtual time is observed. Because virtual time is used only when the virtual processor is executing, or is waiting for an event, and because asynchronous events occur in virtual time, no timing interference from the emulator or other virtual machines is apparent. However, timing measurements are only approximate, since the timing of the target machine's devices are approximated. When the resources are available, virtual machine emulation provides a useful way of evaluating a system.

4.7 Workload characterization

The performance of a system depends heavily on the demand for hardware and software resources by the workload. Therefore, the quantitative characterization of the resource demands of the workload is an important part of performance measurement. We can distinguish three types of workloads that are used in measurement experiments:

1. live workloads - the actual work performed by the system,
2. executable workloads - a portion of a real workload suitable for an experiment, and
3. synthetic workloads - a reproducible workload, often generated automatically.

Workload characterization studies generally involve the following steps (Heidelberger and Lavenberg, 1984):

- Select the workload component to be characterized, where a workload component is a module that results from a natural decomposition of the workload.
- Select the parameters which will be used to characterize the workload component. These parameters are the hardware and software resource demands of the component.
- Obtain values for each of these parameters by measuring a real workload. Typically, data is collected over a period of several weeks, often with accounting programs.
- Calculate values for these parameters by statistical analysis of the collected data. Calculate the distribution and range of each parameter and transform or scale them to get data suitable for comparison. At this point, values outside the common range are discarded.
- Partition the measured components into clusters so that components in a cluster have similar parameter values (Hartigan, 1975). The purpose of clustering is to consider all components in a cluster to be identical, so that compact workload characterization is obtained.

Using the above workload characterization, an analyst can construct a synthetic workload representative of the actual system. The components of the synthetic workload can be parameterized, and values chosen to match the parameter values of the clusters. The above approach is also used to obtain parameter values for workload models.

4.8 Statistical methods

Whenever large volumes of data are to be analysed, engineers and scientists use statistical methods. In performance measurement, statistical methods are used in the design of measurement experiments, as well as in data reduction and analysis (Heidelberger and Lavenberg, 1984). For example, they are used to validate the data collected with sampling tools.

The measurements made with a sampling tool can be described as a discrete-time stochastic process, where the time separating the sampling instants can usually be described with a sampling law or function. A stochastic process is a function of time whose values are random variables, in this case the measured values. If each random variable may take only a finite or countable number of states, we have a discrete-state process. If the time instants at which state transitions may occur are finite or countable then the process is a discrete-time one. If the variable we are measuring has a binary value, such as CPU busy, then the utilization of the parameter this value represents is the mean of the samples.

Sampling relies heavily on the assumption that our measurements are statistically independent. The larger the number of samples, the closer our sample mean is to the actual value. If there is a functional relationship between the observations, the sample mean may not tend toward the actual mean as the number of samples increases. The minimum number of observations that must be made to ensure a reasonable estimate of the mean is proportional to the variance of the data and inversely proportional to the square of the confidence interval (Ferrari, 1978a).

Statistical methods are also used to estimate values for unmeasurable parameters from measured parameters. To estimate the relative influence of different sources of variation on a performance index, analysis of variance methods are used when all factors are not quantitative, where factors are the parameters which influence appreciably the value of a performance index. These methods decompose the total variation of the index into components which correspond to the sources of variation being considered. When all factors in an experiment are quantitative, regression analysis techniques can be applied.

Regression analysis can be used to approximate the functional dependence of one or more dependent variables on another collection of independent variables. Each dependent variable is expressed as a postulated function of the independent variables and a collection of parameters plus a random error term. This relationship is used to predict values for dependent variables from the measured values of the independent variables. Usually, a linear relationship is postulated, and the parameters are estimated from measurements of the independent variables. These techniques are used to construct an empirical model which estimates the performance index as a function of the values of the factors.

Chapter 5
Using a Logic State Analyser

In the early seventies, traditional fault-finding tools were found to be inadequate for monitoring parallel digital circuits, a problem accentuated by the increasing complexity of those circuits. Oscilloscopes can monitor up to three high speed repetitive digital signals and, if equipped with storage facilities, can catch single events. Logic probes can monitor low speed digital signals and detect short duration pulses. Both of these instruments can monitor individual signals on a computer bus, but not the traffic on that bus.

Logic timing analysers were developed to assist in finding faults in complex high speed logic circuits (Allan, 1977; Hill, 1974). These tools monitor many signal lines; search for specific data patterns; and read, store, and display data when triggered by an external clock. When used to monitor a computer bus, readings are triggered by a clock signal derived from a bus synchronization signal or a processor clock signal.

Figure 5.1 HP 1610A logic state analyser.

Thus, because the analyser is synchronized to the bus, the data read by the analyser is identical to the data latched into the device at the receiving end of the bus. Some analysers have been enhanced to indicate the occurrence of bus activity between measurements.

Logic timing analysers met with success when used to find circuit faults, and it was not long before they were used to monitor program flow. From this beginning, manufacturers developed the logic state analyser (Figure 5.1), claiming it to be a valuable tool for monitoring software, for code optimization, and for performance analysis (Hewlett-Packard, 1978b). Many of the features included in logic state analysers were initially developed in the design of customized memory-bus monitors (Fryer, 1973). In this chapter, we discuss the effectiveness of using a logic state analyser as a performance measurement tool, the analysis of the interrupt-handling routines of the UNIX operating system, and the improvement in performance that resulted from redesigning the common interrupt program to use architectural features of the Perkin-Elmer computer.

5.1 Performance measurement

Traditional hardware tools provide limited information and, if not designed into the computer hardware, are difficult to implement. Logic state analysers are the latest development in the stored-program class of hardware tools. They have programmable event filters and hence are flexible, but are they effective performance monitors? An effective tool is one that can be easily attached to a data path, and can collect user selected information at different levels in the object hierarchy. Other desirable features are: accuracy, ease of use, powerful event filtering, and a range of measurement methodologies.

I wanted to evaluate the change in the performance of interrupt handling which resulted from modifying the common interrupt program in the UNIX operating system. This performance evaluation experiment was an ideal environment in which to evaluate the effectiveness of the logic state analyser as a hardware performance monitor (McKerrow, 1983). UNIX was moved from the Digital Equipment Corporation PDP-11 series of computers to Perkin-Elmer 32-bit series machines by Richard Miller (1978) at the University of Wollongong. As this was the first time UNIX had been ported to another machine, I wanted to evaluate its performance in its new environment, one it was not designed for.

I started my evaluation by measuring the low level routines running in the computer, commencing with a completely idle system. When no user programs are active, the operating system is occupied solely with housekeeping functions, mainly the time of day clock. Following this, I measured the system while it executed a single CPU bound program. The philosophy behind this approach is:

- These routines are relatively small, and thus easy to modify and measure.
- Many of the routines constitute fixed overheads, which have to be taken into account when measuring higher-level behaviour.
- Only a small part of the operating system is written in assembler; the majority of the operating system is written in the 'C' programming language. To enable the transfer from PDP 11 to Perkin-Elmer the assembler code had to be rewritten, making it an area of interest. The assembler code includes the common interrupt handling program.
- The heart of any operating system is the scheduler and its associated interrupt handling routines. I felt it was imperative to understand these before we made more extensive measurements.

5.2 Interrupt handling

All processes running under UNIX are started in response to interrupts generated by external events. External events include: clock ticks, user input from a keyboard, character output to a video display, and the completion of disk operations. A common interrupt program performs actions common to all interrupts, including saving user registers, and then calls the appropriate interrupt handler. Information required by the handler is passed to it from the common interrupt program via a standard stack linkage. Thus, interrupt handling software is modularized, and adding new handlers is reasonably simple. When processing is complete the system returns to idle, where it remains until the next interrupt.

A variety of interrupts occurs within a Perkin-Elmer 7/32 system, all of which can be inhibited by masks in the program-status word (Figure 5.2). External devices interrupt the processor through the single level immediate interrupt. When an interrupt occurs, the processor completes the current instruction, saves the current program status word, and sets the status portion of the new program status word: to select the supervisor register set (the Perkin-Elmer 7/32 has two sets of sixteen 32-bit general-purpose registers), to disable interrupts, to allow the execution of privileged instructions, and to disable memory relocation and protection. After the interrupt is acknowledged, the processor loads the device number and status of the interrupting device into registers, and from the device number calculates the address in the interrupt service pointer table where the start address of the interrupt handler is located. Finally, the start address of the handler is loaded into the location counter and program execution commences.

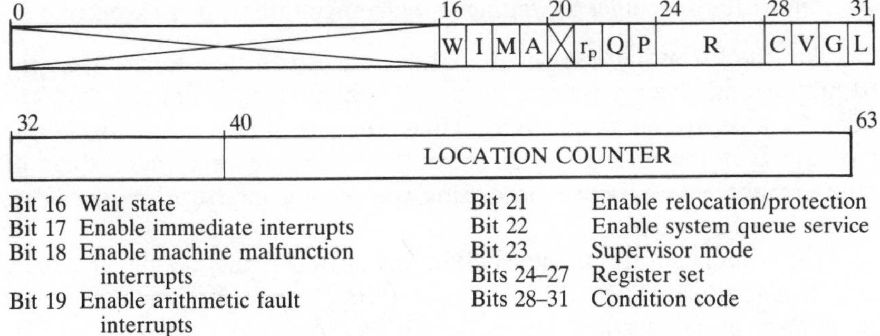

Figure 5.2 Program status word.

5.2.1 Clock interrupt handling

To illustrate the general principles of interrupt handling, the clock interrupt handler is included in this discussion. The following description of the clock handler is included to provide the reader with enough background to understand the discussions about performance in later sections. When the clock interrupts the processor every ten milliseconds, the handler performs the following operations:

- The contents of the memory location addressed by the front panel switches are displayed on the front panel.
- The callout queue is scanned, and any functions ready to be executed are called. A function can arrange to be called after a time delay by placing an entry into the callout queue, where an entry consists of an incremental time, a function address, and a parameter. At every clock tick, the incremental time of the first entry in the queue is decremented, and when this time reaches zero, the function is executed and the entry removed from the queue.
- User time or system time for the current process is updated, and the total CPU time used by the current process is incremented.

At the end of every second, additional operations are performed by the clock interrupt handler, including:

- The time of day, measured in seconds since the beginning of the year, is incremented, and the process time of each currently defined process is updated.
- A flag is set to instruct the common interrupt program to switch to a higher priority user process if one is waiting.
- The priority of the current process is reduced, and if it goes below a set level the priority of all currently defined processes is recalculated.
- Any sleeping processes that are ready to wake up are prepared for waking.

- And if the scheduler is waiting to rearrange things, it is executed.

The clock routine is a small routine, but it can take longer than the 10 milliseconds between clock ticks. So that interrupts are not lost, the clock is able to interrupt itself while doing callouts, and during the processing at the end of every second. To ensure that these areas of code are not entered when processing the second interrupt, a flag is set by the first interrupt.

The regular nature of the clock interrupt makes the handler relatively easy to monitor. When the computer is idle, only the clock interrupt handling routine uses any system resources. Also, two cleanup routines are started by the clock at regular intervals (0.5 and 5 minutes). Thus, measuring and modelling the clock routine characterizes an idle system.

5.3 Common interrupt handler

When UNIX was transferred to the Perkin-Elmer computer, the design of the original version was maintained, and the code was written to match the functions of the PDP 11 code as closely as possible. The common interrupt handling program was no exception (Figure 5.3).

When an interrupt occurs, the processor obtains the corresponding vector from the interrupt service pointer table and then executes a vector routine, which obtains the desired processor status and the start address of the interrupt handler. Then all interrupts and software traps (supervisor calls) branch to the common interrupt handling program (CALL in Figure 5.3). If the system was in user mode prior to the interrupt, the common interrupt program loads the memory relocation registers to switch to the kernel's address space, and re-enables memory relocation and protection. Any information to be passed to the device interrupt handler is saved on the stack, the user register set is selected, user registers are saved, and if a trap handler, as opposed to an interrupt handler, is to be called, interrupts are enabled.

Next, the appropriate handler is called to service the interrupt. If a one second period has just ended, or if the processor was executing a user process prior to the interrupt, a check is made on return from the handler to see if a higher priority process is waiting for service. If so, the process dispatcher is called to switch to that process. Then the common interrupt program returns to a higher priority user process, or to the process which was executing prior to the interrupt.

5.3.1 Modifying the common interrupt handler

UNIX is a multi-tasking operating system designed to support a number of programmers in an interactive environment. A common interrupt handling system is adequate for this application, and has the advantages of modularity and ease of modification, mentioned earlier. For real-time

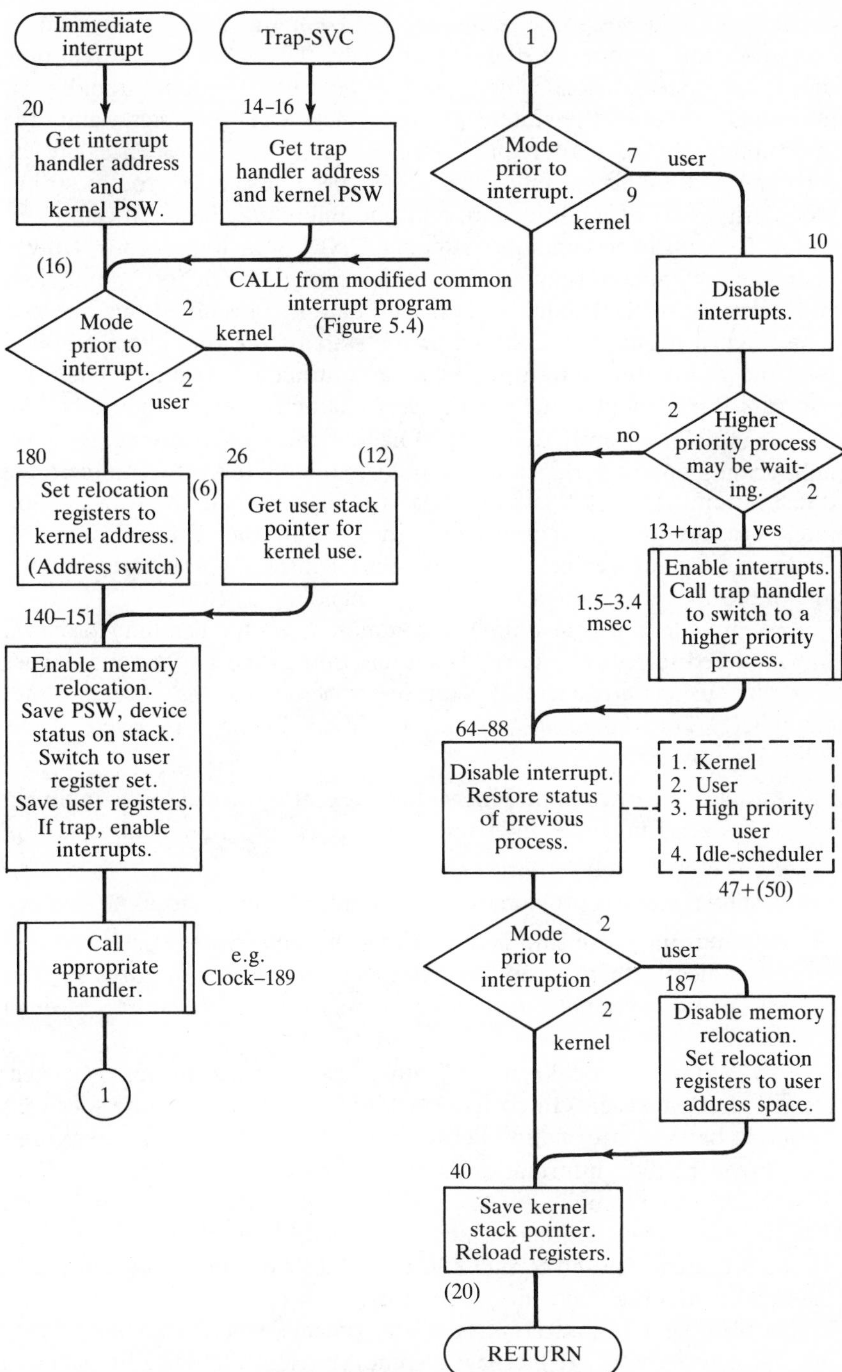

Figure 5.3 Common interrupt program. Numbers above boxes are the execution times in microseconds. Numbers in brackets are the execution times of the software monitor that can be added.

applications, the response time of the common interrupt system is excessive; this is one of the reasons why UNIX is not a real-time operating system. Real-time systems have to respond rapidly to interrupts because the interrupt frequency can be high, and the interrupting device may require fast service. Rapid response can be accomplished by using individual high speed assembler routines; but modularity, ease of modification, and portability may be sacrificed.

A Perkin-Elmer computer running UNIX was linked to a Univac mainframe computer running Exec 8 for remote batch job submission. A synchronous RS232C link is used, and data is transmitted one line at a time. Synchronism is established at the start of the first character, and then the whole line is transmitted as a continuous stream of bits. An interrupt is generated at the end of every character - every eight bits. An 80-character line, transmitted at 4800 baud, generates 80 interrupts, 1.667 milliseconds apart, during the 134 milliseconds it takes to complete the transmission. The data transfer rate is effectively half the transmission rate, because of the cumbersome design of the Univac protocol. Protocol handling requires complex, time consuming software; but the high interrupt rate requires fast interrupt handling software.

To provide a usable link, the common interrupt handling program was modified to reduce interrupt handling time in most situations (Figure 5.4), by using architectural features specific to the Perkin-Elmer computer. Trap handling was not modified. Time was saved in the following ways:

- An address switch is no longer done. Memory relocation is inhibited while servicing the interrupt, and thus program addresses are physical addresses.
- A special stack is provided for the interrupt routines to use.
- All interrupt processing is done using the supervisor register set, and consequently there is no need to save and restore the user register set, or to pass data from one register set to the other through memory.

An additional architectural feature was utilized to make system reconfiguration easier. Interrupts no longer vector to separate locations to obtain handler information before branching to the common program, but instead handler information is placed in tables, and interrupts from all devices vector to one address, except the auto-drive channel interrupt. The physical device number, which has already been placed in a register by the processor, is used to index into the tables to obtain the address of the handler and the minor device number.

In the case of an interrupt to a user process, where a higher priority process may be waiting, the new common interrupt handler branches to the entry point of the original program (CALL on Figure 5.3).

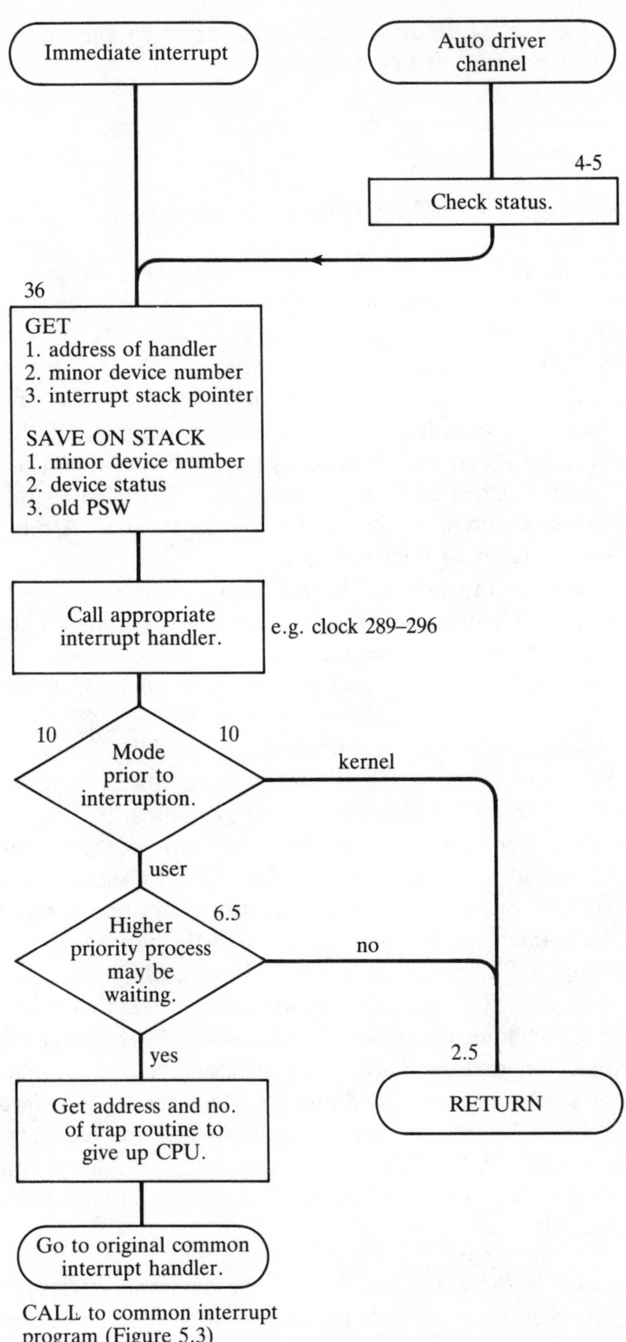

Figure 5.4 Modified common interrupt program.

Otherwise, the system returns to the state prior to the interrupt: user process, kernel process, or idle.

5.4 Performance improvements

We studied the execution of the common interrupt program with the logic state analyser, by measuring execution paths and times before and after modification of the program (Figures 5.3 and 5.4). In two sections of the flow chart in Figure 5.3, a time range is shown. This time range is a consequence of variations in the time taken by the processor to calculate the effective addresses of indexed instructions. If the machine is idle when interrupted, the interrupt is serviced, and then the scheduler is entered, where, depending upon the action of the interrupt handler, either a process is started or the system returns to idle. A return to idle via the scheduler takes 47 microseconds.

Times shown in brackets on these figures are the execution times of a software monitor, which can be added to the program. This monitor measures system time, user time, and idle time to the nearest millisecond. For every interrupt to a user process, this tool costs 42 microseconds, and for every interrupt to a kernel process it costs 48 microseconds. When the common interrupt program returns to idle, the monitor costs an extra 50 microseconds. The counters maintained by this software monitor are recorded by system accounting programs.

Execution times for the common interrupt program, for various processor states, are summarized in Table 5.1. In the initial program, interrupts to user processes are more expensive than interrupts to kernel processes (654 microseconds compared to 303 microseconds), because when servicing an interrupt to a user process, the common interrupt program must switch from user address space to kernel address space before calling the interrupt handler, and switch back again afterwards. To accomplish an address switch, the memory relocation registers are loaded from a table in memory, a process which takes 174 microseconds. In the modified program, the address switch to user space was eliminated, accounting for 60% of the reduction in execution time.

Performance improvements arising from modifying the common interrupt program are:

- a reduction in the execution time of the common interrupt program from 654 to 55 microseconds for interrupts to user processes, and
- a reduction in the execution time of the common interrupt program from 303 to 49 microseconds for interrupts to kernel processes.

Table 5.1 Execution time of the common interrupt program, before and after the program modifications. All times in microseconds.

Exception type	*Previous mode*	*Return mode*	*Execution time*	
			Before	*After*
Interrupt	Kernel	Kernel	303-336	49
Interrupt	User	User	654-687	55
Interrupt	User	Higher priority user	667-700	689
Interrupt	Idle	Idle	350	96
Trap	Kernel	Kernel	297-332	no change
Trap	User	User	648-683	"
Trap	User	Higher priority user	661-693	"

The time taken to handle traps has not altered, and the time taken to handle an interrupt to a user process which returns to a higher priority user process has not changed, because the modified common interrupt program calls the original program to achieve the address switch. For the majority of interrupts, processing time has been significantly reduced. Adding the software monitor to the modified program increases the execution time by 40 microseconds, making it an expensive tool.

The total time taken to handle an interrupt is the sum of the execution time of the common interrupt program and the execution time of the appropriate interrupt handling routine. The latter time varies from handler to handler, and is affected by processor status. Prior to the modifications, when the system was idle, the time taken to service a clock tick was 541-548 microseconds. This time was made up of: common interrupt program, 306 microseconds; clock handling, 188-195 microseconds; plus return to idle via the scheduler, 47 microseconds. If the software monitor was included an additional 92 microseconds were used. When the processor was executing a user process, servicing a simple clock tick took even longer, 843-849 microseconds (Table 5.2).

The clock handler is the only handler which had to be modified to compensate for memory relocation being turned off. In order to access user area structures, the clock handler must calculate the physical address of the user stack from the virtual address, using the kernel segmentation table. This calculation increased clock handler time from 189 to 292

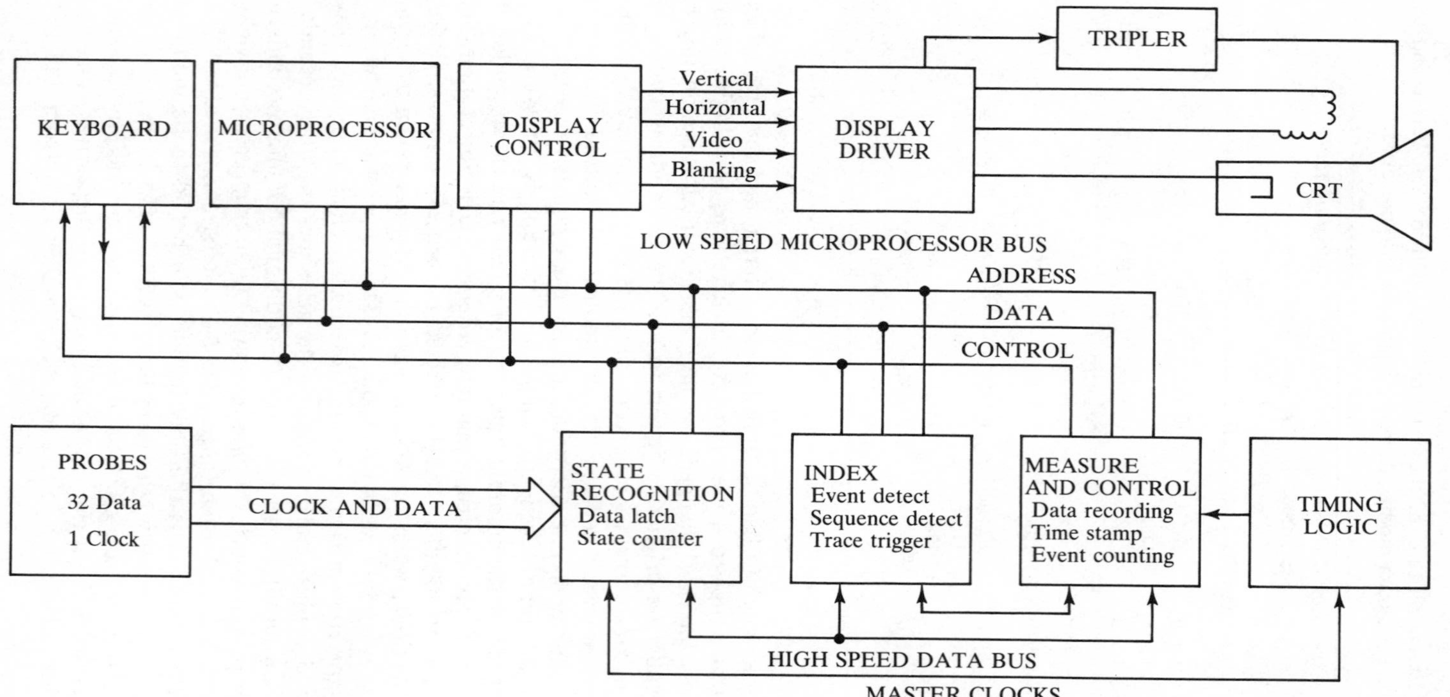

Figure 5.5 HP 1610A logic state analyser block diagram.

microseconds (Table 5.3) negating some of the savings in the common interrupt handler.

For a clock tick during a user process, clock service time has been reduced from 843 to 347 microseconds. For a clock tick during a kernel process, clock service time has been reduced from 492 to 341 microseconds. This improvement in clock handling is a saving of 1.5% of CPU time during kernel processes, and a *saving of 5% of absolute CPU time* during user processes.

During the processing of interrupts from other devices, the time saved is the reduction in the execution time of the common interrupt program. For a synchronous link running at 4800 baud, *the saving is 36% of absolute CPU time,* for transmissions during user processes. For asynchronous devices, the saving depends upon the frequency of the interrupts.

5.5 The logic state analyser

The logic state analyser which we used to make these measurements (Figure 5.5) can monitor 32 digital signals simultaneously, at a maximum sampling rate of 10 megahertz (Hewlett-Packard, 1978a). It can store 64 readings, and display any sequential group of 24 of these. This analyser can be set to trigger on a sequence of data patterns and, once triggered, it will record the occurrence of specified data patterns until its memory is full.

Table 5.2 Representative times for clock handling, before and after program modifications. All times in microseconds.

Clock function	*Execution time*	
	Before	*After*
Clock tick during idle	541-548	388
Clock tick during a kernel process	492	341
Clock tick during a user process	843-849	347
Clock tick during a user process, and return to a higher priority process	3031	3151
Clock tick during a user process with 1 callout - printer new line delay	1970	1475
1 second period, kernel process, and no callouts	5784	5634
1 second period, user process, and callouts pending	6517	6022

Table 5.3 Comparison of clock handler execution times, before and after program modification. All times in microseconds.

	Kernel process		*User process*	
	Before	*After*	*Before*	*After*
Common interrupt program	303	49	654	55
Clock handler	189	292	189	292
Total	492	341	843	347
Time saved	150		495	
Saving in CPU time	1.5%		4.95%	

Unlike traditional hardware monitors, event filters cannot be manually selected on a patch board; instead an interactive video display is used to split signals into logical groupings, to define triggering sequences, to specify states to be traced, and to enable counting functions. A microprocessor internal to the analyser sets electronic switches and counters to perform the tasks normally done by a patch board.

The event filter in this tool can be set up to trace a path through a complex branching network before recording is commenced (Figure 5.6); to record all states, or only selected ones; and to record the time between states, or the frequency of occurrence of a specified state. An event filter set up to monitor the network in Figure 5.6 is shown in Figure 5.7. The input signals have been split into three groups: A is the address bus, D is the least significant byte of the data bus, and B is status information. This event filter specifies a series of states that must occur in sequence before tracing starts, and specifies four states to be traced. As only four states are traced the analyser will record several passes through the code, but only trigger once, so subsequent passes may not necessarily follow the same path. To indicate path variation, a state from the alternative path is also traced (State 4A20). A measure of interrupt activity during the measurement period is obtained by counting the entries to the common interrupt program (State FC4).

The analyser was connected to the backplane of a Perkin-Elmer 7/32 processor (Figure 5.8). Insulated connectors, supplied with it, push onto wire wrap pins, making a convenient and safe connection. Eight bits of the data bus, sufficient to read the operation code, the 18-bit address bus and some status lines were connected to the analyser (Figure 5.9). To establish confidence in the operation of the analyser, we compared data bus information to a machine code listing of the program we were monitoring.

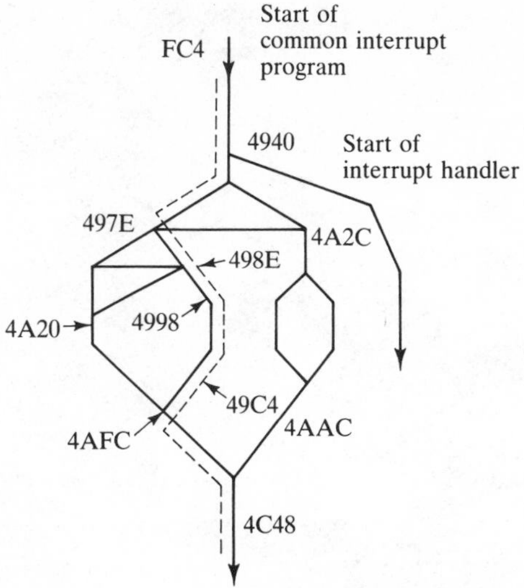

Figure 5.6 Complex network branching requires high-level, sequential trigger capability; e.g.: trace states from 498E only after dashed path is executed.

A clock signal, derived from the bus control logic, was connected to the analyser to synchronize it to the correct phase of the memory access cycle of the minicomputer. The chosen signal was activated when an instruction fetch was initiated by the microcode. A consequence of selecting this signal is that other memory cycles, such as data fetch, were not seen by the analyser, effectively filtering out much bus activity. When analysing the common interrupt program, we were solely interested in tracing the execution path of the program, so this filtering was desirable.

5.5.1 Measurement methodology

At the machine-code level, we can trace the execution path of a program by triggering on the start address of the program and recording the first 64 instruction addresses. By repeatedly updating the trigger address to the last address recorded on the previous trace, we can record the execution of the whole program. If we compare several recordings, taken at each trigger point, we can find most program branches. Then, by comparing these recordings to a machine code listing, we can extract a flow chart of the program, and detect any missed branches. Finally, we can calculate the execution time for each section of the code from the timing data recorded by the analyser.

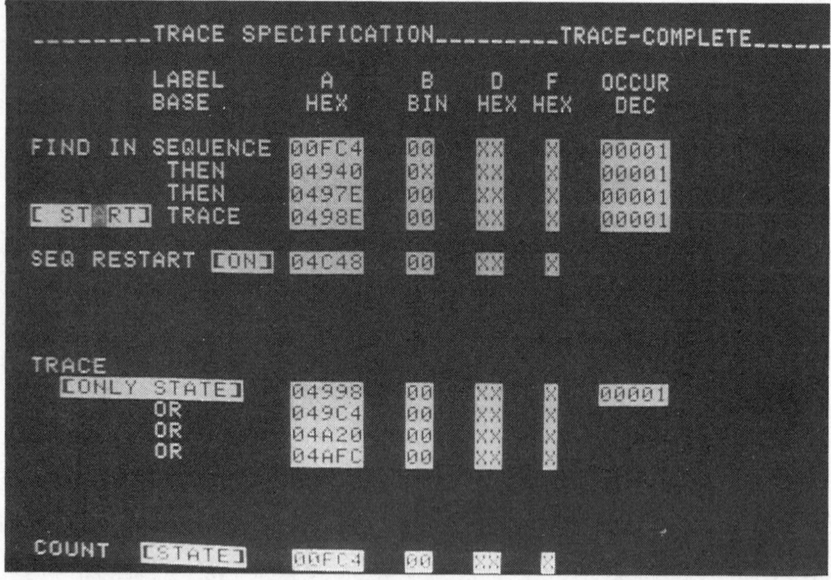

Figure 5.7 Event filter set up to trace the states after address 498E in the program graphed in Figure 5.6.

With large, complex programs the above method can become tedious, and may provide too much detail. Important information, such as execution path and execution time, can be obtained using a simpler approach. In the analysis of the clock handler, we set the analyser to trigger on a clock interrupt, and to trace the entry address, exit address, and an address in each program branch of the clock routine. Execution path was indicated by the occurrence of a branch address in the recording, and execution time was the time period between the occurrence of entry and exit addresses. In this way, the program level object was decomposed into block-structure level modules.

The clock routine was written in the 'C' programming language. The 'C' compiler produced assembler mnemonics, which were assembled to machine code, and an assembler listing was produced. We used this listing in conjunction with symbolic debug to find program entry, branch and exit addresses for state analysis. If the entry and exit addresses of the called routine are not known the addresses of the call and return statements of the calling routine can be used.

Modifications to the common interrupt handler created some problems for state analysis. In the modified program, all interrupts vector to the same location, making it difficult to distinguish one interrupt from another, and interrupt specific information is contained in memory locations and registers. We overcame this problem by setting the analyser to trigger on the entry point of the interrupt handler rather than on the interrupt vector address.

Figure 5.8 Connection of the analyser to the backplane of the computer.

If processor status information is available to the analyser, we can devise even more powerful methodologies, and decompose the system object into task-level modules. When an interrupt occurs, the processor switches from user to supervisor mode, and indicates this by setting a flag in the program status word (Figure 5.2). This signal is available on the backplane, and we connected it to the logic state analyser (Figure 5.9).

We measured the total time taken to handle an interrupt to a user program by triggering the analyser on an address unique to the desired handler, and tracing only user-mode instructions. The time difference between the user-mode instructions located immediately before and after the interrupt is the time taken to handle the interrupt. Again, specific execution paths can be monitored by tracing addresses in branches of the program. To simplify initial measurement, we had only one user process running on the system: a BASIC program in an infinite loop.

5.5.2 Limitations

A lot of useful information is provided by the preceding measurements (Table 5.2), but to model the clock routine completely, we need to investigate two areas further: the callout section, and the process table update section. Execution time for the callout section depends on the number of callouts, and the functions called. For example, a function called to provide newline delay on a line printer took 1068 microseconds.

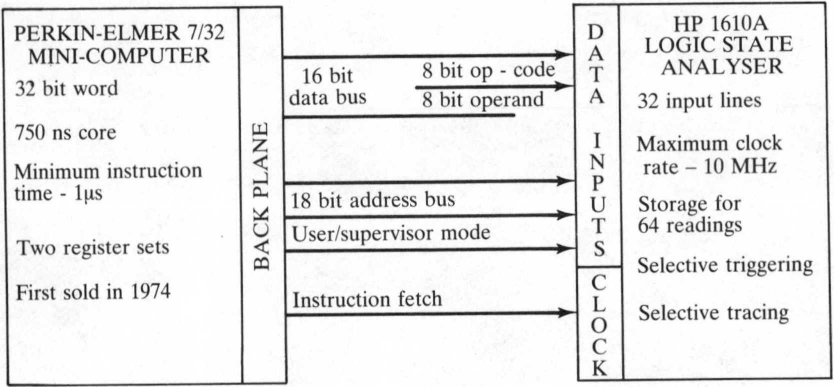

Figure 5.9 Backplane to analyser signal connections.

Execution time for the process table update section depends on the number of current processes, the priority of the current process, and the number of processes ready to wake up. If we could use the state analyser to read memory locations, we could determine this stimulus information during the trace, thereby simplifying measurements. In this study, we determined this stimulus information both by measuring the current system state with software tools and by controlling the workload of the system.

Hardware monitoring tools are inherently limited to measuring information that can be interpreted at the hardware level without knowledge of software activities. In the case of the logic state analyser, there is a solution to this problem if the information is stored in fixed known memory locations, and if memory contents are updated regularly. The solution is to use the memory cycle as an analyser clock signal, and to connect memory access status information to analyser inputs, information such as instruction fetch and data write. Then we could use the analyser to obtain program specific information by tracing memory data writes to specified memory locations.

Whether we can do the above depends on the availability of the desired memory access status signals, the width of the analyser, and the triggering capabilities of the analyser. The analyser we used in this study is 32 bits wide, has one clock input, and has only eight registers available for specifying triggering sequences and states to be traced. If a second clock input were available, a dual clocking system - one for data write, and one for instruction fetch - could be used as an alternative to the above solution, freeing up some of the analyser inputs.

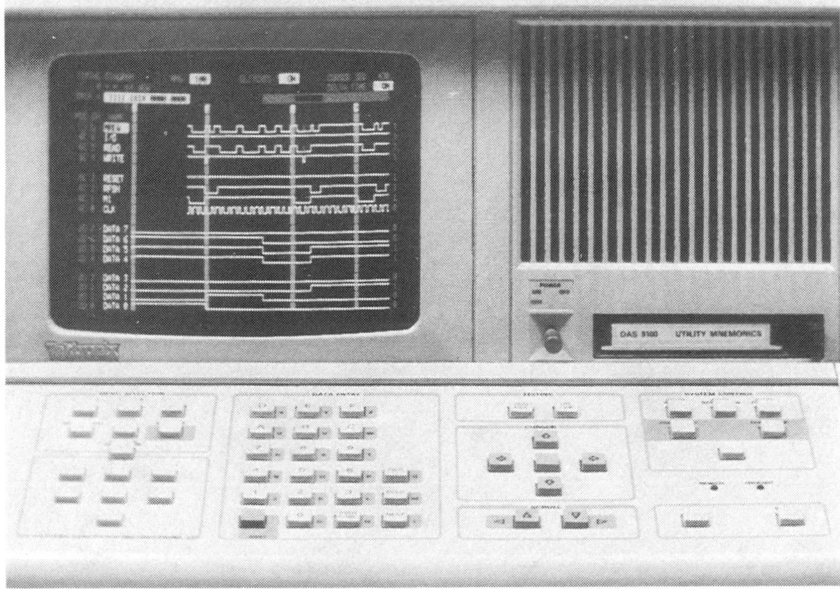

Figure 5.10 Colour display on the Tektronix 9129 digital analysis system.

5.6 Newer logic state analysers

The logic state analyser used in this case study is obsolete. A range of new analysers, from a number of manufacturers, has been released onto the market (Comerford, 1981; Brampton, 1982; Guteri, 1982; Corson, 1983). Their principle of operation is the same; however, advances in technology have enabled the designers to increase the power of these tools. All have increased resolution, more inputs and more storage, and many combine the facilities of both state and timing analysers in the one instrument. In addition, event filtering facilities have been enhanced and some analysers can handle multiple clocks. Optional plug-in modules extend the range of the basic instrument and provide new facilities; for example, a programmable pattern generator for stimulus generation.

Considerable emphasis has been placed on improving the user interface and data presentation features. Tektronix (Figure 5.10) use a colour display to highlight areas of interest. Hewlett-Packard (Figure 5.11) have included a histogram display, and enable the user to label measured signals.

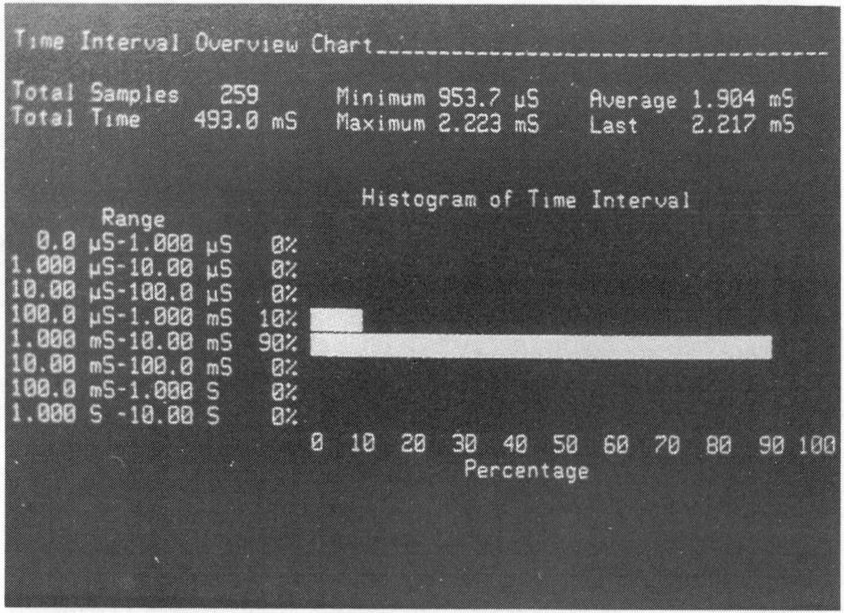

Figure 5.11 A time histogram display on the HP 1630 logic analyser.

A major application of logic analysers is the analysis of microprocessor software. One problem when measuring most microprocessors is that no signals are available to separate instruction fetch memory cycles from other memory cycles. When using one of these analysers to measure the execution of programs on a microprocessor, either the microprocessor is replaced by an emulator or a state machine is used to model memory bus activity. These facilities are built into microprocessor specific personality modules, to enable easy connection of bus signals. If an emulator is used, the microprocessor is removed from the target system and an interface connector is inserted in its place. If a personality module is used, an IC clip is used to connect the microprocessor to the personality module. Software running on the logic analyser maps the machine operation codes into mnemonics. These mnemonics are displayed together with the address of the instructions. Memory activity between instruction fetches is also indicated on the display. Thus, very powerful assembler debugging tools are available.

Hewlett-Packard (Corson, 1983) have also included some performance evaluation tools in their logic analyser. The time period between two user defined events (module execution time) and the number of times that path was taken can be measured and displayed as a path utilization histogram (Figure 5.11). A second display presents a histogram of address space usage (Figure 5.12). The user can quickly identify the location of maximum system activity by defining the address space in terms of program labels. These tools are both useful and powerful, but require an address map of the program being analysed, limiting their usefulness in high-level language and dynamic memory allocation applications.

Of more interest to performance analysts is the trend toward user programmable analysers (McLeod, 1986). Such analysers are equal in power to many hardware monitors, and enable users to write their own analysis software. Measurements are recorded in memory which can be directly accessed by the monitoring processor, eliminating the data link used to connect a stand alone state analyser to a controlling computer. Thus, the data transfer overhead is eliminated, and analysis software can examine the data as soon as the measurements are made. With stand alone analysers, the data is not transferred to the controlling processor until the measurement buffer is full, creating a delay between measurement and analysis. Also, data recording stops until data transfer is complete, introducing discontinuities into the trace.

One such user programmable instrument is the μAnalyst from Northwest Instrument Systems (Figure 5.13). The μAnalyst contains the probes, event filtering circuits, and storage of a traditional logic state analyser, and plugs into a host personal computer, which provides processing power. It costs one third of the cost of an equivalent stand alone instrument, plus the cost of the personal computer.

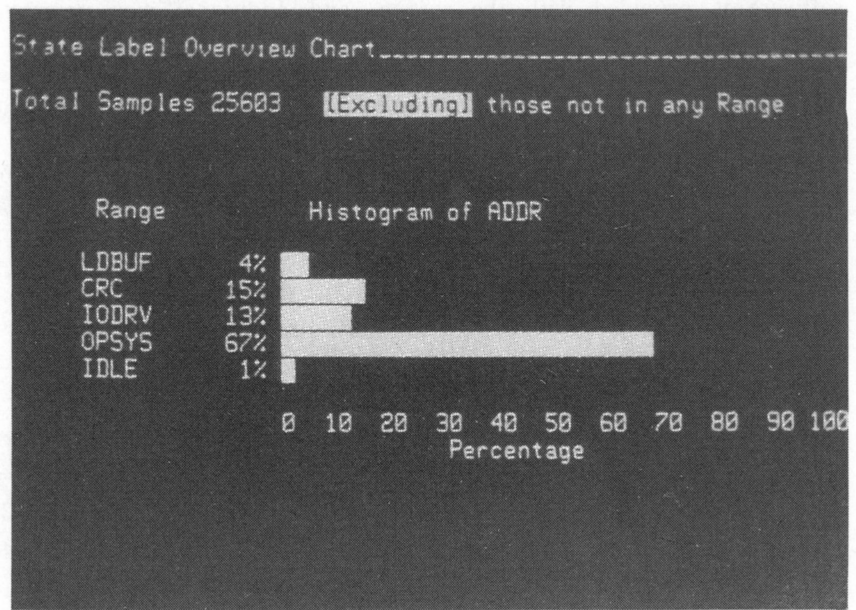

Figure 5.12 A label histogram display on the HP 1630 logic analyser.

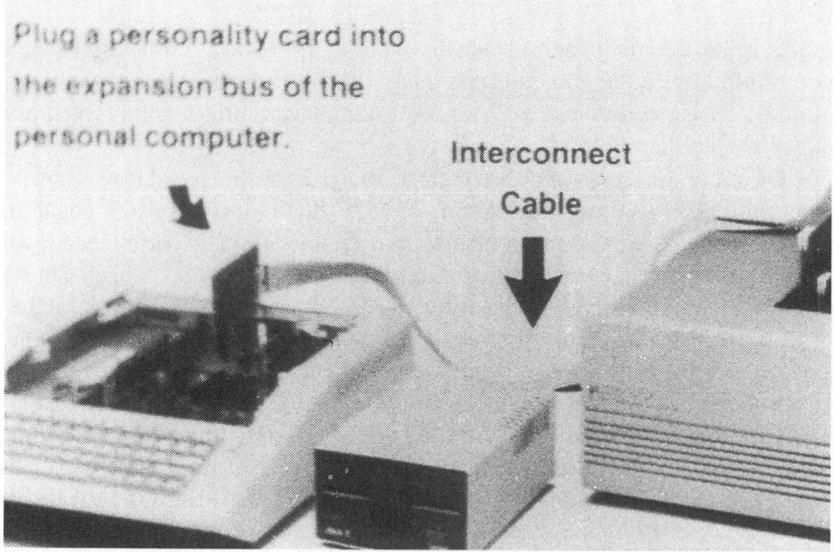

Figure 5.13 A logic analyser controlled by a personal computer.

Software running on the personal computer controls data collection, event filtering, data analysis, and data display. Some measurement software is provided with the system, and additional measurement software can be written by the user as needed. Each probe card can connect to 16 data signals (up to five cards can be used), with a resolution of 10 MHz, and can store up to 4096 measurements.

5.7 Conclusion

Code written to be portable and easily modifiable often does not make use of specific features of the target architecture. Modifying code to use these architectural features improves performance at the cost of portability. Performance improvements which resulted from modifying the common interrupt program include a reduction in its execution time from 654 to 55 microseconds, when servicing interrupts to user processes. During transmission over a synchronous link running at 4800 baud, this reduction in execution time is a saving of 36% of absolute CPU time. Surprising amounts of CPU resources are consumed by clock handling, 3.41% of CPU time with the modified handler, making the selection of the clock interrupt rate an important consideration in system design.

The logic state analyser is a useful performance evaluation tool, because of its ability to measure object execution paths and execution times. Objects can be examined in great detail - down to machine-code level. Program-level objects can be monitored by tracing program entry points, exit points, and branch paths. The execution time of interrupt handlers can be measured by measuring the time spent in supervisor mode servicing the request. State analysis is a powerful and accurate measurement method which does not interfere with the software under study; however, the logic state analyser has the limitations of a traditional hardware tool: it cannot read program specific information.

Chapter 6
Measurement Methodology and Tool Design

In the Introduction, we discussed the need for a measurement methodology based on the scientific method (Section 1.4). One of the corollaries of the formulation of performance measurement is that the formulation provides a general overall context within which measurement and evaluation can take place (Section 2.13). In this chapter, we will develop a measurement methodology from the formulation (Figure 6.1), and we will design a hybrid measurement tool to implement this methodology.

In the formulation of performance measurement, we defined the set of measurements which can be made on an object. Which measures an analyst wants to record during a performance evaluation study depends upon the hypothesis he wants to test. However, a comprehensive monitoring tool will measure all parameters, and enable the analyst to select those measures he desires. When commencing a performance study, the analyst should define clearly the purpose of the study, and the results he expects; for example, is there a system bug to be found? From this information, he can propose an initial hypothesis, formulate a measurement experiment, and in the case of a bug, collect all the symptoms. Once he has delineated the object to be measured, he can study it until he understands its operation (or expected operation). With this understanding, he can refine his hypothesis.

At this stage, the analyst should know enough about the system to define clearly the object to be studied, the level of the object in the measurement hierarchy, the depth of decomposition required to give the desired measurement resolution, and the decomposition of the object into modules. Once he has defined the modules, he can select a method of instrumentation suitable for that level of the object hierarchy. To measure these modules, he inserts probes into the system, to detect their start and termination and to record stimulus information. If the object decomposition is more than one level deep, then the probes must also detect the start and termination of lower level objects. As the system is instrumented, he constructs a module map, which includes module name, module identifier, module function, and stimulus variables.

Once the system is instrumented, the analyst runs tests to verify the accuracy of the instrument. Then he can select the measurements to be made, run the measurement experiment, and analyse the data.

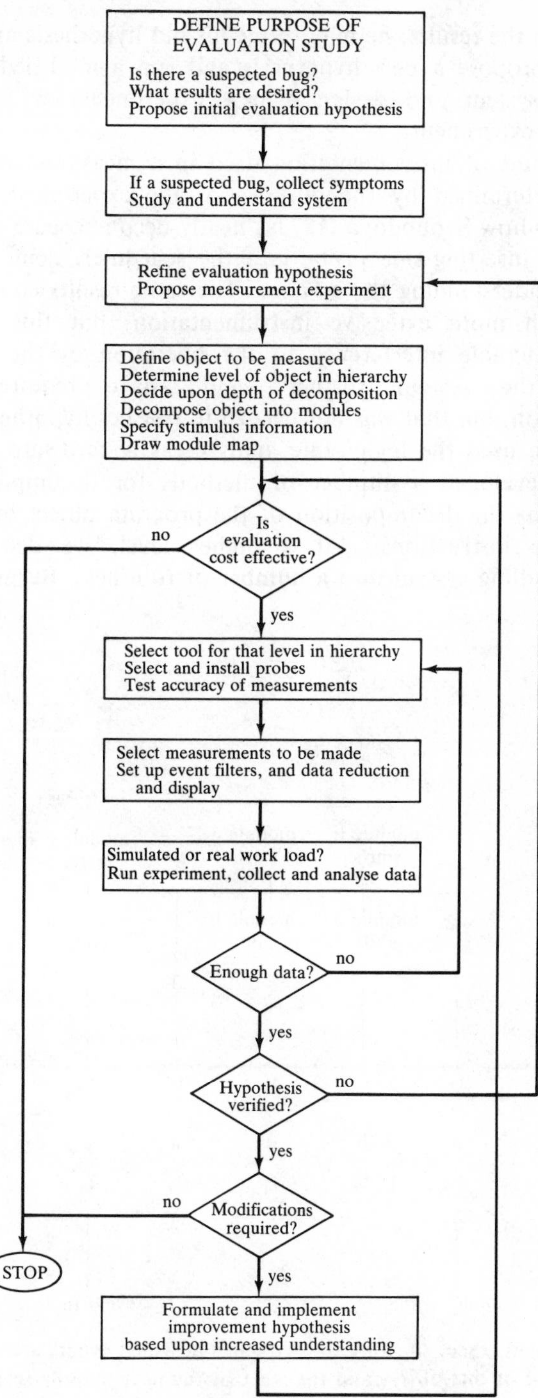

Figure 6.1 Measurement methodology.

Depending on the results, he may refine his old hypothesis and re-run the experiment, propose a new hypothesis and run a modified experiment, modify the system and design a new experiment, or terminate the measurement experiment.

The amount of instrumentation used in a measurement experiment should be determined by the purpose of the experiment. In Section 4.5.1, we saw how Svobodova (1973a) neatly decomposed a system to the task level by inserting one probe into the scheduler, demonstrating the benefits of understanding the system. The same results could have been obtained with more extensive instrumentation, but this would have caused considerable interference to the operation of the system. To decompose the system further would have required extensive instrumentation, but that was not needed to test her hypothesis.

When we used the logic state analyser as a hardware tool (Section 5.5.1), we developed a number of methods for decomposing objects. The finest was the decomposition of the program object into individual machine-code instructions. At a higher level, we decomposed the interrupt handling system into a number of routines. By monitoring the

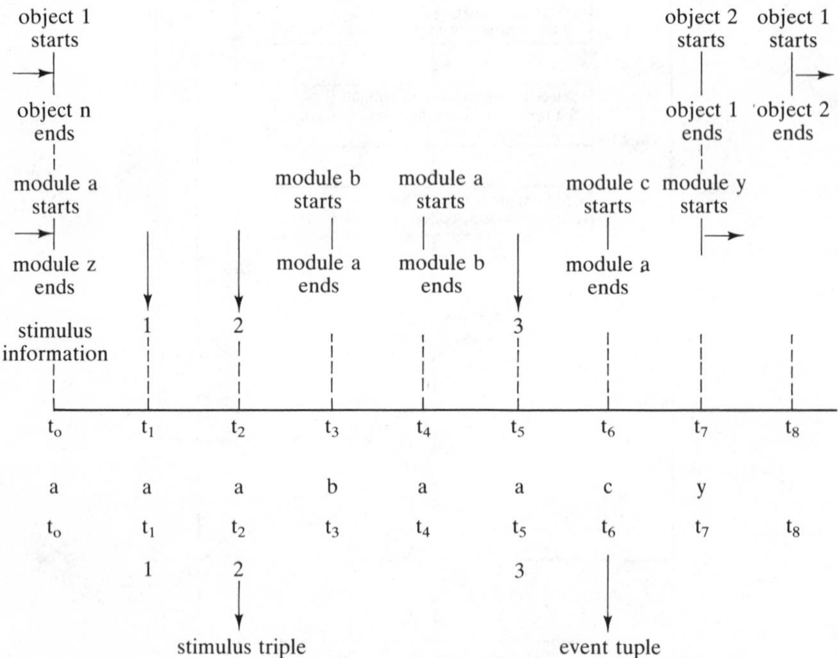

Figure 6.2 Event trace, showing the sequence in which events are recorded. The end of one object and the start of the next may be seen as two views of the same event; similarly, the start of an object and the start of the first module in that object are also two views of the same event.

processor-mode status flag, we decomposed the system into a kernel-mode module and a user-mode module, and then, by selecting suitable experiments, we were able to monitor individual process modules. Other methods of decomposition are discussed in the case studies in Chapters 7 and 8.

6.1 Measurement of objects

6.1.1 Event detection

In Chapter 2, we developed a theoretical method for decomposing objects into modules. This method is based on a conceptual model of an object: a sequence of modules, where the modules are started and terminated by events. In this section, we will develop a practical method for object decomposition based on event detection. We will detect events by inserting probes into the software, probes which produce a continuous stream of event information, from which the execution of the modules can be traced. This module event trace and associated stimulus information (Figure 6.2) should be recorded by our monitoring tool. The event trace is a sequence of tuples, each containing a module identifier and the time at which the module commenced execution, relative to the start of the measurement period. Stimulus information is recorded in the event stream as a triple: current module identifier, time relative to start of measurement period, and one item of stimulus information.

To achieve the desired decomposition, an object must be instrumented to detect the following events:

- start of object execution,
- pause in object execution (if the module is interruptible),
- resumption of object execution, and
- termination of object execution.

These events must be detectable both for the object and for all the modules into which it is decomposed during the measurement experiments. Instrumenting a system to detect each of these events is a fairly complex task.

Usually, a significant reduction in the number of event tuples (and hence the number of probes and the interference) is achieved by one tuple signifying more than one event. The termination of one module and the start of the next occur at the same instant, and can be recorded as one event tuple rather than two. The start of an object and the start of a module always occur at the same time, and a pause in a module and the start of another occur at the same time, as do the end of the latter and the resumption of the former; hence, all these pairs of events can be recorded with single event tuples.

This data compression causes an apparent loss of information which must be reconstructed either by the analysis section of the tool or by extending the information in the event descriptor (for example: old module identifier, pause; new module identifier, start; time relative to start of measurement period). In either case, the analyst must have a reasonable understanding of the system to be able to do the reconstruction. This understanding can be built into the probes, or into the analyser. The latter has two obvious advantages: there is less interference, and event probes can be added before the system is understood. Understanding can be built up through analysis of measurements. During the analysis of experiments, the analyst has two options: either he can manually reconstruct the information, interactively, from his own knowledge, or he can build the information into a database in the analyser. Ultimately, by combining this database and the measurement database, he can construct an expert system.

6.1.2 Measurement algorithms

Measurement algorithms massage the data in the event trace to produce an **object record** for the object under study. An object record (Figure 6.3 to Figure 6.8) is a data structure in which all the information measured during the execution of an object is stored. From the data stored in the object record, we can derive values for all the calculated parameters (Section 6.1.3). An object record (Figure 6.3) consists of an object descriptor and a set of path records. A **path record** (Figure 6.4) consists of a path descriptor (a sequence of modules and their execution times) and a set of path execution records.

Every time a path is executed, a **path execution record** (Figure 6.5) is generated. The path execution record includes a **stimulus record** (Figure 6.6), a **variable usage record**, a **variable data record** (Figure 6.7), and a **memory usage record** (Figure 6.8) for that invocation of the path. The set of path execution records can become very large, very quickly. If the experiment doesn't require data about individual path executions, then path execution records should be left out of the path record. An object record that doesn't include the set of path execution records grows to a fixed size, and consequently, we can use it to collect data over an extended period of time (until the values assigned to count variables overflow).

These data structures can be implemented in a number of ways, although the diagrammatic representation used here implies a linked list of variable sized structures. With this set of structures, an analyst can record all measured data, and some measured values derived from the data, without data loss. As a consequence, these structures can become

Object name	Number of object executions (N_e)	Measurement period (T_p)	Object class (J_c)	Object address
Path record for path I	One path record for each path through the object – sorted in ascending order of execution time			Path record for path K

Figure 6.3 Object record – data structure for recording information about an object during a measurement experiment.

large and cumbersome. To minimize this problem, an analyst should use only those data structures needed for an experiment, and should employ data reduction in situations where data loss is not a problem. I have not implemented a full set of these data structures in any experiment, and in some experiments, I have generated and recorded the values manually. In the construction of a hybrid monitoring tool, based around a logic state analyser (Section 6.6), I implemented a subset of the object record (Figure 6.16).

The object record for the event trace in Figure 6.2 is shown in Figure 6.9. This display of an object record is an additional data display which is added to the set of displays described in Section 2.8. Methods for setting up the memory usage record and the variable access record are discussed in Section 6.3, because they require extensions to the event trace.

Measured values can be obtained from the event trace, and stored in the object record, using the following algorithms:

Path number (P_k)	Path execution time (t_k)	Number of path executions (C_k)
Module name	One tuple (name, duration) for each module in the path – in order of invocation	
Module execution time	Other information about modules can be found from their object records	
Path execution record 1	One execution record for each time the path is executed in order of execution	Path execution record (C_k)

Figure 6.4 Path record – data structure for recording information about individual paths through an object during a measurement experiment.

Path execution number	Memory usage record	Stimulus record	Variable usage record

Figure 6.5 Path execution record – data structure for recording information about individual path traversals during a measurement experiment.

A6.1 To calculate the measurement period (T), subtract the time recorded in the first tuple of the event trace from the time recorded in the last tuple (e.g. $t_8 - t_0$ in Figure 6.2).

A6.2 To find an execution path (p_k) through an object record, list the sequence of modules between initiation and termination of the object (e.g. a, b, a, c for object 1 in Figure 6.2).

A6.3 To calculate the execution time (t_k) for an execution path, subtract the time recorded in the start tuple from the time recorded in the finish tuple of the path (e.g. $t_7 - t_0$ in Figure 6.2).

The names of objects, modules, and variables can be obtained from the analyst, interactively, or from a database of information about the target system, which the analyst has previously constructed.

A6.4 To generate an object record:

```
Go to the start of the trace
Initialize object record
Measurement period start time = time in first tuple
While there are still invocations of the object to be counted do
    initialize a temporary path record
    move to the next object traversal to be analysed
    object start tuple = first tuple
    module start tuple = first tuple
    while object traversal not complete do
        read next record on event trace
        if stimulus information then
            calculate time since start of object
            save a triple in stimulus record
        else {event information}
            if end of an object traversal then
                calculate module execution time
                save module tuple
                calculate object execution time
                if a new path then
                    add a new path record to object record
                    copy temporary path record to new path record
                    set path counter to one
```

```
                else
                        copy appropriate data from temporary path
                          record to actual path record
                        increment path counter
                else {end of a module}
                        {expand here to detect interruption
                         by foreign modules}
                        calculate module execution time
                        save module tuple
                        update module start tuple
        {end of measurement trace}
        Sort path records in ascending order of execution time
        Calculate measurement period
        Calculate total number of path executions
```

During one pass through the event trace, the **object record generation algorithm** records the module sequence and stimulus information, and calculates the set of execution paths (P_e), the set of execution counts (N_c), and the set of execution times (T_e). As data is collected, it is stored in the stimulus record, the path execution record, the path record, and the object record. Using this algorithm, a measurement tool can analyse the event trace in real time, as event tuples and stimulus triples are generated.

Algorithm 6.4 does not detect the pause and resumption of modules due to interruption. The section of the module before the interruption and the section of the module after the interruption are treated as separate invocations of the same module, unless a module continuation flag is set (Section 6.5.2). The modules which are executed during the interruption are recorded as part of the module sequence in the object. If the analyst wishes to study the activity during the pause in the execution of a module, he can record this sequence of foreign modules. Alternatively, once he has established the cause of the interruption, he can study the interruption as a separate object.

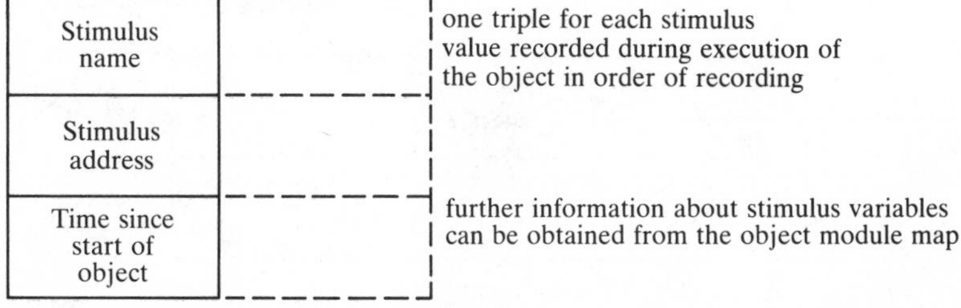

Figure 6.6 Stimulus record – data structure for recording information about individual stimulus variables for an individual path traversal during a measurement experiment.

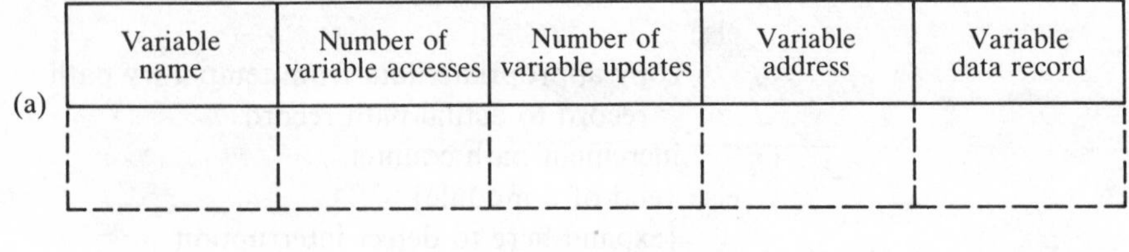

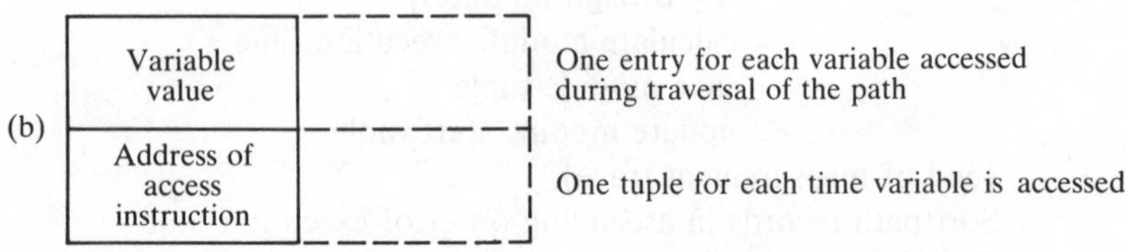

Figure 6.7 (a) Variable usage record and (b) variable data record – data structures for recording operations on a variable during an individual path traversal.

If the analyst is not interested in the activity during pauses in module execution, he can insert a **foreign module handler** into Algorithm 6.4 (Algorithm 6.5). However, to use this handler he must know which modules are in the object, information which should be available from the module map of the object. If this information is not readily available, he will have to make several measurements to determine which modules are in the object. A switch is included to allow the analyst to select foreign module removal as required.

```
A6.5 To detect foreign modules:
     If foreign-module-removal switch is set then
         if next module is a foreign module then
             if foreign-module-detected flag not set then
                 set foreign-module-detected flag
                 save tuple time as foreign start time
             else {not a foreign module}
                 if foreign-module-detected flag set then
```

Code/data	Start address	Size

One entry for each memory segment used during path traversal

Figure 6.8 Memory usage record – data structure for recording usage of memory segments during an individual path traversal.

{end of foreign module sequence}
clear foreign-module-detected flag
calculate execution time of foreign modules
add execution time to time in module start tuple
add execution time to time in object start tuple
else {end of a normal module}

By applying Algorithm 6.4 at lower levels in the hierarchy, we can obtain the set of execution times (T_m), the set of execution paths (P_m), and the set of execution counts (N_a) for each module; and the total number of module executions (N_m). Algorithm 6.4 records stimulus information, and if we wish to do more than that with stimulus information, we must extend this algorithm, for example we can add counters to count the occurrence of specific values of stimulus variables. One piece of stimulus information that we often record is **object class** (Figure 6.3).

To implement Algorithm 6.4, we require a method of detecting the start and finish of an object, and a way of differentiating between paths through an object. One **object path** can be differentiated from another

Object record	Object 1	1	t_8-t_0	example 6.2	× 8000
Path record	1	t_7-t_0	1		
	a	b	a	c	
	t_3-t_0	t_4-t_3	t_6-t_4	t_7-t_6	
Path execution record	1				
Memory usage record	Memory usage not recorded				
Stimulus record	exl	ex2	ex3		
	1	2	3		
	t_1-t_0	t_2-t_0	t_5-t_0		
Variable usage record	Variable usage not recorded				

Figure 6.9 Object record for the event trace in Figure 6.2.

by comparing execution time, module sequence, and the execution times of the modules in these sequences. At times, we may use only one of these to distinguish between paths, or, to reduce the number of distinct paths, we may consider all paths within an execution time range to be one path. However, this should be done with caution, as it is possible for different paths to have the same execution time.

It is also possible for one path to have different execution times, creating a problem for the analyst. However, by investigating the cause of varying execution time for a path, the analyst will increase his understanding of what is actually happening inside the computer. Execution time variations can be due to a number of different causes:

- The execution time of some assembler instructions is data dependent, particularly on older machines (Section 5.4).
- Temperature variations in the processor and the monitoring tool can cause apparent variations in execution time.
- In systems with asynchronous memory buses, memory access time may vary between different memory banks due to the usage of different types of memory. Thus, the place where the program is loaded into memory may cause execution time variations.
- If a direct memory access controller steals memory cycles during the execution of the object, the execution time may increase. We can compensate for this by disabling DMA during the experiment, or by counting DMA cycles and associated dead cycles.
- The device which causes the most headaches is cache memory. The execution time of a program is a function of the cache hit ratio, which may vary from one execution of the program to the next, particularly if the execution of the program is paused to allow the system to handle interrupts or to switch to other processes. The simplest way to overcome cache problems during experiments is to switch it off. However, such measurements may not provide the data required by the performance study, although they do provide a yardstick for studying performance improvement through using cache. The only real solution is to count both the number of instruction cycles and the number of cache hits or misses during the execution of the object, and use these to normalize the execution times. In many studies, cache variations may not be worth worrying about.

When deciding if the current path is a new one, all paths whose execution times lie within a small range can be recorded as one path, to overcome the effect of minor variations in path execution times. This should only be done after the cause of the variation has been established.

6.1.3 Calculation algorithms

From the information stored in the object record, a number of values are calculated. Calculated values can be obtained using the following algorithms:

A6.6 To calculate the set of object execution frequencies (F_e), divide the execution count for each path by the total number of object executions. The set of module execution frequencies (F_m) is obtained in a similar manner.

A6.7 To calculate the object throughput (N_o), divide the number of object executions by the measurement period. Module throughput is calculated in the same way.

A6.8 To calculate the set of relative path execution times (T_r), divide the execution time for each path by the maximum execution time. The execution time of the last entry in the object record is the maximum execution time, because the path records have been sorted in ascending order of execution time (Algorithm 6.4). Due to the recursive nature of the object definition, the set of normalized relative module execution times can be found using the same algorithm.

A6.9 To calculate the set of module to path execution time ratios (E_r), divide the execution time for each module in the path by the execution time of the path.

A6.10 To calculate the set of path utilizations (U_p), multiply the execution time for each path by the number of times it is executed and divide the result by the measurement period. Module utilizations are calculated in a similar manner (Equation 2.42).

6.2 Data display

In Section 2.8, we discussed a number of graphs with which we can display combinations of measured and calculated values. These graphs display the contents of the object record, and values derived from the contents of the object record, in a form that is easy for people to analyse. Most of these graphs are simple histograms and flow graphs; consequently, only the object spectrum requires a special algorithm.

A6.11 To plot an object spectrum:
Determine vertical axis scaling from the range of execution counts.
Determine horizontal axis scaling from the range of execution times.

```
For each execution path
    Draw a vertical line,
        with length equal to the execution count, and
        horizontal position equal to the execution time
        [This is a spectral line.]
    Write the execution time on the spectral line.
    Write the stimulus information on the spectral line.
Add titles etc. to graph
```

As with the production of the object record, data can be displayed by programs running on the monitoring tool or by manual methods. Which method an analyst will use depends upon the available tools, the purpose of the experiment, and the amount of data to be analysed.

6.3 Memory usage and variable access measurement

In some experiments, we wish to monitor variable access, usually by counting reads and writes to individual variables and data structures. We can monitor variable accesses with software probes, but hardware probes create less interference. However, if we want to use hardware probes, we must know the physical addresses of the variables, and our monitoring tool must be able to detect accesses to these addresses.

Before we can measure the access by an object to physical memory, we must extend the event trace to include memory bus activity. This greatly increases the volume of data in the trace, but most of this data is discarded by the event filters. On many computers, control signals can be used to separate data accesses and instruction fetches, simplifying the task of event filtering.

Recording and analysing all address bus activity to determine which memory segments are used gives a very precise measurement, but requires a lot of resources. Often, we do not need this level of precision, and coarser measures can be used. One simplification is to segment the memory into fixed size blocks, and simply record access to any location in a block. Another is to record the address at which probes are inserted when the event tuple is recorded, and use these addresses to determine a coarse measure of memory usage. One problem to avoid is that you may record the probe address instead of an address in the module (Section 7.3.3).

At higher levels in the object hierarchy, we can measure memory usage from the event trace or with stimulus information. At the block-structure level, the routines which access dynamic data structures (e.g. add to list) can be defined as modules. We can calculate the number of data elements in a data structure at any time by counting and comparing module executions as the program executes. Alternatively, we can record the size of the data structure as a piece of stimulus information every time the structure is updated.

At the task level, two modules that a system can be decomposed into are: the page fault module and the memory allocation module. To study the usage of various memory segments in the working set, we can insert a stimulus probe into the memory allocation module, which will write out the identifier of the segment being allocated. This produces a trace of the working set of an object with respect to time and, by counting the executions of these modules, we can measure page fault frequency. Alternatively, we can record the number of pages in an object's working set as a piece of stimulus information, every time the working set is changed. Algorithms for the measurement of working set behaviour are discussed by Spirn (1977) in Chapter 5 of his book on program behaviour.

Measurement of memory usage is one reason for having general purpose probes and counters which are not permanently allocated to the event trace. In a hardware tool, this means extra probes to monitor the bus of the target computer and additional event filters. In a hybrid tool, it means the ability to detect and count specific events or stimulus variables.

The measurements we make of memory usage and variable access are dependent on the experiment. One use of these measures is illustrated in the debugging case study in Section 7.5.2. Kearns *et al.* (1982) report on the study memory usage, and the performance of memory allocation procedures, in the context of dynamic data structures for co-routines. A major use of memory usage measures is in the performance evaluation of virtual memory systems (Ferrari, 1976), particularly in the areas of program referencing behaviour and page fault replacement algorithms.

6.4 Hybrid tool design

In the rest of this chapter, we will discuss the design of hybrid tools (Figure 6.10), both ideal tools and an actual tool. In the previous sections, we detailed the functions performed in the data reduction, data analysis, and data display sections of measurement tools. In this section, we will look at questions relating to the class of tool, selection of probes, insertion of probes, method of event detection, synchronization of the monitor to the target process, and the realization of a monitoring tool, all within the framework provided by the measurement formulation.

We chose a hybrid tool for a number of reasons. They have demonstrated their superiority over purely hardware or purely software tools (Section 4.5). Although many of the measures indicated by the performance measurement formulation can be made with independent tools, a hybrid tool is required to implement the full set. Also, when discussing a hybrid tool, features of both hardware and software tools are examined.

By using hybrid tools, we can minimize the modifications that we have to make to the target system. The software added to the system is reduced to probes, a probe insertion tool, and a program to generate an object database. By careful design, the hardware probes can often be reduced to electronic cards which plug into the backplane, without any modifications to the circuitry of the computer. Consequently, the cost of the required modifications is reduced, and the bulk of the measurement tool can be used on other systems, amortizing the tool cost over a large number of measurement experiments. As all new computers are being designed with LSI and VLSI chips, many of the signals that were available to hardware tools are no longer available. Software tools have to be used to compensate for this reduction in hardware information.

The availability of sophisticated low cost logic state analysers will dictate their increased use as performance evaluation tools. As the research discussed in this book is about formulating a unified body of performance measurement knowledge, tools discussed in this context should be constructed from readily available components. Otherwise, the application of the research will be restricted to the few who can afford specialized tools. Also, by using off the shelf components, the cost can be kept down, and obsolescence can be overcome, simply by stepping up to the next generation of tools. Finally, such research should impact the design of new tools and improve them.

6.4.1 Philosophy of hybridization

A workable philosophy of hybridization should take into account the implications of the performance measurement formulation and practical considerations arising from the complementary nature of hardware and software tools. Obviously, we need to use software meters to gauge software specific information, and hardware meters to gauge hardware specific information. Also, hardware tools must be involved when measuring parallel information. In each situation, probe selection is guided by the availability of signals, the permissible interference, the required precision, and the desired resolution.

From the measurement formulation, the event trace and stimulus information are produced by the probes, and the time stamp is added by the data reduction section. At different levels in the hierarchy, different probe realizations and placements are needed. Also, a simple way of determining which level in the hierarchy an event in the trace represents is required. Part of the problem here is the requirement of high precision (hundreds of nanoseconds) over a wide range of resolution, from microscopic modules (individual instructions) to macroscopic objects (complete systems).

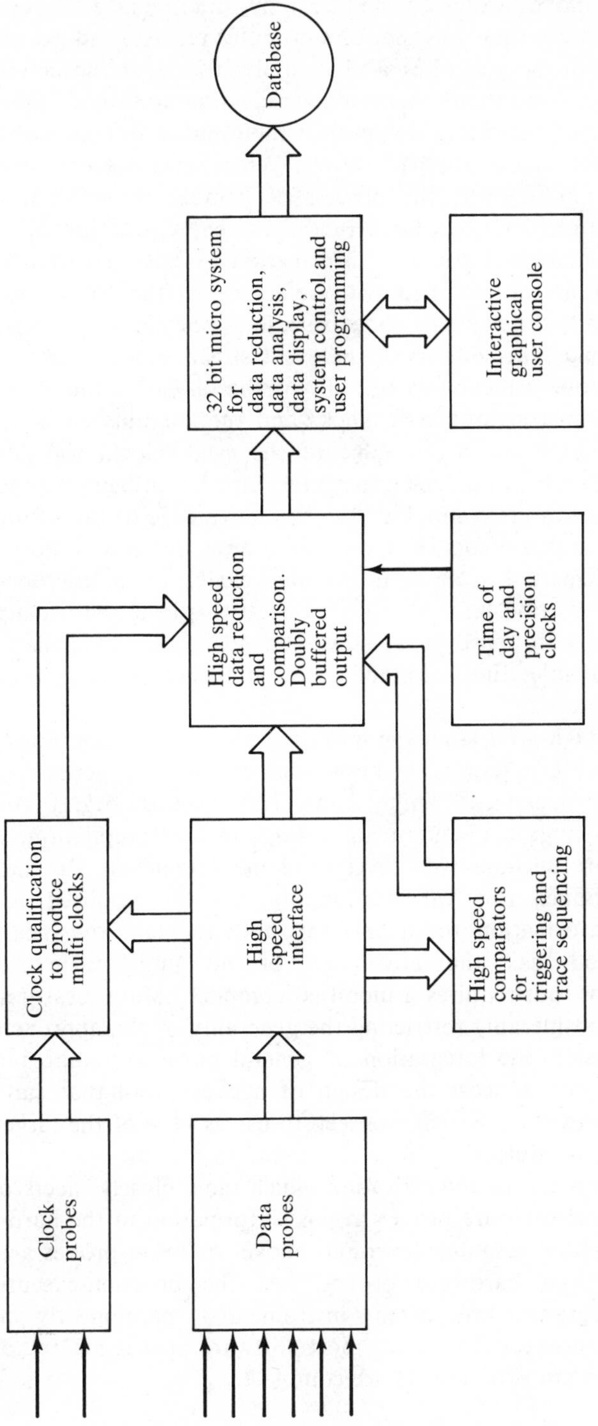

Figure 6.10 Hybrid real-time performance analyser.

As you move further up the hierarchy, the rate at which events occur decreases. Every time an event or a stimulus record is added to the event stream, the probe generates a clock pulse to signal the arrival of new information at the input to the data reduction section of the tool. An obvious way of indicating the level of the event in the hierarchy is to use separate event clocks for each level. When several events occur at the same quantum in time, the process of data compression in the event stream (Section 6.1.1) requires that the event clocks are synchronized, and the event record contains information pertaining to all the events. Time quantums are defined with reference to the finest clock in the system, usually the machine-code execution-cycle clock.

At the **machine-code level**, the event stream can be measured with a hardware probe attached to the bus of the target computer. The event clock is the instruction fetch clock, and the stimulus clock is the data fetch clock. On the active edge of the event clock, the address and operand code of the current instruction (instruction being fetched) are on the bus of the target computer. On the active edge of the stimulus clock, the address and contents of a variable are on this bus. The problem of generating separate event and stimulus clocks on a microprocessor is discussed in Section 8.3. Measurements at this level are usually made in conjunction with a program listing and a program load map. If these are not available, the techniques used at higher levels in the hierarchy must be used.

At the **high-level language level**, the above approach is very difficult to use, because it requires a knowledge of the code generated for each high-level instruction. Some compilers (Section 5.5.1) produce an assembler listing at an intermediate stage in the compilation, which can be used for machine-code level type measurements. If the compiler doesn't produce this information, it can be modified to produce sufficient information for a hardware tool to make the measurements. This method has the advantage of no interference during the measurement, but requires a modified compiler before measurements can be made, considerably restricting the generality of the approach. As our ultimate goal is the integration of general purpose monitoring tools at design time, or at least the design of a cheap tool that can easily be added to an existing system, we seek to use as little of the target system's resources as possible.

The approach to hybridization which most closely meets our design goals is to use software probes to pass information to the hardware tool. At the high-level language level and above, software probes are easier to implement than hardware probes. At the program-execution level, system programs are often instrumented permanently with low interference probes. However, most software probes are removed when the measurement experiments are complete.

High-level language programs can be compiled and then executed, compiled into an intermediate code which is interpreted, or interpreted statement by statement. Probe insertion depends upon the method of program execution. When a program is to be compiled, probes have to be inserted between each high-level statement to achieve complete decomposition. This is tedious and creates considerable interference; hence, it is only done for special experiments - for example, measuring high-level language instruction usage and debugging. Also, if an optimizing compiler is used, measurements made of individual instruction execution times may not sum to the same value as measurements made at the block-structure level because the probe code will interfere with the optimizer.

Instrumenting an interpreter is easier, because an interpreter will execute a piece of common code every time an instruction is executed. Placing a probe in this piece of code will instrument the program without modifying the program. An obvious choice for module identifier is the line number of the high-level statement. A code representing the type of high-level instruction could be written as stimulus information.

For compiled code, measurement at the **block-structure level** makes more sense. Sequential pieces of code are considered as a block, and probes are inserted at the start of each block. Stimulus information is usually related to the function of the program. A case study involving measurement at this level is discussed in the next chapter. Once the extent of the object has been measured, and related to the function of the object, probes at this level should be removed as they create considerable interference. Measurement techniques designed for the block-structure level can be applied to machine code programs as well as to high-level language programs.

At the **program-execution level**, individual programs, processes, and routines are instrumented, by inserting probes to indicate the start and end of each routine. At this level, we can observe the operation of a system as a sequence of events. This level is low enough to give a good clear view of system operation and high enough not to get bogged down in detail. An assumption we make here is that routines are structured properly with one entry and one exit point. An operating system written in unstructured code can be a measurement nightmare.

Stimulus information plays a very important role at this level. Many routines within an operating system can be called by any one of the currently active processes. Stimulus information can be used to determine which active process called a routine. For example, the stimulus information for a reentrant terminal driver would be the terminal number, and the characters handled by the routine. The stimulus information for a run time library routine would be the identifier of the calling process; and the stimulus information for a disk file handler includes the file name, calling process identifier, and the track number. In the latter case, stimulus information gives meaning to the operation being performed by the handler.

At the **task level**, we wish to study the system as it executes a user or system task. The instrumentation at the program-execution level records the sequence of modules in the task object. Under normal system operation, the permanently installed system probes automatically provide information about user programs for task-level measurement and accounting, and probes do not have to be inserted into user processes. These permanent probes must be able to identify the start and termination of tasks. During the life of a task it can exist in a number of states, all of which are initiated and terminated by the scheduler. Thus, the appropriate place to insert a probe is in the scheduler (for example the OASIS task monitor, Section 4.5.1). The module identifier in the event tuple is the process number allocated to the task by the system. Task state and job class are stimulus information. Other resource control programs can also be instrumented, for example the program which controls the allocation of memory pages.

With this instrumentation, we can study individual tasks, study tasks of a specific job class, and measure system resource usage by task. Thus, we can also use it for accounting purposes. A task can be viewed as a collection of modules which interact to perform a desired operation. Measurement at this level can give the analyst insight into the complex web of interactions which occur inside an operating system.

At the **system level**, the lower level instrumentation can be used to study overall system operation. The system object decomposes into a collection of tasks. Resource usage by job class, impact of multiprogramming level, and detection of bottlenecks are typical of analysis done at this level. At this level, we can use hardware probes once again. Signals such as CPU busy and CPU mode (kernel or user, etc.) can be monitored with hardware probes, and used to measure CPU utilization and system overhead. Software probes can also be used for CPU busy type measures. For example, in an interrupt driven operating system, we can measure these parameters by placing probes in the idle loop and in the interrupt handlers. Another use for software probes is the measurement of stimulus information, for example the length of resource queues.

6.5 Desirable features of a hybrid tool

An ideal tool is one with infinite precision, infinite resolution, zero interference, a friendly user interface, and enough power to handle any measurement situation with ease. Unfortunately, the gap between the ideal and the actual is so large that a study of the ideal gives us little help in improving actual tools. But bearing the ideal in mind does fix desirable goals in our mind, and gives direction to our work. We will now look at desirable tool features that can be achieved with the current generation of technology.

6.5.1 Hardware section

The hardware probe to be added to the target system is a simple digital output port (Figure 6.11), and some connectors. The output port consists of a 16-bit module-number monitor register and a 32-bit stimulus monitor register, each with a cable, a connector, and an optional light emitting diode display. The stimulus monitor register can be used to store a single 32-bit variable, two 16-bit variables, or four 8-bit variables. The light emitting diodes are for visual analysis and user confidence.

We can use software probes to store information in these registers pertaining to program operation. As the module-number monitor register is updated when a module starts, the register always contains the number of the currently executing module. When either probe register is updated a clock pulse is sent to the analyser. Other hardware includes connectors for a serial communications port, a direct memory access channel (only necessary in some situations), and state-analyser signals, including the address bus and processor status lines, such as user/supervisor mode, interrupt level, and type of memory access.

Two **clock signals** are included: a memory access clock and a probe update clock. The probe update clock is synchronized to the memory access clock. The active edge of the probe update clock occurs during the next instruction fetch when the buses of the target computer are stable. Thus, an external hardware tool reading the probe in response to the probe update clock can also read the address of the next instruction.

The **external hardware tool** is able to handle multiple clocks in parallel. These clocks can be generated externally or, preferably, they can be generated from the above clocks using appropriate state signals as clock qualifiers. If signals which describe bus activity are available, we can decompose the memory access clock into a number of clocks, each representing different bus activity. Typical bus activity includes: instruction fetch, operand fetch, data fetch, data write, I/O operation, interrupt vector, dead cycle, and DMA activity.

We can decompose the probe update clock into event and stimulus clocks, either with a flag generated by the probe or by comparing successive events to see which monitor register changed: module identifier or stimulus data. The former is simpler to implement. Also, we can decompose the probe update clock into separate clocks for each level of the hierarchy (block-structure, program, and task) by using the high order bits of the module identifier as level descriptors.

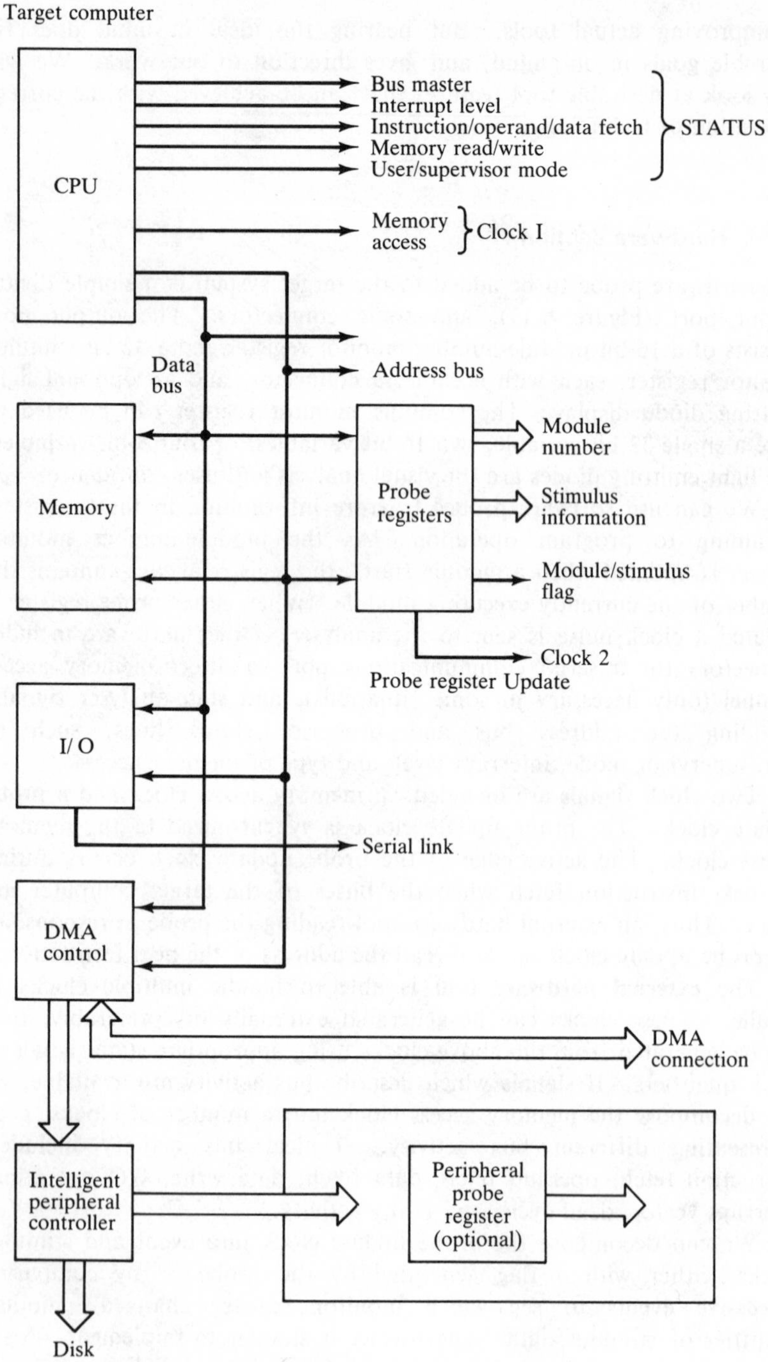

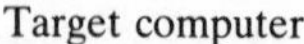

Figure 6.11 Hardware probes.

Thus, the clock qualification section of the hardware tool should be able to read two synchronized clocks and decompose them into a number of slower synchronous clocks. In addition, it should be possible to combine any of these clocks using standard logic functions, or counters, to produce the desired measurement clocks. These clocks are used to synchronize the data capture circuits with their associated data values in the continuous event stream presented to the hardware probe. This stream is monitored by event filters which trigger the recording of data. Captured data is analysed in the data reduction circuits to detect events of interest to the current measurement experiment.

Data recording is triggered by detecting sequences of events. Sequence detection may involve counting the number of occurrences of events in the sequence. Sequence detectors and counters should be available for each clock in use, so that a number of parallel triggers can be generated. These triggers are used to initiate data recording, either separately or in combination. Data recording is controlled by comparators and counters associated with a particular clock. When an event of interest is detected, it is recorded. The clock used for data recording may not be the clock used by the event filter which triggers recording, allowing events at one level to be recorded after the occurrence of events at another level. Parallel data recording filters enable the recording of events from various levels, and events of different types, from the one event stream. Obviously, to make this power available to an analyst, the hybrid monitor must include user friendly tools for easy set up of clock qualification, and definition of events of interest.

Another desirable feature of an event filter is the ability to record events near the event of interest. For example: record six events before the event of interest, or record the seventh event after the event of interest. I do not know of a logic state analyser that has this level of event filtering and clock qualification. Some of the newer models have a few of these features. However, this is the direction the design of future logic state analysers should take.

With advances in technology, the depth of the data storage buffers in logic state analysers has increased considerably. Early models had limited storage (typically 64 words) and limited width (16-32 bits). Data was stored in the buffers until they were full, and then transferred to a separate analysis computer. During the transfer, incoming data was lost. By analysing the data as it is recorded, and with reasonably deep or double buffers, continuous recording over long periods of time is possible. This requires a high degree of parallelism in the analyser and fast transfer to backup storage.

The difficulty of inserting the hardware probe varies from system to system. Usually the probe can be built on a card that plugs into the backplane of the target computer. Using a probe card designed for the system minimizes errors due to faulty connections, eliminates probe placement errors, and considerably simplifies instrumentation. Some systems do not have all the desired signals available on the backplane and may require modification. For one-off measurements, a probe register can be simulated by writing to a memory location.

In systems that do not have a backplane, the probe has to be built into a separate module which is connected to the processor with a logic clip. This module is an extension of the logic state analyser personality module concept. One approach to building a general purpose, system independent, microprocessor specific hardware probe is to add monitor registers to the standard personality module. Such a probe would consist of a personality module, connections to all bus signals, and a method of selecting suitable addresses for the monitor registers in the input-output address space of the target system. The personality module contains processor addressable monitor registers, and a state machine to produce bus status information for clock qualification. The probe electronics could be powered from the target processor.

Memory management and **cache memory** create significant problems for probe connection. The probe should be connected to the address bus after relocation from virtual to physical address space and before cache memory for the recorded addressing information to reflect program execution. Also the memory-read status signals must represent processor requests not cache requests. On some computers, cache memory is an integral part of the processor and the address bus is only accessible after cache. Thus, the address bus does not contain the address of the current instruction during a cache hit. On a cache miss several instructions (which may not be executed) after the current one may be read into cache, and again the addressing signals to main memory may not reflect program execution.

Microprocessors which include integral cache are very difficult to measure at the machine-code level. For example, the Motorola M68020 poses several problems for measurement. First, with a 32-bit data bus, two instructions can be fetched during a single instruction fetch memory cycle. Second, the instructions are pipelined and operations within the processor proceed in parallel, so an instruction can finish execution before the previous instruction does. Third, the instruction cache is located on the chip and an external tool cannot measure the execution path by monitoring instruction fetches on the address bus, without disabling the cache. Fourth, the cache is in logical address space, not in physical address space, but as the memory management unit is on a separate chip it is possible to read the instruction fetch address on a cache miss. Fifth, there is no easy way to distinguish instruction fetch memory cycles from other memory cycles. These problems have made the connection of emulators and logic analysers to M68020 based systems very difficult. In an attempt to overcome these problems, the M68030 includes a status bus from which an emulator can determine the internal state of the processor.

This trend to greater levels of integration is making machine-code level monitoring a thing of the past, just as the trend to high-level languages has made machine-code programming a thing of the past. The hybrid approach, we have developed in this book, is not adversely affected by cache or memory management units, because the probe instructions write information to registers outside the processor. As most software is developed in high-level languages, the loss of machine-code level measurements is of little consequence. However, by using our hybrid tool we can measure machine-code level programs as well as high-level language programs simply by installing probes at appropriate places in the code.

If we connect an additional status signal to our monitor, to indicate whether the current memory reference is a cache hit or miss, we can measure cache performance for instruction fetches, operand fetches and data fetches. Once again, we emphasize the need to define performance measurement requirements at design time, and build them into the system.

6.5.2 Software section

Software probes are used to write module identifiers (event descriptors) to the module-number monitor register, and stimulus information to the stimulus monitor register. A method of probe insertion is required to enable users to instrument their programs, and for the initial instrumentation of system programs. Probes can be inserted into program source manually, automatically, or with an interactive tool. Manual methods can be laborious, but for some experiments the expense of porting a probe inserting program to the target system may not be justified. Automatic probe insertion is possible with sophisticated tools, but the analyst has little control over where they go, and the use of automatic tools may lead to less understanding rather than more.

An interactive tool has the advantages of automation while allowing the analyst complete control over probe insertion. The tool should enable the analyst to search the program text sequentially and insert probes as desired. As probes are inserted, the module identifier should be allocated automatically, and an object module map constructed in the object database. A second tool is required to read and display this database. Probe software can be a standard piece of code, or within certain constraints a user defined routine. Stimulus probes have to be inserted interactively, or manually, because the analyst has to select the stimulus variables. Tools of this nature have been included in some of the reported integrated instrumentation environments (Chapters 8 and 9).

In single task operating system environments, all activity during the execution of an object has to do with that object. Simply inserting probes at the start of each module is enough to give accurate measurements. In some closely controlled experiments on multi-tasking systems, instrumentation in this way is adequate also. However, in any system where an object can be interrupted, a mechanism to write the module identifier to the probe register when the interrupted module resumes is required.

To handle the **pause and resumption** of modules, we must save the module identifier of the interrupted module so that it can be written to the probe on resumption of the interrupted module. If we understand the system, we can do this by inserting additional probes at the end of the modules that interrupt other modules. One difficulty here is the possibility of nested interruptions. A more general way to handle interruption, but unfortunately a way that creates more interference, is to use a module identifier stack. This stack may be a separate stack, the stack of the currently executing process, or the stack frame of the currently executing module. The last entry on this stack is the identifier of the currently executing module. Above the block-structure level there are four ways of entering and exiting a module:

- absolute branch in and absolute branch out,
- jump to subroutine and return from subroutine,
- external interrupt and return from interrupt, and
- software interrupt to a trap handler and return.

In well structured code these pairs occur together. At levels higher than the block-structure level, the sequence of modules that an object decomposes into can sometimes be seen as a nested set of modules (Figure 2.4), if structuring is adhered to. At times, the sequence of modules is discontinuous due to process pre-emption (Figure 6.14). These views do not alter the performance measurement formulation; they just provide alternative perspectives on how the modules are ordered.

The algorithms we use to handle the module identifier stack depend on the way the current module is entered and exited. Thus, the probe routine has to be selected according to the method of call and return. The standard probe algorithms are:

A6.12 On entry to a module by an absolute branch
Pop the module identifier of the terminated module
Push the module identifier of the executing module
Write the module identifier to the probe

A6.13 On exit from a module by an absolute branch
Do nothing

A6.14 On entry to a module by an interrupt
Push the module identifier of the interrupting module
Write the module identifier to the probe

A6.15 On exit from an interrupt sequence
Pop the module identifier of the terminating module
Read the last entry on the stack without changing the stack pointer
Write module identifier (of the resumed module) to the probe

A6.16 When calling and returning from a subroutine, use either of the above pairs of probe algorithms, but the members of the pairs cannot be mixed

A subroutine call differs from an external interrupt in that it always occurs at the same place in the code. In this sense a subroutine call is identical to an absolute branch. If we consider that the calling module is resumed on return from a subroutine then we use the algorithms for interruption. Alternatively, if we consider that a different module is started, then we use the algorithms for absolute branches. The choice of how to instrument subroutines is left to the analyst; however, circumstances may dictate which method is to be used. The interference is the same with both methods, but the results may be different.

As soon as we allow the possibility of a module pausing and resuming, we are faced with a measurement difficulty. Should we treat the resumed portion of the module as the same module, as the algorithms for interruption do, or as a new module, as the algorithms for absolute branching do? If we consider it to be the same module, then we have to combine module fragments, otherwise we face the danger of having a module with multiple entry and exit points. If we consider it to be a different module, we increase the number of modules. While the path record is the same in both cases, all calculated values are different with the two methods, except for utilization.

The above discussion points to a problem with the interruption algorithm, which returns to the same module number. Interruption can occur at any time, with the result that we have many entry and exit points for the module. To overcome this problem, we introduce a simple method of combining module fragments: incrementing a module continuation flag.

A6.14a On entry to a module by a subroutine call (alternative algorithm)
Pick up the calling-module's identifier from the temporary variable
Push it on the stack
Write the module identifier of the called module to the probe
Increment the continuation flag
Save the called module's identifier in the temporary variable

A6.15a On exit from a subroutine (alternative algorithm)
Pop the module identifier of the module being resumed
Save it in the temporary variable
Write it (module identifier of resumed module) to the probe

Algorithm 6.14 has been modified to increment a flag in the module number, to indicate continuation (A6.14a), before the module number is written to the probe (Figure 6.14). In this way continuation is easily recognizable, and the module can be treated as two separate modules, as in the absolute branch case, or the data can be preprocessed to combine module fragments before calculation. The disadvantage of this method is the increased interference of the probe. Also, in Algorithms 6.14a and 6.15a a temporary storage variable has been introduced, because in some implementations, it is more efficient to use a temporary storage variable than the top of the stack. If multiple interruptions, or several subroutine calls, are possible the continuation flag becomes a continuation number.

Every system has a **quiescent state**: either the machine goes to idle or it goes to a continuous background process. A special probe is inserted at this point. The purpose of this probe is to clean up the stack, and to assist in the detection of instrumentation errors. If the stack is not empty, or if it underflows during object execution, then an error condition exists in the balancing of probe pairs. The quiescent state always has a zero module identifier. A module identifier consisting entirely of ones is the first entry on the stack. If this identifier appears at the probe then an underflow error has occurred. By examining the module identifiers immediately prior to the quiescent identifier, unbalanced instrumentation can be detected. Also, this probe is required for system-level measurements of idle time.

```
A6.17 When going to the quiescent state (separate module-identifier stack)
      While stack not empty do
          Pop module identifier
          If module identifier not zero or all ones
              then write identifier to probe
      Push module identifier of all ones
      Push module identifier of zero
      Write module identifier to probe
```

Algorithms 6.14a and 6.15a will work on a single address space, non pre-emptive system using one module identifier stack. However, in **multi-address space systems** a process cannot access memory in the address space of another process, and hence a separate module identifier stack is needed for each process. Also, a separate module identifier stack is needed for each process in **pre-emptive systems**, where processes can have their execution paused by pre-emptive scheduling. When an executing process requests service from the kernel, the kernel may not return to the calling process, because the process may be waiting for an input-output operation to complete, or a higher priority process may be waiting to be dispatched.

When pre-emption can occur, algorithms 6.14a and 6.15a will only work if a separate module identifier stack, or stack frame, is used for each process; just as a separate stack, or stack frame, is used by each process. For example, in the character handling task shown in Figure 2.3 the input handling process asks the kernel to send a message to the terminal administrator process. After the message is sent, the input handling process is blocked, waiting for a reply, and the terminal administrator process is dispatched to reply to the message. If only one stack was used, the module identifier popped off the stack on exiting the kernel would be the identifier of the paused module in the input handling process, not the identifier of the resumed module in the terminal administrator process (Figure 6.14).

An obvious question here is: why is a module identifier popped off the stack, indicating a resumption of the terminal administrator process, and not a new module identifier pushed onto the stack, indicating the start of the first module in this process? The terminal administrator process is in an **infinite loop**, and was blocked waiting for someone to send a message to it. User processes are often created to execute once, after which they die; in contrast, system processes are often created to be eternal, and thus have to be instrumented accordingly (Section 8.4). The entry path to a newly created process is different from the entry path for a resumed process (Figure 8.4). Hence, in the former case, a new module identifier is pushed onto the stack; and in the latter case, a resumed module identifier is popped off the stack.

Instrumentation involving several stacks has to be inserted carefully, to avoid interference with normal program execution, and to maintain the balance between pushes and pops. One way to minimize these problems is to store the module identifier of the calling process in a fixed slot in the stack frame of the called process. In this way, the module identifier is always stored in a fixed location relative to the return address of the module (Figure 8.9), and stack balance is maintained automatically.

When entering the kernel process, the module identifier of the paused module must be saved, either by stacking it or by storing it in the process descriptor of the paused process, so that, when the process is dispatched again, the module identifier of the resumed module can be written to the probe. Obviously, on return to the quiescent state of the system there is no longer any need to clean up the stack, and a stimulus probe is sufficient.

A6.18 *Stimulus probe algorithm*
Read stimulus variable
Write it to probe

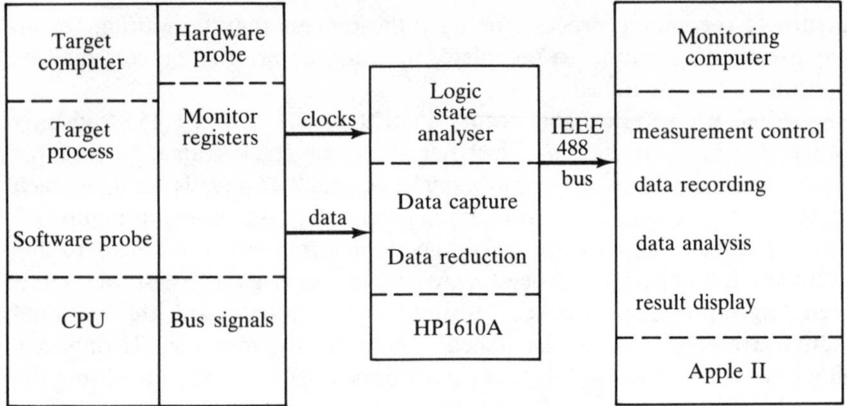

Figure 6.12 Hybrid monitoring tool.

Two other types of programs require special consideration during instrumentation: **recursive programs** and **re-entrant modules**. In both of these cases, the same module can be invoked many times. Probe placement must be considered carefully to avoid multiple events with the same module identifier in the recursive case, and to avoid event confusion in the re-entrant case. A number of approaches can be taken; however, the easiest seems to be to use stimulus information. When a recursive program bottoms out, the depth of the recursion can be written as a stimulus variable. When a re-entrant module is entered, the process number of the calling task can be written as a stimulus variable. This stimulus variable can then be used to separate out invocations of the re-entrant module.

If an **optimizing compiler** is used, measurements may not match expectations. During optimization, source code statements may be relocated, removed, or split apart. The result is that we may not be able to map directly from high-level language level to machine-code level, and hence we may not be able to compose machine-code modules into higher-level objects easily. These problems may force the analyst to measure at higher levels only.

If the optimizer is poorly designed, or the source code is poorly written, the optimizer may shift a probe, resulting in incorrect measurements. Alternatively, insertion of probes into the code may change the results of optimization, again giving incorrect measurement results, due to increased interference.

6.6 An actual tool

During the course of this research, I built a hybrid tool and used it in a variety of experiments. This tool is now obsolete, and I only implemented a subset of the desired features, but enough to validate the performance measurement formulation, and to test the measurement algorithms. The tool is constructed from a logic state analyser and an Apple II personal computer. We discussed its use as a purely hardware tool in Chapter 5. In Chapter 7, we will illustrate monitoring program execution at the block-structure level with a case study which occurred during the development of this hybrid tool. And in Chapter 8, we describe the instrumentation of a small system.

```
PROCEDURE GENOREC;
BEGIN (* GENERATE OBJECT RECORD FROM TRACE BUFFER*)
I := 1;
WHILE I<63 DO (*trace buffer is 64 entries long*)
  BEGIN (* INITIALIZE PATH RECORD*)
  FOR J := 1 TO PLENGTH DO
    BEGIN
    TPATH.MNAME[J] := 0;
    TPATH.MSTIM[J] := 0;
    TPATH.MTIME[J] := 0;
    END;
  WHILE (PROBE[I] <> SMOD) AND (I < 63) DO I:=I+1;
  J := 1; (* FOUND AN OBJECT *)
  MSTIME := I;
  TPATH.MNAME[J] := PROBE[I];
  OBJTRAV := FALSE;
  LMOD := FALSE;
  WHILE (OBJTRAV = FALSE) AND (J < PLENGTH) AND (I < 63) DO
    BEGIN (* TRAVERSE OBJECT ONE MODULE AT A TIME *)
    I := I+1; (*GO TO NEXT TUPLE*)
    IF PROBE[I] = PROBE[I-1] THEN
      TPATH.MSTIM[J] := STIM[I] (* STIMULUS*)
    ELSE
      BEGIN (* EVENT TUPLE *)
      IF LMOD THEN
        BEGIN (* END OF OBJECT *)
        OBJTRAV := TRUE;
        TPATH.MTIME[J] := TIME[I+1] - TIME[MSTIME];
        TPATH.PETIME := 0; (* PATH EXECUTION TIME *)
        FOR K := 1 TO J DO
          TPATH.PETIME := TPATH.PETIME + TPATH.MTIME[K];
        FOUND := FALSE;
        K := 1;
        WHILE (OBJECT[K].PETIME <> 0) AND (NOT FOUND)
                AND (K < OSIZE) DO
          BEGIN (* LOOK FOR A KNOWN PATH *)
          IF TPATH.PETIME = OBJECT[K].PETIME THEN
            BEGIN (*FOUND A KNOWN PATH*)
            OBJECT[K].NOEX := OBJECT[K].NOEX + 1;
```

```
          FOUND := TRUE;
          END
        ELSE K := K + 1;
        END;
      IF NOT FOUND THEN
        BEGIN (* NEW PATH, COPY PATH RECORD *)
        OBJECT[K] := TPATH;
        OBJECT[K].NOEX := 1;
        END;
      END
    ELSE (* END OF MODULE*)
      BEGIN
      J := J + 1;
      TPATH.MTIME[J-1] := TIME[I] - TIME[MSTIME];
      MSTIME := I;
      TPATH.MNAME[J] := PROBE[I];
      IF PROBE[I] = EMOD THEN
        BEGIN (*LAST MODULE IN OBJECT*)
        LMOD := TRUE;
        I := I - 1; (*STAY AT THIS TUPLE*)
        END;
      END;
    END;
  END;
 END;
MPERIOD := MPERIOD + TIME[64] - TIME[1];
END;
```

Figure 6.13 Code of a subset of the object generation algorithm (Algorithm 6.4) used in the hybrid monitoring tool.

The tool consists of: a probe card (Figures 7.1-7.3), a logic state analyser (Figure 5.1), an IEEE 488 bus, and an Apple II personal computer. The interconnection of these components is shown in Figure 6.12. As we can see from Figure 7.3, the amount of hardware needed to probe a personal computer is very small. Several software probes are shown in Figure 7.4.

Event filters are set up from the keyboard of the logic state analyser. The measurement software (Figure 6.15) starts the recording of the event trace (Figure 6.14), monitors the trace buffer in the state analyser (which is 64 words long), and, when it is full, transfers the trace to the Apple II, and then restarts event recording. This sequence is continued until the experiment is halted from the keyboard of the Apple.

TRACE LIST TRACE-COMPLETE

REMOTE-LISTEN 15

LABEL BASE	A HEX	B HEX	C DEC	D HEX	TIME DEC
START	09BB	0	003	00	
+01	0901	0	002	00	572.9 US
+02	0964	1	003	00	220.0 US
+03	0A28	1	001	00	3.847 MS
+04	1BF7	1	032	00	121.0 US
+05	1BFC	1	032	24	11.0 US
+06	1C4B	1	001	00	393.9 US
+07	0C1E	0	021	00	100.0 US
+08	08A8	0	026	00	68.0 US
+09	08D2	1	021	00	92.0 US
+10	0860	0	006	00	158.9 US
+11	0893	1	021	00	103.0 US
+12	0979	0	024	00	101.0 US
+13	09A6	1	021	00	107.0 US
+14	0901	0	002	00	107.0 US
+15	0964	1	021	00	219.9 US
+16	0CB5	1	001	00	45.0 US
+17	1BF7	1	034	00	141.0 US
+18	1BFC	1	034	21	11.0 US
+19	2F27	0	039	21	177.0 US

Figure 6.14 Logic analyser display showing the sequence of modules (event trace) during the first four processes of the character handling task (Figure 2.3) prior to modifications. A: address bus; B: continuation flag; C: module number; D: process number.

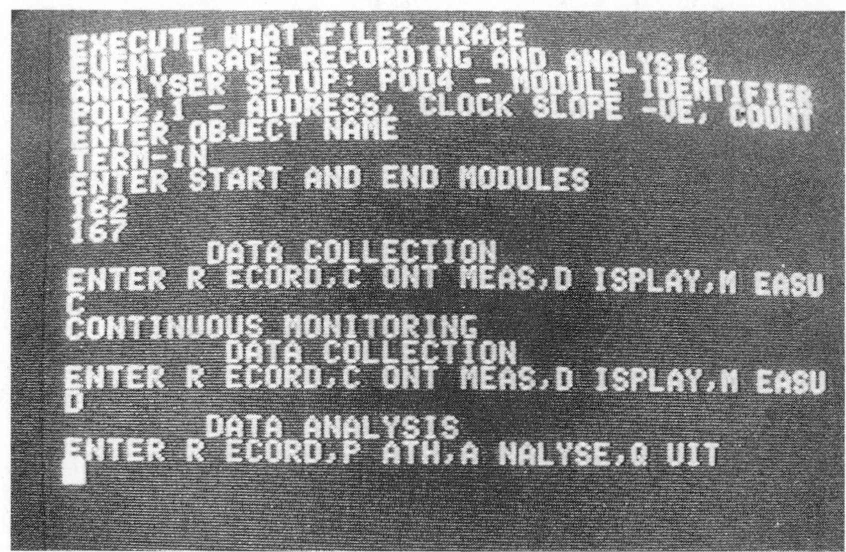

Figure 6.15 Menu display for measurement program used to select the terminal administrator object (Figure 2.4).

```
ENTER R ECORD,P ATH,A NALYSE,Q UIT
R
OBJECT TERM-IN MEAS PERIOD 1261896
PATH 1 TIME 24396 NOEX 9
MOD      162     39     36     37
TIME    1879   2580   4239   1830
STIM      33      0      0      0
MOD      182    172    165    164
TIME     540    660   1289    810
STIM       0      0      0      0

PATH 2 TIME 22417 NOEX 1
MOD      162     39     36     37
TIME    1880   2580   3939   1830
STIM      33      0      0      0
MOD      165    164    167      0
TIME    1289   1280   2040      0
STIM       0      0      0      0

        DATA ANALYSIS
ENTER R ECORD,P ATH,A NALYSE,Q UIT
```

Figure 6.16 Object record for the terminal administrator (Figure 2.4), produced by the hybrid monitoring tool – procedure GENOREC (Figure 6.13). Times in microseconds times ten.

During the time when the trace is being transferred, no monitoring takes place, so the trace is discontinuous. To minimize the impact of these discontinuities, Algorithm 6.4 was modified (Figure 6.13), so that only object execution paths which are completely recorded within the trace buffer are stored in the object record; and consequently, fragments of objects are discarded. The measurement period is the sum of the periods during which the analyser was actually tracing. Thus, this hybrid tool may not record all object executions during the period of the measurement experiment. Also, it could be subject to aliasing if an event triggered several executions of the object and only the first few were recorded in the limited trace memory.

When measurement is terminated, the software enables the analyst to look at a number of tabular displays, or resume measurement. The analyst can look at spectrum data, at selected path records, at calculated values (Figure 6.17), or at the complete object record (Figure 6.16). This implementation records the object record to the path record level only. Individual path traversals are not recorded, but some stimulus information is. Graphical displays are hand drawn from the information contained in the object record.

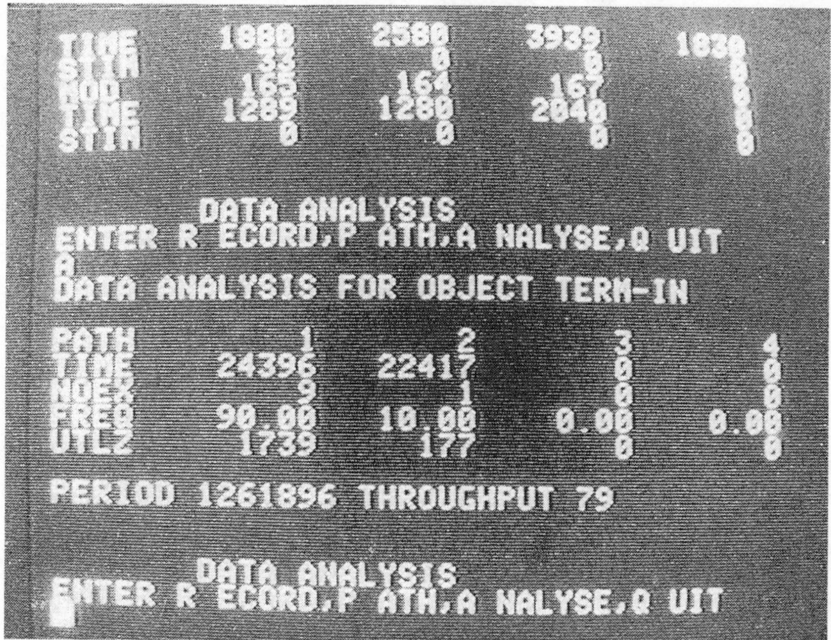

Figure 6.17 Values calculated from the object record (Figure 6.16) by the hybrid monitoring tool.

A number of people have used this tool for debugging software, for system development, and for performance measurement (Section 8.4). We have found it to be easy to use, and that through using it we can save a lot of debugging time. More importantly, we found that measurement increased our understanding of the systems we were studying, and quickly destroyed our misconceptions about their operation.

Chapter 7
Monitoring Program Execution

Personal computers are being used for an increasingly diverse range of applications, including computer aided instruction in schools, accounting systems in small businesses, and bible translation on remote mission stations. However, manufacturers of these systems seem to place more emphasis on games software than on program debugging aids, as apparently games sell computers. Lack of debugging aids, often accompanied by inappropriate documentation, considerably increases the development time of software, and the frustration of programmers.

Parallel to this revolution in the use of personal computers is an exploding use of microprocessors in manufactured goods, such as process controllers, instruments, household appliances, and cars. The software for these systems is normally developed on a host system and downline loaded into the target system. Host systems range from the in-house computer to general purpose microprocessor development systems. The latter, through the inclusion of sophisticated in-circuit emulators, place powerful hardware for execution monitoring in the hands of those who can afford them. The former often provide little more than a monitor, in the target system, which can set breakpoints, examine registers, and single step through machine code. Debugging is often complicated by undetected faults in prototype hardware, and by poor understanding of the software/hardware interrelations in the target system.

In recent years, most research effort has been in the area of good design methodologies with the aim of producing programs which work correctly the first time, and hence require little debugging effort. Plattner and Nievergelt (1981), in their survey of the field, state:

> 'Program execution monitoring has been neglected as a research topic ... [, and] ... program execution monitoring has not kept up with the rapid progress of programming languages.'

Glass (1980) has described the development of software for real-time computing as: 'the lost world of software debugging and testing.'

In this chapter, we discuss our second case study: using a hybrid performance measurement tool to monitor program performance at the block-structure level. The programs we monitored in this case study handle the transfer of commands and data between the controlling computer and the logic state analyser in our hybrid performance monitor. In this study, we will see a variety of debugging techniques, all of which are applicable at the block-structure level.

7.1 Programming tools

Researchers have developed tools to assist the mental activities of the programmer during all stages of the programming process. Systems analysts use design tools to divide a problem up into intellectually manageable portions, to devise a structured solution to the problem, and to express the solution in a human understandable form. Programmers use coding tools to convert these designs into a machine understandable form. Up to this point in the programming process, testing and debugging consist of a static analysis of the design and program text. Consistent application of these tools, combined with an understanding of the problem and a working knowledge of the implementation language, should result in a 'nearly' correct program.

Once the program has been compiled it is executed with selected test data - a dynamic program analysis procedure. During execution, the output of the program is recorded with a program execution monitor, and the programmer studies the execution history of the program to determine the correctness of the program. Program execution monitors are tools which either take a snap-shot of the program at a particular point in its execution or record a complete execution history. Simple execution monitors are the insertion of breakpoints into machine code and the addition of write statements to program source code (Huang, 1980).

7.2 Static evaluation and simple timing

In the absence of monitoring tools, a programmer is forced to use static analysis of the program text, and simple timing measurements. Simple timing measurements are performed by executing the program a known number of times, measuring the total execution time with a stop watch, and calculating the average execution time. This technique is useful for tight loops, but the loops must be executed many many times to get accurate results (often of the order of 100 000 times).

In static analysis, a programmer maps expected execution paths and calculates expected execution times from the text of the program without executing the program. He can determine the execution path by drawing a flow chart of the program, a chart showing every branch and the conditions under which each branch is taken. Expected execution time is calculated by decomposing the program into machine code and adding the execution times for each instruction. The accuracy of this calculation is affected by the programmer's estimate of memory access time, which may vary due to hardware causes, such as cache hit ratio. Finally, execution time can only be calculated if the manufacturer has provided instruction execution times.

Static analysis is usually only used as a last resort in debugging, because it is time consuming, prone to error, and is a prediction of what may happen not a measurement of what actually happens. Static timing calculations cannot be done above machine-code level, and at machine-code level are subject to variations in instruction execution time, particularly with branch instructions.

7.3 Microprocessor development systems

Many large program development teams use microprocessor development systems (Rafiquzzaman, 1984). These systems provide an environment where a designer can develop and debug hardware and software separately, and then progressively integrate them. Initially, the software is debugged with an in-circuit emulator running on the development system, and as the hardware is debugged, sections of the software are transferred to the target hardware until the two are completely integrated.

The in-circuit emulator acts like the target microprocessor, but gives the designer complete control over the action of the microprocessor. Two main techniques of software debugging are available: single stepping and tracing. Both use symbol table information to simplify debugging. In single step mode, one instruction is executed and the contents of registers and selected variables are displayed, in response to each step request from the operator. In trace mode, the operator specifies the data to be displayed after each instruction, and then starts the trace at a specified location. After each instruction is executed, the data is displayed. Tracing slows the execution of the program, and thus real-time operation cannot be examined with an in-circuit emulator.

For real-time debugging, when the software is running on the target processor, a logic state analyser is available. At the machine-code level, microcomputer personality modules are used to disassemble the code; address traces and breakpoints are used to monitor program flow; timers are used to measure the execution time of code segments; and symbol table information is used to detect variable accesses.

At higher levels, these tools suffer all the limitations of hardware monitors, and thus they can be improved by the hybridization techniques discussed in Chapter 6. A microprocessor development system would require the same extensions that we made to the logic state analyser before it could be used to solve the problems in the following case study.

7.4 Program execution monitoring

The fundamental question faced by both the programmer and the designer of a program execution monitor is: 'What information should the monitor capture for it to be a useful tool?' This question can be refined into two further questions: 'What questions can be asked about the execution of a program?' and 'What properties should a program execution monitor have if it is to answer these questions?' We can find answers to these questions by applying the formulation of performance measurement at the program-execution level of the object hierarchy. At this level, an object is a whole program, or sub-program, which we decompose into block-structure modules, and sometimes into individual instructions.

The questions we ask about a program object depend upon the function of the object and the context in which the object is found. The function of the object depends on the problem it is designed to solve, and context includes the mode of execution of the object (stand alone, interactive, etc.), and any programs or events which call for the object to be executed. For example, an object might be a mailing list program, or a search procedure called by that program.

However, even though the questions we ask about a particular program depend upon its function and context, these questions can be generalized to a standard set which apply to all programs, of any function, in any context. For program execution monitoring, the measures defined in the formulation of performance measurement (Section 2.6) provide answers to the following questions:

- In what order were the statements, or blocks of statements, in the program executed?
- How long did the program, or a section of it, take to execute?
- How often is the program, or a section of it, executed?
- Does the program spend an excessive amount of time in one section?
- What information gives meaning to the action of the program, e.g. what condition causes it to loop?

The hybrid monitoring tool described in Section 6.6 was designed to collect the information needed to answer these questions. We can use it on any computer system, once a simple hardware probe has been inserted into that system and software probes have been added to the target program. With it, we can collect and analyse program execution data on-line.

7.5 Hybrid monitoring tools

Program execution monitors are constructed from the same basic components as performance measurement tools; in fact a well designed tool can be used for both. Some researchers have used software tools for program execution monitoring, for example Grishman's debugging language (1971); others have used hardware tools, for example Fryer's memory-bus monitor (1973). Most of these tools, with the exception of microprocessor development systems, have been designed for specific applications, and thus they are not available for general use.

As with performance monitors, the integration of hardware techniques and software techniques in hybrid program execution monitors gives them the flexibility to handle situations where purely hardware or software tools are inadequate. When measuring some programs both software specific information and hardware specific information are needed to understand what the program is doing - for example, measuring the execution time of a keyboard handler in response to a variety of inputs. Other programs include sections where hardware techniques are easier to use - for example, an assembler procedure stored in read only memory - together with sections where software techniques are easier to use - for example, measurement of a high-level language program at the block-structure level.

We used the hybrid performance monitor (Figure 6.12) as a program execution monitor. It consisted of:

- a hardware probe plugged into the backplane of the target computer (Figures 7.1-7.3),
- software probes inserted into the target process (Figure 7.4),
- a logic state analyser to monitor and record the signals from the hardware probes (Figure 5.1), and
- a monitoring computer to control the measurement, and analyse the collected data.

7.5.1 The logic state analyser

Event filtering and data recording were done with the logic state analyser. Event filters to trigger program execution traces, and event filters to select data for recording, were set up from the keyboard on the analyser. The analyser could be armed either from its own keyboard or from the monitoring computer (once the communications software was debugged). A state analyser is a purely hardware tool and suffers from the limitations of traditional hardware tools.

Figure 7.1 Apple II hardware probe with logic analyser connectors pushed onto probe pins.

The latest generation of logic state analysers contains very powerful facilities for monitoring program performance, but these are difficult to use on any language other than assembler, and cannot be used if a memory map is not available. A static memory map of the program may not be adequate either, because the data space may be dynamic. The following comment, taken from a personal computer manual, indicates the difficulties to be faced when using a hardware tool to monitor program execution:

> 'The memory map ... is provided for your curiosity only: a primary task of the transportable Apple Pascal system is to eliminate the necessity for the programmer to know anything about specific memory addresses and use.'
>
> (Apple Computer Inc, 1980; page 254)

7.5.2 Hardware probes

The concept of a monitor register, where all signals of interest are multiplexed through a single register, was introduced by Deese (1974) to overcome some of the problems inherent in connecting a hardware monitor to a computer. In our hybrid monitor, multiplexing is done by the software probes writing data into monitor registers located in the

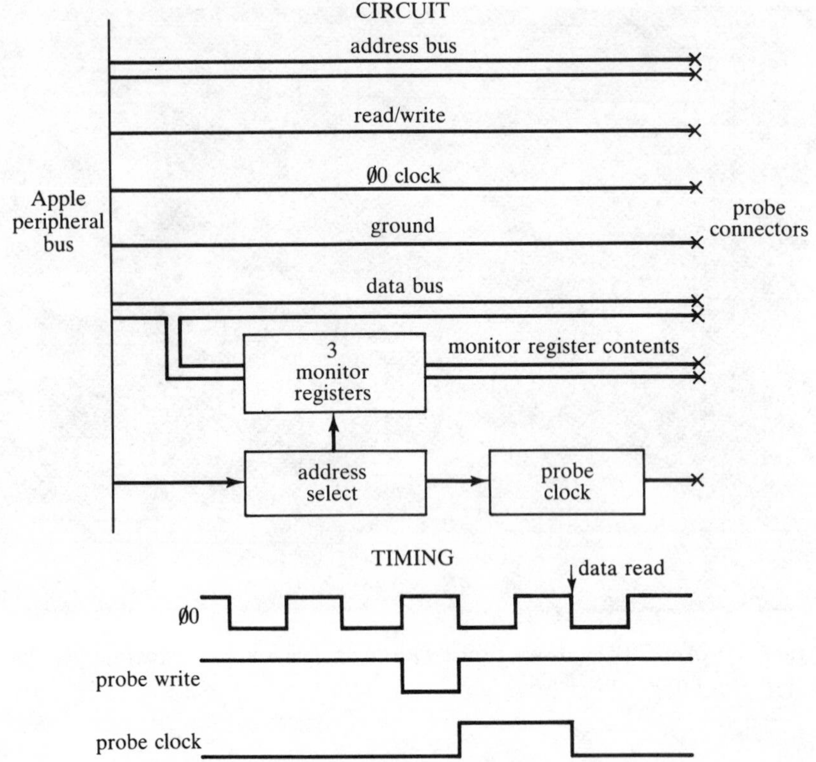

Figure 7.2 Apple II hardware probe – block diagram.

hardware probe (Figures 7.1-7.3). These monitor registers are used to interface between the software probes and the logic state analyser. When an event of interest occurs a software probe writes information about that event to a monitor register, from which it is read by the logic state analyser. The hardware probe also connects signals from the bus of the processor to the logic state analyser.

From this bus information, the monitor can determine what the computer is doing, at the machine-code level, and record its execution path, memory accesses, and data transfers. All signals, including the probe clock, are synchronized to the memory cycle clock of the target processor. When one of the monitor registers is updated, its probe clock is pulsed, with its active edge occurring at the end of the next memory cycle. Consequently, the analyser's reading is synchronized with an instruction-fetch memory cycle. This synchronization is important when monitoring microprocessors, which do not provide external signals to distinguish instruction-fetch memory cycles from other memory cycles.

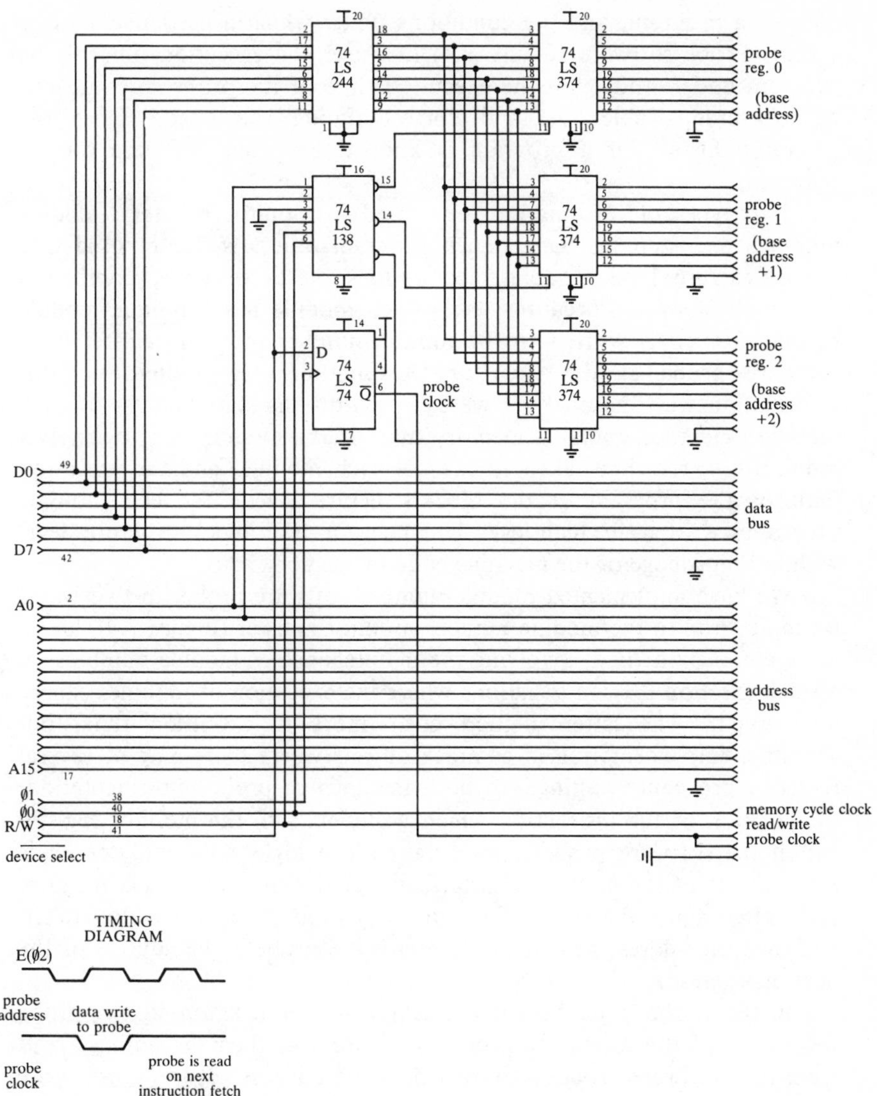

Figure 7.3 Apple II hardware probe – circuit diagram.

7.5.3 Software probes

Determining why a program has taken a particular path, and recording the execution path of a program at the block-structure level, cannot be done with a hardware monitor. We can use information stored in the monitor registers by the software probes to determine both the execution path of a program, and the conditions under which a particular path is taken. Probe software (Figure 7.4) increases the execution time of the program under study, but the execution time of the probe software can be measured (Table 7.1) and correct timing calculated. Once the execution history of a program is known the probe software can be removed.

Two types of information are stored in monitor registers: module numbers and stimulus data. Each program object is decomposed into block-structure level modules: contiguous pieces of code, compound statements, loops, procedures, etc. Each module has a unique module number, which is written to the module-number monitor register by a software probe at the start of the module. By monitoring this information with the analyser we can record: the start address of each module (and thus obtain a memory map of the modules for lower-level monitoring), the time taken to execute each module, and the execution path of the program at the block-structure level. We can monitor programs written in high-level languages at the block-structure level without knowledge of the machine code or memory map.

We have implemented module number software probes in two ways: a simple write to the module number monitor register (Figure 7.4), and a more complex method, involving the maintenance of module numbers on a stack (Section 8.4), in situations where the execution of modules can be interrupted. The latter method costs more in execution time, but simplifies implementation in complex objects where there may be several levels of procedure nesting. In both methods of probe implementation, the position of the instruction which writes data to the monitor register within the software probe is important. The logic state analyser reads the contents of the monitor registers, etc, at the end of the next memory cycle after the probe write. This memory cycle is an instruction fetch, and thus the address read from the hardware probe is the address of the next instruction.

If the probe write instruction is the last instruction in the probe software (see the assembler probe in Figure 7.4) then the address read from the hardware probe is a target program address. If the probe write instruction is not the last instruction in the software probe (see the assembler poke procedure in Figure 7.4) then the address read from the hardware probe is not in the target program, and is of no use to the analyst. One way to guarantee that the address read from the hardware probe is a target program address is to use hand crafted macro routines instead of subroutines (Figure 8.9), if the implementation language will allow it. By using macros we can obtain memory map data for the target program with both methods of probe implementation, at the cost of increased memory usage by the probe software. Having target program addresses available, in addition to module identifiers, is of considerable advantage when debugging programs, and when running

Table 7.1 Cost of the software probes in Figure 7.4 – measured on an Apple II.

Implementation		*Time in microseconds*		
Language	*Code*	*Before*	*After*	*Total*
Assembler	two instructions	6	0	6
Assembler procedure	poke(data,address)	427	25	452
Pascal variant	probe.ptr∧[0]: = data	609	12	621

monitor verification programs.

Stimulus information can be written to the stimulus-probe monitor register at any time. An object **module map**, which includes module name, module number, module stimulus information, and the order in which stimulus information is written, must be documented when the probes are inserted into the software.

7.6 Program execution history

Data collected by the logic state analyser is analysed, by programs in the monitoring computer (an Apple II), to find answers to the questions raised in Section 7.4. Prior to making any measurements, the programmer decides what he wants to know about the program under study. Then he arms the trigger circuits of the logic state analyser to start recording the execution history when the program reaches the section he wishes to monitor, and he sets up the data reduction circuits in the logic state analyser to record only data of interest. As the target process executes, data stored in the hardware probe by the software probes is recorded until either the target process terminates or the trace buffer in the analyser is full. At the completion of the measurement, this data, which is the execution history of the object under study, is transferred to the monitoring computer for analysis. Recorded data is also displayed on the screen of the logic state analyser for manual analysis.

One program studied with the program execution monitor was that used to develop the Apple to analyser communication link. The Apple IEEE-488 bus interface included a driver in read only memory. Calling this firmware routine from Pascal programs proved to be very difficult. Consequently, the hybrid performance measurement tool was used as a program execution monitor to debug the software (Section 7.7), and to measure what the firmware was doing.

The execution path of part of the program (Figure 7.5), and the time each module took to execute, were read directly from the execution

Assembler Probe

(*Probe for insertion into assembler program*)

```
ADDR EQU 0C0D0 ; PROBE ADDRESS
    LDA #02   ; MODULE IDENTIFIER
    STA ADDR  ;WRITE TO PROBE
```

Assembler Poke Procedure

(*Pascal calling sequence*)

```
ADDR := -16176; (*PROBE IS IN SLOT 5*)
POKE(2,ADDR);
```

(*Assembler code for poke procedure*)

```
      .PROC POKE,2
; PROCEDURE POKE(DATA,ADDR:INTEGER)
;PROCEDURE TO WRITE TO ADDRESS
RETURN .EQU 0
ADDR   .EQU 2
      POP RETURN   ;SAVE RETURN ADDRESS
      POP ADDR     ;MEMORY LOCATION
      LDX #0
      PLA          ;GET OUTPUT
      STA @ADDR,X  ;POKE
      PLA          ;CLEAN UP STACK
      PUSH RETURN
      RTS          ;GO BACK
```

Pascal Variant

(*Variant record declaration*)

```
TYPE MAGIC = RECORD
        CASE BOOLEAN OF
        TRUE : (INT:INTEGER);
        FALSE : (PTR:∧PA);
        END;
VAR CHEAT:MAGIC;
```

(*Probe for insertion into Pascal program*)

```
CHEAT.INT := ADDR;
CHEAT.PTR∧[0] := 2;
```

Figure 7.4 Variety of software module identifier probes.

history, and then drawn as a flow graph (Figure 7.6). A **module spectrum** (Figure 7.7) was produced for the firmware routine which handles output to the IEEE bus and sets up the mode of operation of the interface card, by plotting the time taken to execute the module versus the number of module executions which take each path. As there is a discrete number of paths through a module the spectrum consists of a vertical line for each execution path. Stimulus information, also recorded on the spectrum, defines the conditions under which different paths are executed. The most frequently used execution paths, and execution paths which take excessive amounts of time, can be read directly off the spectrum. The most frequent operation performed by this program was writing data to the IEEE bus. From the module spectrum (Figure 7.7), this operation took the path through the firmware transmit routine with the longest execution time.

Full characterization of a module is possible only if all execution paths are taken. Monitoring the execution paths of a module at the machine-code level, for all known execution paths, will show up any areas of the program address space that are not used, and thus indicate the presence of additional execution paths. Alternatively, at the block-structure level, comparing the modules in the event trace to the module map will indicate any blocks that are not executed.

When monitoring execution-paths at the machine-code level (Section 5.5.1), we need a method of isolating instruction fetch memory cycles from the larger set of memory cycles. On minicomputers, signals indicating the type of memory cycle (instruction fetch, operand fetch, data fetch, and data write) can usually be found. Unfortunately, these signals are internal to most microprocessors and, as a result, data reduction has to be done by one or several of the following methods: separating data and address space and recording only address space cycles, comparing the execution history with a machine code listing, emulating the processor (as is done in microprocessor development systems), or using a state machine to simulate processor operation (as is done in many personality modules used on logic state analysers).

Monitoring the execution path of a module, written in a high-level language, at the program-instruction level can be done by inserting stimulus probes between program statements. The cost, and tedium, of this exercise are such that it would only be considered as a last resort in program debugging, or as a means of determining the execution time of individual high-level instructions.

```
'T' : BEGIN (* APPLE TO TALK*)
      POKE(3,ADDR); (* module identifier probe *)
      OUTPUT(TALK,5); (* talk statement module Figure 7.6 *)
```

```
PROCEDURE OUTPUT(VAR STR:STRNG;N:INTEGER);
(* SENDS A STRING TO IEEEBUS *)
VAR I,STIM:INTEGER;
   DAT:CHAR;
BEGIN
POKE(8,ADDR); (* character output procedure probe Figure 7.6 *)
FOR I := 1 TO N DO
  BEGIN
  DAT := STR[I];
  STIM := ORD(DAT);
  POKE(STIM,ADDR + 2);
  PUTCHAR(DAT);
  END;
POKE(7,ADDR); (* return to talk statement probe Figure 7.6 *)
END;

      .PROC PUTCHAR,1  ; PROCEDURE PUTCHAR(DOUT:CHAR);
      .PUBLIC PSTATUS,PHZWD,PPOSN,POUT,PIN,PDELM,PCCLN
RETURN .EQU 0
DATA   .EQU 2
STAT   .EQU 7
HZWD   .EQU 21
POSN   .EQU 24
OPHK   .EQU 36
INHK   .EQU 38
XREG   .EQU 46
DELM   .EQU 5FB
CCLN   .EQU 7FB
ADDR   .EQU 0C0D0
OUTPUT .EQU 0C32B
      POP RETURN
      POP DATA
      LDA #0F0 ; assembler probe
      STA ADDR ; first save restore module Figure 7.6
      PUSH OPHK
      PUSH INHK
      PUSH XREG
      PUSH DELM
      PUSH CCLN
      MOVE PSTATUS,STAT
      MOVEB PHZWD,HZWD
      MOVEB PPOSN,POSN
      MOVE  POUT,OPHK
      MOVE  PIN,INHK
      MOVEB PDELM,DELM
      MOVEB PCCLN,CCLN
      LDA #0F1
      STA ADDR ; firmware transmit module Figure 7.6
      LDA  DATA
```

```
JSR OUTPUT ;write a character to IEEE bus
LDA #0F0
STA ADDR ; second save restore module Figure 7.6
MOVE STAT,PSTATUS
MOVEB HZWD,PHZWD
MOVEB POSN,PPOSN
MOVEB DELM,PDELM
MOVEB CCLN,PCCLN
POP CCLN
POP DELM
POP XREG
POP INHK
POP OPHK
LDA #08
STA ADDR ; return to character output procedure Figure 7.6
PUSH RETURN
RTS
```

Figure 7.5 Instrumented test program.

7.7 Program debugging – case study

To illustrate the applicability of the hybrid tool for monitoring program execution, we will describe the debugging of the IEEE488 communications program, a program running in the monitoring computer. The documentation for the IEEE488 interface card (Kayin Peripherals, 1979), which we bought for the Apple II, included the following specification:

> 'The IE-01-79 [interface card] comes with on board firmware (listing in Appendix D) and requires no additional machine code software or memory space to operate. The firmware was written to enable the user to invoke communications with the IEEE bus from a high level language and programming examples presented in this manual are in Applesoft or integer BASIC.'

7.7.1 Traditional methods

We wrote several BASIC programs to test the operation of the card, and these worked in all but one mode. For a number of reasons the analysis software had to be written in Pascal, but our attempts to drive the interface from Pascal failed because the card was designed to be driven from BASIC. Pascal and BASIC handle input/output in a different

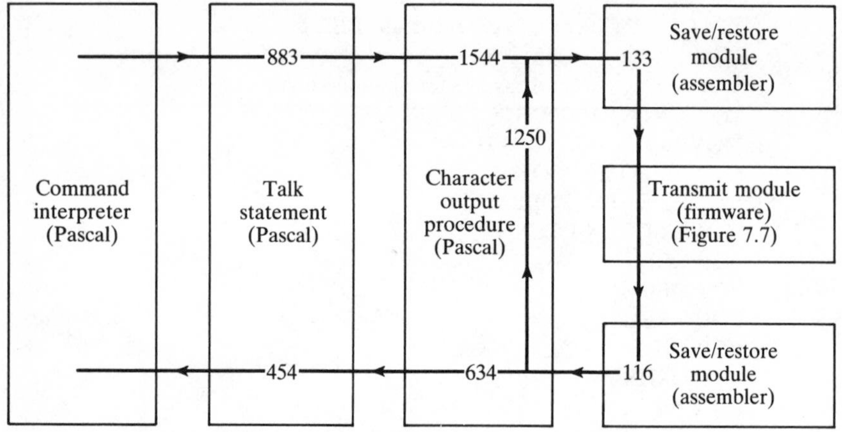

Figure 7.6 Execution path flow graph for the program in Figure 7.5 showing the flow of program execution when the Apple is talking. Times in microseconds.

way: BASIC has only one input device and one output device, requiring only one input and one output vector; Pascal can have a number of input and output devices each with its own vector. We compensated for these differences with an assembler routine, which also handled the bank switching of interface firmware - firmware on all interface cards resides at the same address. The modified program appeared to initialize the IEEE bus, with the Apple to talk and the analyser to listen, but as soon as data transfer was attempted the program crashed and the Apple rebooted.

By examining the listing of the program, we found that the firmware was using additional memory space for the storage of variables, despite the comment in the above quotation. The memory locations used were valid temporary locations in BASIC but not in Pascal. We added assembler routines before and after the calls to the interface card firmware to save and restore these memory locations (Figure 7.5), but the fault remained. Using the disassembler, in the Apple monitor, we disassembled the firmware and found it to be different from the listing: one mode of operation had been left out completely, and minor changes had been made to the rest of the code.

7.7.2 Hybrid methods

Having exhausted traditional debugging methods, we decided to use a program execution monitor, so we plugged the hardware probe into the Apple and inserted software probes into the program. We chose the character being written to the interface card by the Pascal program as

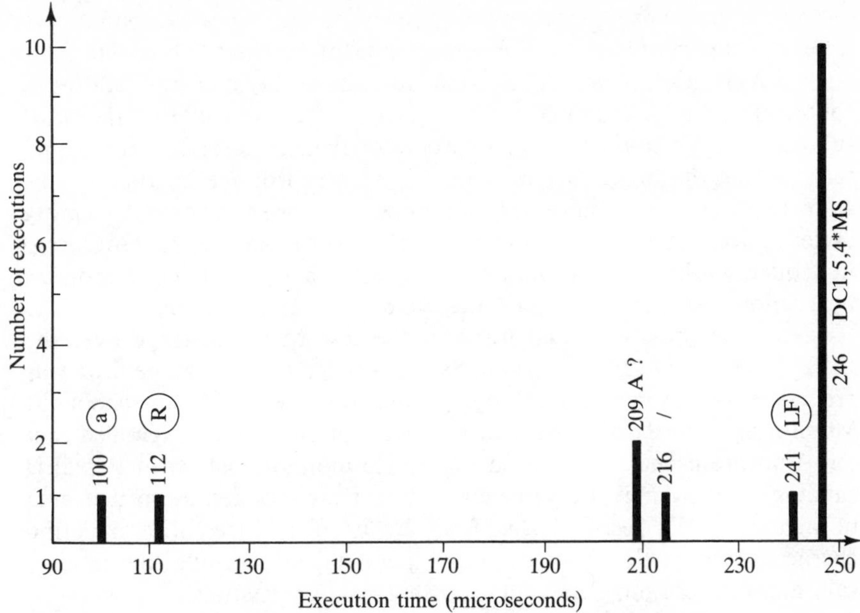

Figure 7.7 Module spectrum of the firmware transmit routine in the IEEE-488 interface, for the command string: @?A/ R followed by the data string: DC1,5,4*MS LF

stimulus information. With this instrumentation, we monitored the firmware execution path for each character written to the IEEE bus, and built up an execution history (Figure 7.6). We monitored the Pascal code at the block-structure level, but because we could not insert probes into the firmware, we monitored it at the machine-code level. The firmware could be monitored as a block, but it could not be decomposed into block-structure level modules. Dynamic analysis of the program was considerably faster than static analysis of the code, which had proved to be difficult due to the complexity of the code.

From the execution history, we determined that: the interface was being set up correctly; the interface was switching from command mode to data transmission mode, when the terminator of the command string was processed; the first data character was being transmitted, but the execution path included a routine which de-selected the firmware memory bank; and, consequently, during the attempt to transmit the second character the crash occurred, when a call to the firmware routine jumped to a non-existent memory location and fetched the code for a software interrupt, which caused the Apple to reboot. We overcame this problem by reselecting the firmware memory bank before the firmware was called.

While examining the execution history of the firmware routine, we were initially confused by the appearance of isolated subroutine start addresses in the trace. The confusion arose because the addresses following each subroutine start address were not in the indicated subroutine. We studied the 6502 processor manual carefully, and found that, during the processing of a return from subroutine instruction, the address of the next memory location appears on the bus for one memory cycle. There were many subroutines in the code, and as these occurred in sequence, the next memory location after a return from subroutine instruction was usually the start address of another subroutine.

Now the program could transmit the text of the message over the IEEE bus, but when the termination character (a carriage return) was processed the Apple did strange things, and we had to reboot it. Monitoring the execution path of the termination character revealed that the firmware called a routine in the Apple monitor, but when Pascal is running on the Apple a completely different monitor resides in that area of memory. We rectified this fault by using a different termination character (line feed) whose execution path did not include the monitor call, and then the program could transmit data successfully.

Next, we attempted to receive data from the IEEE488 bus. The program initialized the interface correctly, but as soon as it attempted to transfer data, the Apple appeared to die. Monitoring the execution path revealed that the program had hung up in an infinite loop. By comparing the execution path to the listing we found that the path should not have been possible, because the program was branching on the state of a variable to a routine which reset that variable. Obviously the variable was being modified elsewhere. We wrote this variable to the stimulus probe and confirmed that it was being modified in the save/restore routine between the Pascal host and the firmware. This module worked in the call to the output firmware routine, so why didn't it work in the call to the input firmware routine?

The save/restore routine uses global variables declared in the Pascal host, and references to these variables are resolved when the assembler routine is linked to the Pascal host. The linker had not reported any errors, and the documentation (Apple Computer Inc., 1980; page 181) does not explain how to interpret the information in the link map. We confirmed the existence of a linkage fault by monitoring the execution path, and the data space accesses, of the save/restore module in both the working and the non-working cases. We fixed the fault by changing the order of the assembler procedures in the library which was linked into the program - a rather unusual fix. Now the program could receive data, but it failed to detect the termination character. By writing the received characters to the stimulus probe, we discovered that the most significant bit of the incoming characters had been set, a change which caused the Pascal test for equality to fail. Several other problems were caused by reducing the data from eight to seven bits, so we replaced the firmware input routine with a modified version, which does not mask the input data and is stored in volatile memory. The new routine used permanently allocated variables, and hence the calls to the save and restore routines were no longer needed. After all these modifications, we finally had a working communications link.

7.8 Conclusion

During the development of a program, there are many occasions where the process of identifying program faults can be simplified by examining program execution histories. However, program execution monitoring has been a neglected research topic, and consequently few general purpose tools are available for dynamic program analysis.

The foregoing case study demonstrates that a powerful, easy to use, hybrid program execution monitor can be built from readily available components - components which are becoming cheaper and more powerful. Only minor additions are required to the hardware of the target computer, and the cost of the software probes can be measured, eliminating errors in timing measurements. We introduced a method of measuring program execution histories at the block-structure level, which removes any need for the programmer to know details of the machine code or the memory map of the program. This methodology is consistent with modern philosophies of programming, in contrast to many techniques in common use, which require an intimate knowledge of low-level implementation details. Low-level details can be measured by the tool, if required.

Chapter 8

Computer System Design for Measurement

Increasingly, computer users are faced with black boxes which have been built without regard for the user's need for information about system operation. In many ways, computers complement human intelligence, but if a computer fails to provide information that is easy for the user to assimilate, confidence in the computer is diminished. Computers are excellent at handling numbers and tables; humans at recognizing patterns and pictures. Often, when executing a copy command on a dual floppy disk system, one wonders if the copy is going the correct way. Using lights to indicate reading and writing operations would give the user increased confidence in the operation of the system, through more rapid feedback.

The removal of speakers and front panels from computers has made them less friendly. These components were regularly used in system debugging. For example, the operating system used in a real-time control project was modified to illuminate an individual light on the console for each process, when that process was active (McKerrow, 1978). As many of the processes were cyclic, due to the nature of the external machines, a regular pattern could be observed on the lights when the system was operating correctly. This enabled the operation of a complex control system to be analysed visually. On a number of occasions, control system problems were diagnosed by observing the light pattern.

Simple tools like these may not provide very accurate measures, but they do inform the user about what is happening. Some new systems have an icon moving about the screen during program execution to inform the user that the system is working and he must wait for it to finish. These tools all increase user confidence, and should be included at design time. If they are not, they can be difficult to add later. Unfortunately, the majority of performance monitoring tools are added after systems are operational. Consequently, due to the constraints imposed by the organization of the system being monitored, serious problems are often encountered, problems which make measurement difficult and cause measurement errors. These problems include:

- excessive interference;
- inaccessibility of events of interest;

- difficulty in verifying collected data;
- it may not be possible to place the probes where you want them; and
- modifications to the system to provide the required data may be difficult, risky, or expensive.

These problems can be minimized by including a comprehensive set of measurement facilities in the system when it is designed. This practice has not been popular with computer manufacturers, even though such tools could be used during system implementation and debugging. Research projects into tool integration include the instrumentation of Multics (Saltzer and Gintell, 1970) and of PRIME (Ferrari, 1973). One of the main problems faced by the designers of these systems was: 'How do you predict which events will be of interest for measurement purposes once the system is implemented?' As a result, both projects adopted a mixture of ad-hoc fixed tools and general purpose tools.

For performance evaluation to be effective in the long term, it must be considered when the system is designed. Integration of the design of hardware, software, and instrumentation will result in a cohesive system, and eliminate the frantic patching that is often done to interface these sub-systems. However, before an integrated approach can be achieved, performance evaluators have to be able to specify clearly what they want to measure and why, at system design time. One problem faced by designers is the difficulty of specifying measurement needs when the system's specification has not been stabilized. Ferrari (1973) comments:

> '... in the absence of a general theory of performance evaluation, the only way to overcome this difficulty is to build into the system general purpose tools with sufficient power and flexibility to allow the system's evaluators to measure practically any variable they may be interested in.'

One of the corollaries of the formulation of performance measurement is that it provides a theoretical basis for defining measurement needs, hence enabling the inclusion of specific instrumentation in the design of a system. The formulation provides a method for decomposing a system, it defines a set of measures which apply to any code object in a system, and it gives the designer a basis on which to partition measurement functions between hardware and software tools.

However, to apply the performance measurement methodology (Chapter 6) to the instrumentation of a system the designer must understand the system. As the operating system designer understands the system better than anyone else, he is better equipped to instrument it than anyone else. Thinking about instrumentation will force a structure on the design of the system.

If a system is instrumented, it can be measured to see if it is operating in accordance with the design, as each section of code is tested, providing immediate feedback to the designer, who can then evaluate its performance and test improvement hypotheses. Also, measurements made on one system can be used to build models during the design of new systems (Lynch, 1972). In this way, designers can improve the design and performance of operating systems from one generation to the next. Another goal of operating system designers is the adaptive control of system performance (Boulaye *et al.*, 1977; Geck, 1979; Serazzi, 1981). Feedback control requires integrated instrumentation, coupled with an understanding of the impact of parameter changes on performance. This understanding is gained by changing parameters and measuring the resultant performance change. From these measurements, a transfer function for the system can be found. In the next sections, we will look at two systems where measurement tools were included in the design: Multics and MU5.

8.1 Instrumentation of Multics

Multics was developed as part of a research project to create an operating system to support a wide variety of computational jobs, a system centred around the ability to share information in a controlled way (Saltzer and Gintell, 1970). A spectrum of user services characterized the system, and contributed to a complexity that made careful instrumentation mandatory - services such as: parallel processing, a hierarchical file organization, sharing of information in core memory, dynamic linking of subroutines and data, and device independent input/output facilities. Analysts were particularly interested in studying multiprogramming and demand paging.

In their research, they sought to try out new ideas, and new combinations of old ideas. As a result, a large number of design choices had to be made between different algorithms, strategies, parameter settings, and implementations. They presumed, from the start, that some wrong choices would be made, so they emphasized integrated instrumentation. During the instrumentation of Multics, Saltzer and Gintell observed that:

- frequently, the best guesses by system programmers as to the cause of a performance problem are proved to be wrong by detailed measurement;
- many otherwise undetected performance problems are discovered while studying measurements; and
- performance degradation of the order of 20% regularly goes unnoticed by users.

Thus, advantages of integrated instrumentation are:

- the elimination of the non-scientific approach many programmers take to debugging;
- programming effort is reduced, because incorrect hypotheses are spotted, and programmers do not spend time optimizing the wrong code module; and
- performance problems which are not perceptible to the user are detected.

Although the instrumentation in Multics was directed primarily towards the goal of understanding what goes on inside the operating system, it provided an effective tool for detecting system bottlenecks. A second goal of Multics measurement research was to discover what measurement facilities were needed. Consequently, not all the measurement techniques were thought out in advance. Multics included a combination of hardware, software, and hybrid tools.

Three hardware tools came with the GE645 computer on which Multics was implemented: a program readable clock; a memory cycle counter; and an externally driven input/output channel, which enabled an external computer to monitor the contents of the primary memory of the GE645. Associated with the program readable clock was a programmable comparator, which generated an interrupt whenever a match occurred.

Multics did not have a built-in general event tracing package. The designers thought that the volume of data produced by such a package would be too large to analyse. It had a number of software tools which performed the following tasks:

- A general measuring package recorded the time spent executing selectable supervisor modules and their frequency of execution.
- Every 10 milliseconds, a segment utilization meter sampled the segment number of the executing segment, and stored the result in a table. This provided a simple way of detecting how time spent in the system was distributed among the various components.
- The number of missing pages, and segments, encountered during execution in a segment was recorded on a per segment basis.
- The number of procedure calls was counted.
- The sequence of missing pages encountered by a task was recorded. This record frequently indicated poor locality of reference, and hence a higher than necessary use of system resources by a program.
- The effect of the multiprogramming effort of the system on an individual user was traced.
- Feedback was provided to the user about the resource utilization of

the command just typed (time of day, CPU use by program, and number of page misses).

On a separate computer, connected by a channel, a graphics display monitor (Grochow, 1969) provided a variety of standard displays which were used to observe system queues, primary memory usage, and arrays of data constructed by other tools. During system initialization, Multics built a table containing pointers to interesting databases for use by this hybrid tool. Also, the researchers used the monitoring computer to generate simulated workloads for measurement experiments. For this simulation, they developed a number of typical user interaction scripts, which enabled the monitoring computer to simulate up to 12 interactive users.

Saltzer and Gintell (1970) comment:

> '... building permanent instrumentation into key supervisor modules is well worth the effort, since the cost of maintaining well organized instrumentation is low, and the payoff in being able to "look at the meters" any time a performance problem is suspected is very high.'

8.2 Design of the MU5

The design of the MU5 at the University of Manchester was based on measurements of the Atlas computer (Sumner, 1974). The Atlas hardware interrupted the operating system at the end of every 2048 instruction executions, at the end of every tenth of a second, and at the end of every second. In response to these interrupts, software probes collected measurement data and stored it into spare fields in the supervisor log data structure. A logging program read this data structure regularly and wrote the information to a daily log tape.

To measure the dynamic operand accesses of high-level language programs, Sumner modified the compiler to insert a probe into the target program whenever data was accessed. When executed, these probes incremented counters. At the termination of program execution, the counter values were printed out. By measuring a large number of programs, he found that 80% of accesses were to variables, and 20% of accesses were to array elements. Further measurements were made to determine the size of data caches for the MU5.

To get a picture of dynamic instruction usage the interrupt at the end of every 2048 instructions vectored to a program which classified the currently executing machine-code instruction, and incremented an appropriate counter. At the end of the day, these counters were read, printed, and analysed. Because of the long duration of these measurements, a good average of instruction usage over many programs was obtained. The ratio of floating point arithmetic instruction usage to fixed point arithmetic instruction usage influenced the design of the fixed point arithmetic unit of the MU5. They designed a multiplier into the fixed point arithmetic unit so that address calculations could be done without having to interfere with the operation of the main arithmetic unit.

Sumner found that 20% of the instructions executed were branch instructions. This explained why the theoretical maximum throughput of the Atlas was not attained. The Atlas had an overlapped architecture where instructions which took seven microseconds had an effective execution time of two microseconds, due to a five microsecond overlap. However, branch instructions did not take advantage of this overlap, and lost five microseconds, effectively increasing the average instruction time from two to three microseconds, i.e. a 50% slowdown.

To find ways to improve the execution of branch instructions on the MU5, he modified the hardware of the Atlas to generate an interrupt whenever a branch instruction was executed, except for branch instructions in the analysis routine. This interrupt called an analysis routine to count the number of instructions executed between branch instructions. He plotted several histograms of the number of sequential instructions between various types of branch instructions. Very rarely were sequential blocks, and hence loops, more than ten instructions in length, with a median block length of four instructions. Analysis of the histograms showed that 70% of branch instructions do branch, count and test conditional branch instructions branch about 80% of the time, and arithmetic test conditional branch instructions branch only 50% of the time.

Also, he found that on any particular test the branch goes the same way 80% of the time, and 30% of jumps span a distance of less than four instructions. In the MU5, a buffer is used to store the jump from and jump to addresses for up to eight branch instructions. The first time a piece of code is executed, these addresses are calculated and stored in the buffer. When it is executed again, as each branch instruction is fetched, the jump to address for the branch is loaded into the address register and an instruction fetched, while the test is evaluated. If the branch goes the same way as last time, the next instruction is already in the pipeline, and no time is lost. If it does not, the fetched instruction is discarded and another fetched, and time is lost.

Eighty per cent of the time the assumption that the program will branch the same way it did last time is correct and the pipeline runs at full speed. Twenty per cent of the time the assumption is incorrect, and the extraneous bus activity generates a large gap in the pipeline. Careful programming can reduce the number of gaps encountered. For a comprehensive study of branch behaviour on modern machines, see the article by Lee and Smith (1984) on branch prediction strategies.

Sumner also attempted to measure the optimum page size for the Atlas, but the right signals were not available. When the MU5 was built, performance measurement tools were included to measure the operation of the pipeline (Yannacopoulos *et al.*, 1977). These tools were the same in function as those on the Atlas, but as they were included in the design they were integrated into the system. The performance of the branching mechanism was at least as good as expected, but the data cache did not perform as well as expected. This case study illustrates the usefulness of performance measurement in hardware design.

8.3 Microprocessor design for measurement

The design of microprocessors involves many compromises between the desirable and the achievable. Higher packing density has enabled the introduction of more powerful architectures, but many desirable features are still left off. Some designers have implemented reduced instruction set architectures to free up chip area for use by other circuits. No microprocessor has had performance measurement tools included in it, and compromises on pin count have eliminated a number of useful signals. When designing a microprocessor for measurement, we must consider the following questions:

- What signals should be available for performance measurement?
- What circuits can be added to a processor to reduce the interference of software tools?

The signals needed by an external hardware tool all relate to bus information. They include:

- address bus,
- data bus,
- memory cycle code – instruction fetch, operand fetch, data read, data write, dead cycle, interrupt vector, DMA cycle – used to qualify the memory cycle clock,
- memory cycle clock,
- user/supervisor mode flag,
- busy/wait flag,
- exception processing flag (i.e. interrupts disabled), and
- interrupt priority level.

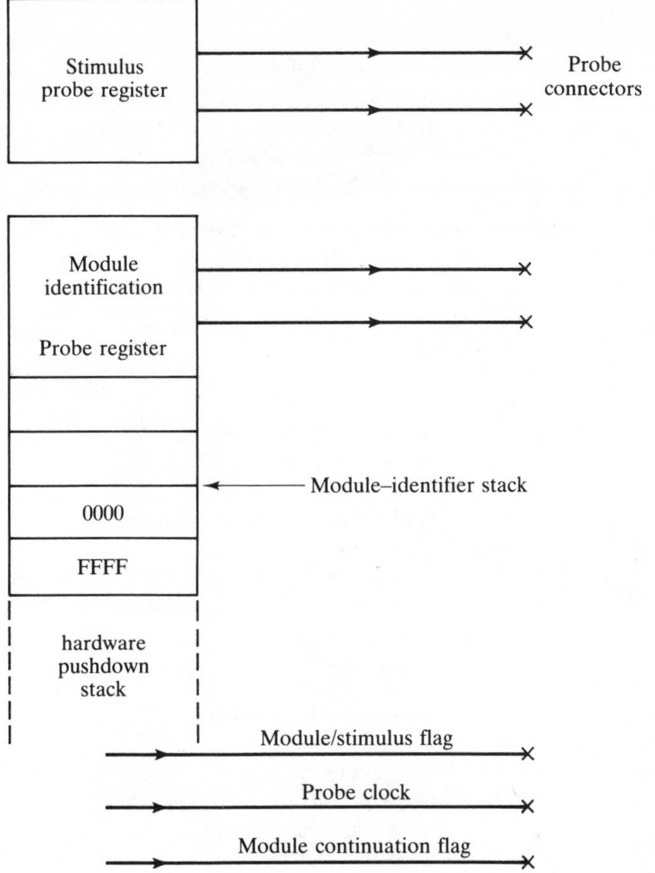

Figure 8.1 Hardware to be added to a microprocessor to reduce probe interference.

Some of these signals are not present on current microprocessors. The most important additional signals are those used to qualify the memory cycle clock. These signals enable bus traffic to be classified in accordance with internal processor activity. If they are not available, it is very difficult to separate out instruction fetches from other cycles. Personality modules used in logic state analysers use complex state machines to separate memory cycles into their categories. The other flags relate to the internal state of the processor, and thus they are useful for object decomposition at the system level.

	Opcodes
probe	writes information to module-identifier monitor-register. {sets module/stimulus flag, and generates probe clock}
stim	writes information to stimulus monitor-register {resets module/stimulus flag, and generates clock} {sets process and task flags as required}
	Probe instruction opcode modifiers
abe	absolute branch entry - A 6.12 writes new value into module register {overwrites old value} stack is not operated on continuation flag reset
inten	interrupt routine entry - A 6.14a push new value into module register continuation flag reset
intex	interrupt routine exit - A 6.15a pop stack {old value into module register} continuation flag set
idle	return to quiescent state - A 6.17 pop stack until zero in module register clock generated after each pop continuation flag reset on last pop
	Stim instruction opcode modifiers
proc	this is a process number write to first stimulus register
task	this is a task identifier write to second stimulus register
num	number of stimulus register to write to
	Operand
	value address of value {normal instruction addressing modes}

Figure 8.2 Probe machine instructions - used in conjunction with monitor chip.

Software probes write data to the monitor registers in the hardware probe, but they interfere with the target software. This interference can be reduced by including monitoring features in the microprocessor. An obvious way to do this is to store module identifiers in a hardware push down stack (Figure 8.1). The top of this stack is the module identifier monitor register. When a probe instruction writes to the monitor register, a new value is pushed onto the stack or an old value is popped off the stack, depending upon which probe algorithm is executed.

Stimulus information is stored in on chip registers too. As all these registers are implemented on the microprocessor chip, they are at fixed addresses, and implicit addressing can be used by special probe instructions.

Two probe instructions must be added to the assembler instruction set (Figure 8.2): one to write to the module identifier monitor register, and one to write to the stimulus monitor register. These instructions include opcode modifiers to specify which probe algorithm is to be executed by the hardware. The instruction operand has all the addressing modes available on the microprocessor, although intermediate (operand is value) and direct (operand is address of value) will be most commonly used. In these addressing modes, only one instruction is needed to implement probes, considerably reducing probe interference. Addressing modes involving registers will create more interference because the register has to be loaded with the address of the probe value. A probe instruction is able to execute in one instruction cycle because:

- the probe addresses are fixed and thus can be implicit,
- the operand of the instruction is either the value to be stored into the monitor register or the address of the value,
- stack handling, probe clock generation, and status flag settings are all implemented in hardware as selected by the opcode modifiers, and
- the processor latches the data directly into the monitor registers.

Implementing the additional hardware inside the microprocessor chip is no problem, but getting the signals out is. The probe requires at least 40 pins, assuming 16-bit monitor registers, pins which cannot be found on an existing microprocessor. Also, the defined hardware will not handle pre-emption, which requires separate stack areas for each process, considerably complicating the hardware. Therefore, the probe hardware has to be implemented on a separate monitor chip (Figure 8.3).

Two additional buses connect the microprocessor to the monitor chip: a 4-bit monitor bus and a 4-bit status bus. Some microprocessors already have a status bus, for example the 8085 and the Z8000. By multiplexing information over these buses, the number of pins required for monitoring is reduced to eight. The status bus contains information about the current status of the processor: busy or idle, user or supervisor mode, etc. This information can be used for system level measurements.

During normal operation, the monitor bus carries information about the current bus cycle, such as the type of cycle - instruction fetch, data write, etc. This bus is decoded by the monitor chip to produce the memory cycle clock qualifiers. When a probe instruction is executed, the monitor bus contains the probe opcode modifier, which instructs circuits in the monitor chip to execute the desired probe algorithm. At the end of the instruction cycle, the data on the data bus, which has been fetched by the probe instruction, is latched into the appropriate monitor register. When a return from interrupt probe is executed, a continuation number is incremented, but all other probes reset this number. Thus, module fragmentation can be detected by monitoring the continuation value.

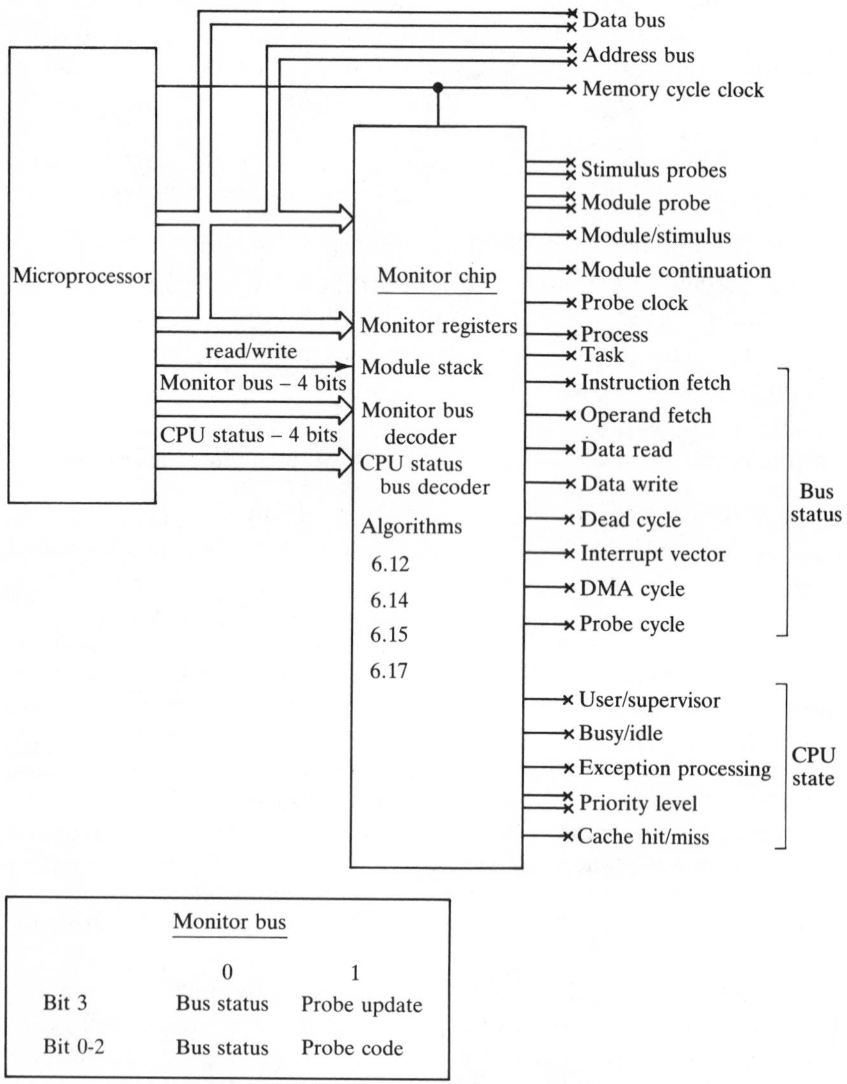

Figure 8.3 Microprocessor to monitor chip interface.

The monitor chip can handle process pre-emption by allocating a separate stack frame for each process. When a process is dispatched, a stimulus probe writes the number of the new process to the monitor chip. The opcode modifier instructs the monitor chip to relocate the top of stack pointer to the stack frame for that process if a stack frame exists, or to allocate a new stack frame and relocate the top of stack pointer to it. Research into the nesting depth of high-level languages (Patterson and Sequin, 1982) indicates that nesting depth is greater than eight for less than 1% of procedure calls. Thus, a stack frame 16 entries long will handle the majority of nesting situations. If a stack overflow does occur, a special event marker can be inserted in the event trace (or a control flag set) to indicate this. This condition is of considerable interest to an analyst who is trying to understand the program. By incrementing a counter each time a stack overflow occurs on module entry, and then decrementing it on module exit, the chip should be able to maintain probe balance, and correctly instrument the process, except for the loss of those probes below the maximum stack depth.

The outputs of the monitor chip are connected to probe connectors, in parallel with the address bus, the data bus, and the memory cycle clock. The probe clock is synchronized to the next instruction fetch, and as the fetched instruction is from the instrumented program, the current program counter can be read in parallel with the monitor registers. By reading the address and data buses during a probe cycle, the placement of probes can be checked.

A computer system built from these components could be instrumented permanently with very little interference to the software. In fact, removal of accounting programs from the computer to the external tool would more than compensate for probe interference. In addition, the outputs of the monitor chip could be used for hardware fault diagnosis.

In the design of a RISC chip (Patterson and Sequin, 1982), a number of constraints were placed upon the architecture so that the goals of simplicity and effective single chip implementation could be met. These constraints were:

- execute one instruction per cycle,
- make all instructions the same size,
- access memory with only load and store instructions, and
- support high-level languages.

The first constraint eliminates variations in the execution time of a path due to variations in instruction execution time. Thus, removing variations in the execution time of machine code is not only desirable from the measurement point of view, but also simplifies the design of the processor. Other causes of path execution time variation can be detected

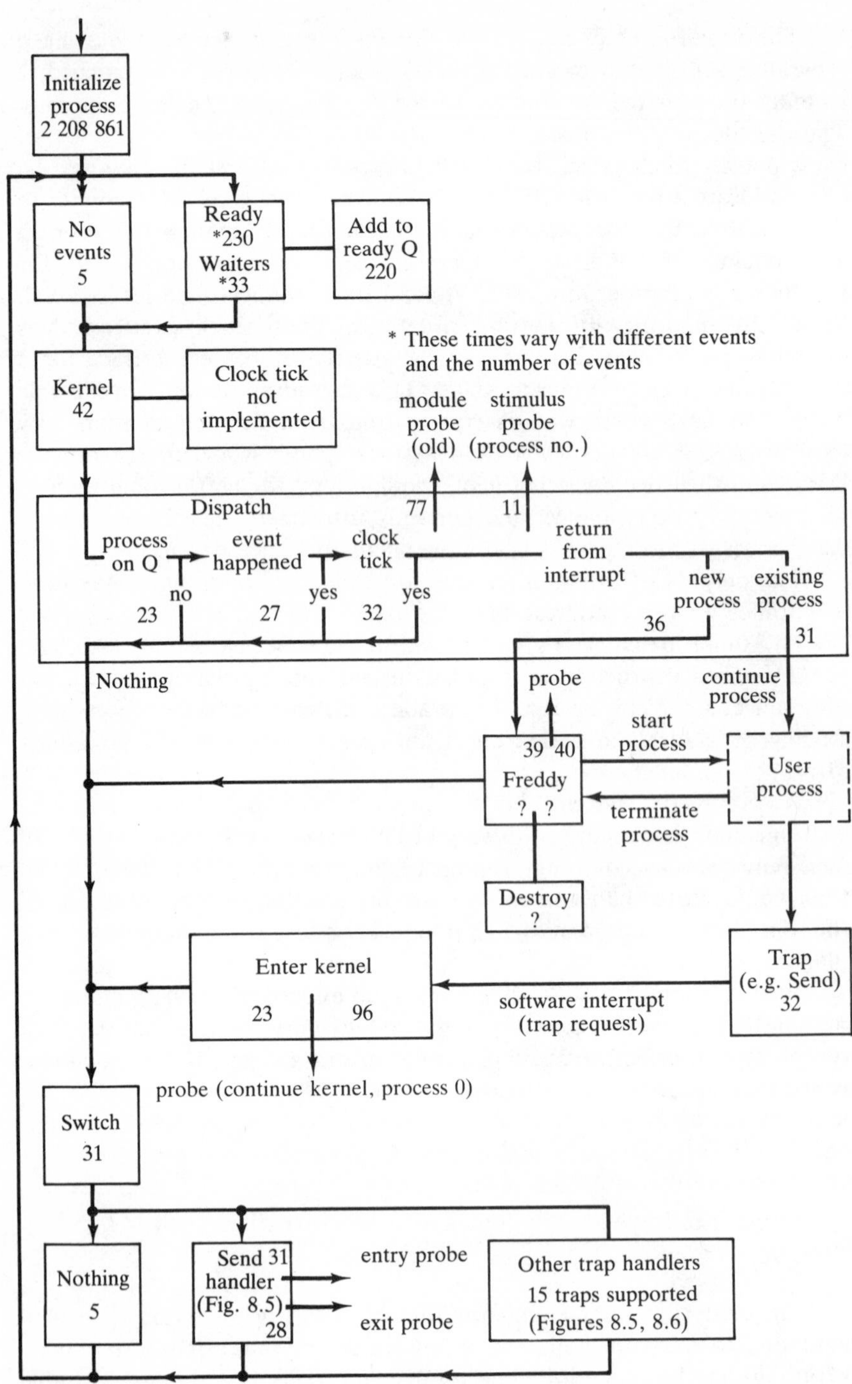

Figure 8.4 Execution path flow graph of the kernel of a message passing operating system (after modification to ready waiters). All times in microseconds.

and compensated for by attaching counters to appropriate status signals on the monitor chip. The cache hit/miss signal is supplied by the cache circuitry, when a cache is used.

8.4 Instrumentation and measurement of a small computer system – case study

We built a small computer system to handle terminal multiplexing to a UNIX system over a Cambridge Ring local area network. From the start, we included performance measurement tools in both software and hardware, in accordance with the methodology developed in this book (Figure 8.7). The hardware includes an M6809 microprocessor, and can transfer data to the network under status loop, interrupt request, or DMA control. We used the hybrid monitoring tool to measure system performance, monitor program execution, find areas of poor performance, and identify the cause of hardware and software bugs.

The operating system is a single address space message passing system similar to Thoth (Cheriton *et al.*, 1979). Sixteen primitive requests are supported by the kernel (Figures 8.4-8.6). Four of these are message passing primitives (Figures 8.5 and 8.6). When a process requests a message to be sent, the message is passed to the receiver (by exchanging pointers to message fields), the sending process is blocked waiting for a reply, and the receiving process is added to the ready queue. When the receiving process replies, the pointers are swapped again, and the sending process is added to the ready queue. The receive and await-sender primitives enable a process to block waiting on either a message from anyone or a message from a specific process. The other primitives handle requests like create a process and allocate memory (Figure 8.6).

When a process requests service from the kernel, a software interrupt vectors to the enter kernel procedure (Figure 8.4), which handles the process switch. Then the appropriate primitive is executed to perform the requested service. After this, a check is made of the event vector to see if any events have happened, and, if so, the process waiting for that event is added to the ready queue. Then the dispatch process procedure switches to the first user process on the ready queue. This may not be the process which requested the service; for example, when a process makes a request for a message to be sent, the sending process is removed from the ready queue so that it can wait for a reply.

This system is built with a large number of small procedures (30 in the kernel, 27 for terminal handling, etc.) which are executed in sequence to form a process (Figures 2.4 and 8.10). A sequence of processes forms a task to execute some operation (Figure 2.3). The system consists of a number of terminal handling tasks (two for each terminal) and three network handling tasks (input, output, and protocol). Many of these

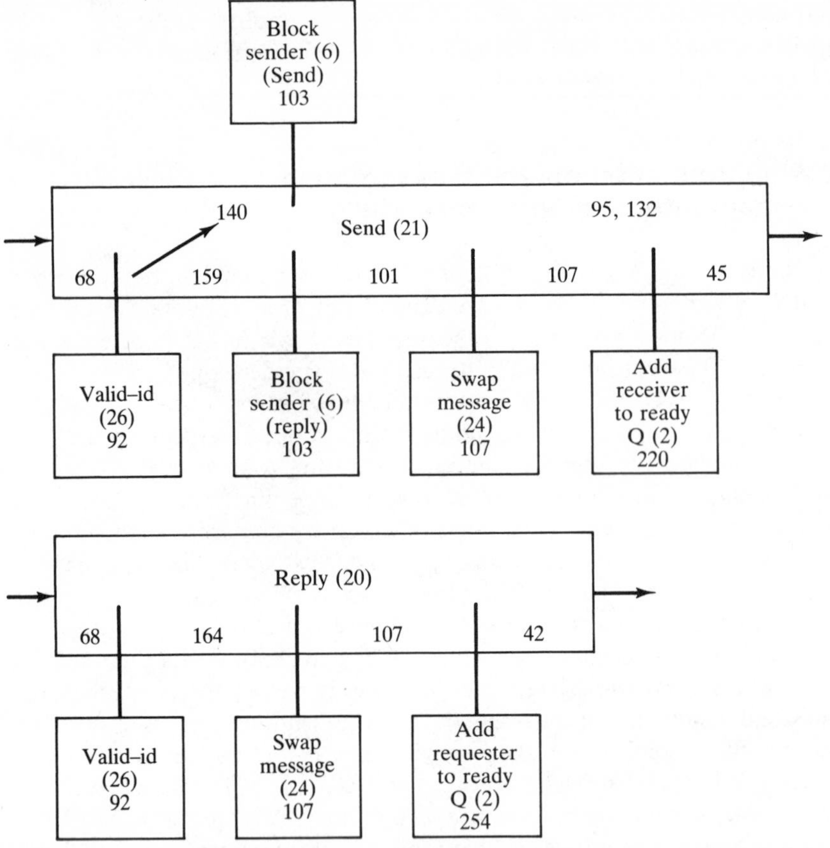

Figure 8.5 Execution path flow graph for the send message and reply trap handlers (before modifications to valid id, block, and swap message). All times in microseconds. Numbers in brackets are module numbers.

tasks use the same processes (which use the same modules), and thus instrumentation at the task level must be sufficient to enable the interleaved tasks to be separated out.

In the discussion of instrumentation that follows, procedures are at the module level (block-structure level), processes are considered to be at the program-execution level, and tasks at the task level. First, we discuss the method of instrumentation, then we describe how we used this instrumentation to measure the system.

8.4.1 Instrumentation

We used a hardware probe (Figure 8.7) which had three monitor registers, based on the same basic circuit design as the Apple probe (Figure 7.3). This probe was plugged into an input-output slot on the terminal multiplexer. We used the hybrid performance monitor in two modes: as a logic state analyser for fault finding, and as a hybrid monitor for performance measurement and evaluation.

We found a minor design error in the probe during these measurement experiments. As designed, the circuit will produce a clock pulse (Figure 7.2) every time a value is stored in a monitor register.

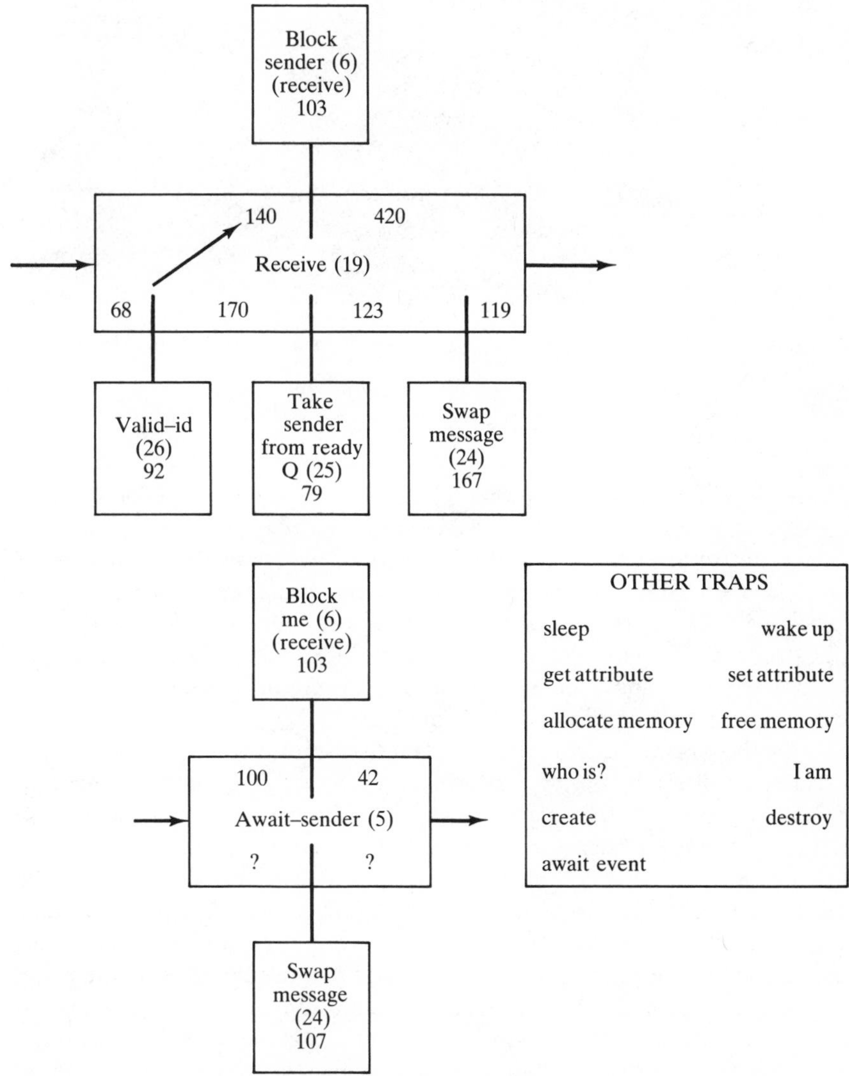

Figure 8.6 Execution path flow graph for the receive message and await sender trap handlers (before modifications to valid id, block, and swap message). All times in microseconds. Numbers in brackets are module numbers.

Figure 8.7 Hardware probe plugged into experimental terminal multiplexer.

However, if data is stored in two monitor registers on successive memory cycles (for example a 16-bit store over an 8-bit bus) only one clock pulse occurs not two. This reduces the number of events in the event stream, without data loss, but it can confuse the measurement tool if it is expecting separate module and stimulus clocks. One solution is to AND the probe clock with the memory-cycle clock. Other solutions are to have a separate clock for each monitor register, or a single probe clock with the register number as a clock qualifier.

As the operating system is pre-emptive, the process number of the executing program is an important piece of stimulus information. Stimulus probes in the dispatch and enter kernel modules (Figure 8.4) wrote process numbers to the second monitor register. With this information, and a clock derived from an address decode signal on the probe, we were able to measure at the process level (Figure 2.3). The ability to obtain a separate clock for each monitor register is important, and the hardware probe (Figure 7.3) should be modified to provide either separate clocks or clock qualifiers, depending on the clock qualification abilities of the logic state analyser. Except for some assembler routines, all procedures in the system were instrumented with software probes which wrote module numbers to the first monitor register, using Algorithms 6.14a and 6.15a.

```
static_Freddy()                          Example of an instrumented program
 {
  Entry( 26 );                           call ______en routine to write module no 26
  (*__________uo)( Who_sent(), Active_pd->msg );
  Destroy( Active_pd->id );
  Exit();                                call ______re routine to write old module no
 }

*     line 500, file "KERNEL/Basics.c"     Entry(26) - Compiler output
      ldb    #26
      stb    0                           write to probe - to here 7 microseconds
      ldd    #26                         3 microseconds
      pshs    d                          10 microseconds
      jbs    ________en+0                call entry routine - 19 microseconds
      leas   2,s                         5 microseconds
*     line 501, file "KERNEL/Basics.c"
      "      other assembler instructions
      "
*     line 503, file "KERNEL/Basics.c"
      "
*     line 504, file "KERNEL/Basics.c"     Exit()
      jbs    ________re+0                call exit routine - 19 microseconds
      tfr     u,s
      puls    x,y,u
      rts                                return to routine which called _Freddy

          .globl ________en              Code of probe used at routine entry
          .text
________en:    pshs   x                  execution time 93 microseconds
          ldd    modstack
          ldx    modindex
          leax   1,x
          stx    modindex
          leax   d,x
          ldd    4,s
          stb    ,x
          tfr    d,x
          leax   d,x
          ldd    #1
          addd   _Mod_ref,x
          std    _Mod_ref,x
          puls   x,pc                    return to _Freddy

          .globl ________re              Code of probe used at routine exit
          .text
________re:    pshs   x                  execution time 60 microseconds
          ldd    modstack
          ldx    modindex
```

```
leax  -1,x
stx   modindex
lda   d,x
ora   #x'80
sta   0          write to probe - instruction time 5
puls  x,pc       instruction time 11 microseconds
```

Figure 8.8 Software probes added to experimental terminal multiplexer. A separate stack is used as a probe stack. All times in microseconds.

We implemented **module-number probes** in two ways: the first (Figure 8.8) used a separate stack as a module identifier stack, and the second (Figure 8.9) used the first local variable in the stack frame of each procedure. The execution time of the second implementation is considerably shorter than that of the first (Table 8.1). The probes in the first implementation were called as procedures, which added 30 microseconds to their execution time (most of this time was spent saving and restoring registers during the procedure call and return). Also, the probes in the first implementation have to find the stack frame and stack pointer for the module stack, all of which is eliminated in the second implementation, because the stack frame of the current procedure is used. However, as the probes in the second implementation are written as macros, execution time is reduced at the cost of increased memory usage. The first implementation was discarded in favour of the second (Figure 8.9).

Four pieces of code are shown in Figure 8.9: the module entry code for a procedure call, the macro used as a module entry probe, the macro used as a module exit probe, and the module exit code for a return from procedure. The **module entry probe** obtains the module number of the calling module from the global temporary variable (T1), saves it on the user's stack, writes the module number of the new module to the monitor register, sets the continuation flag, and saves the module number in the global temporary variable. The **module exit probe** retrieves the module number of the calling module from the user's stack, saves it in the global temporary variable, and writes it to the probe.

These probes differ from Algorithms 6.14a and 6.15a by using a global temporary variable instead of the top of stack. We chose this implementation because the probes only have to access the current stack, where a direct implementation of the algorithms would have to access the stack of the calling module as well. This simplified probe implementation, but created problems when process pre-emption occurred. As the module identifier of the currently executing module is

Table 8.1 Cost of software probe – on the experimental terminal multiplexer. Probe code is given in Figures 8.5 and 8.6.

Implementation		*Time in microseconds*		
		Before	*After*	*Total*
Entry	separate stack	7	125	132
Exit	separate stack	68	11	79
Entry	process stack	16	7	23
Exit	process stack	14	0	14

held in the global variable, it must be saved when a process switch occurs, or the module probes in the next process will overwrite it. With Algorithms 6.14a and 6.15a, the module identifier of the currently executing module is already saved on the stack when pre-emption occurs.

We modified the probes which indicate entry to and exit from the kernel to accommodate for the change in module sequence caused by pre-emption. These probes are located in the enter kernel and dispatch procedures (Figure 8.4). On entry to the kernel, the module identifier of the pausing module is placed in a field in the process descriptor of the pausing process. When a process is dispatched, the module identifier for the resumed module is obtained from a field in the process descriptor of the dispatched process. To be consistent with the approach we used to handle procedures, an area in the stack frame of the current process should be used, rather than a field in the process descriptor of the current process. The cost of instrumenting a system at the module level is reasonably high (Table 8.2), and in the final system the module identifier probes will be removed, leaving only the process number stimulus probes.

Table 8.2 Cost of instrumenting the character handling task at various levels in the object hierarchy.

Probes	*Execution time*	
	Microseconds	*% of task*
Block-structure level only (module probes)	1340	10.6
Program-execution level only (process probes)	198	1.7
Task level only	264	2.2
System level only	264	2.2
Total instrumentation (understanding)	1703	12.8

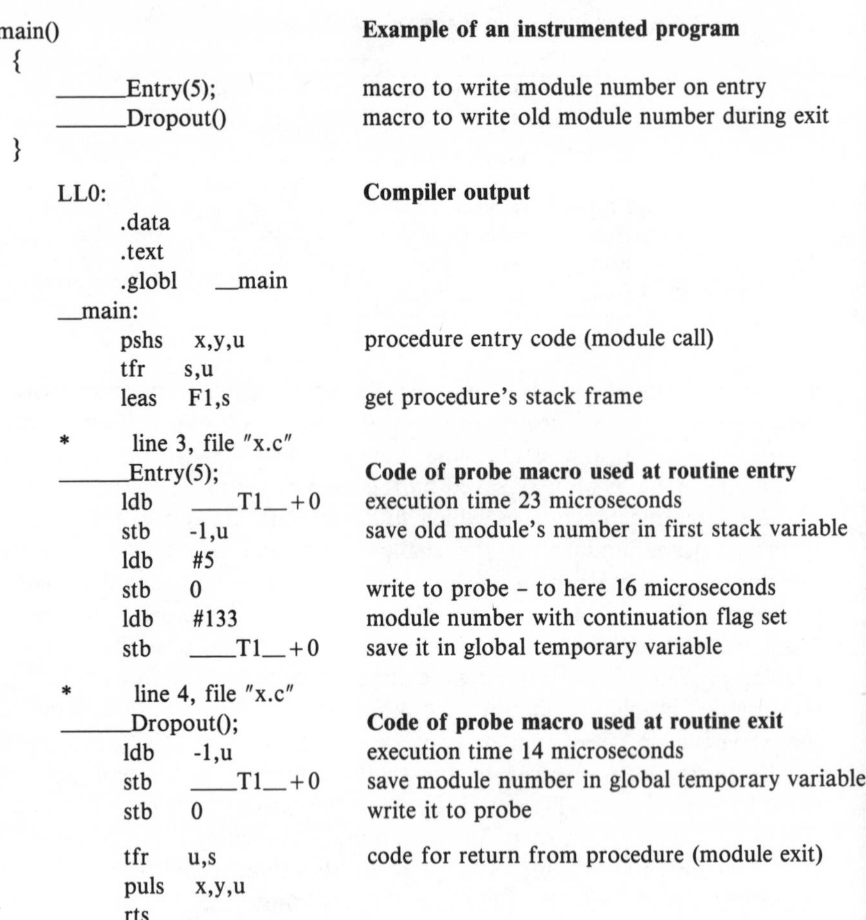

```
main()                                  Example of an instrumented program
 {
        ______Entry(5);                 macro to write module number on entry
        ______Dropout()                 macro to write old module number during exit
 }

    LL0:                                Compiler output
            .data
            .text
            .globl     __main
    __main:
            pshs    x,y,u               procedure entry code (module call)
            tfr     s,u
            leas    F1,s                get procedure's stack frame

    *        line 3, file "x.c"
    ______Entry(5);                     Code of probe macro used at routine entry
            ldb     ____T1__+0          execution time 23 microseconds
            stb     -1,u                save old module's number in first stack variable
            ldb     #5
            stb     0                   write to probe - to here 16 microseconds
            ldb     #133                module number with continuation flag set
            stb     ____T1__+0          save it in global temporary variable

    *        line 4, file "x.c"
    ______Dropout();                    Code of probe macro used at routine exit
            ldb     -1,u                execution time 14 microseconds
            stb     ____T1__+0          save module number in global temporary variable
            stb     0                   write it to probe

            tfr     u,s                 code for return from procedure (module exit)
            puls    x,y,u
            rts
```

Figure 8.9 Software probes modified to use the process and procedure stacks, and to be called as macros, not as subroutines.

One problem with using macros was that while the 'C' compiler has facilities for the inclusion of assembler macros, the assembler does not. Consequently, we had to insert instrumentation into the assembler procedures manually. As a result, a number of the assembler procedures were not instrumented. We had to measure these procedures at the **machine-code level,** using the address map of the system to find entry and exit points. When combining measurements made at different levels in the object hierarchy, we had to align the measurements carefully, because measurements made at machine-code level with a hardware tool are from routine entry to routine exit, where measurements made at a higher level with a hybrid tool are from probe to probe.

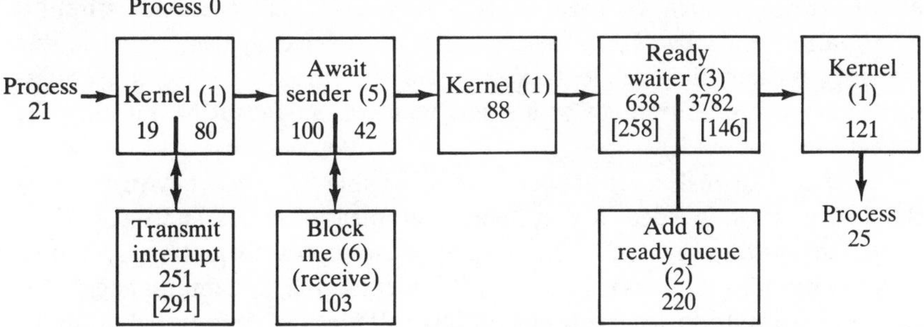

Figure 8.10 Execution path of the kernel process during a transmit interrupt (Figure 2.3). Numbers in square brackets are execution times after modifications to ready waiters. All times in microseconds.

In contrast, the execution path of the kernel process (Figure 8.10) is a combination of machine-code level measurements and module-level measurements. The execution path flow graph of the terminal administrator process was measured at the module level only (Figure 2.4).

To measure the sequence of processes in the character handling task (Figure 2.3), we had to combine measurements made at three levels in the system. At the **process level**, we measured the sequence of processes with the **stimulus probes** placed in the dispatch and enter kernel routines. We measured the first kernel process at the module level, and the interrupt handler at the machine-code level. In retrospect, we would have saved some time consuming machine-code measurements, and some alignment headaches, by taking the time to instrument the machine-code routines manually with assembler probes. To instrument the system completely at process level the following stimulus probes are needed:

- user process number in the dispatch routine,
- kernel process number in the enter kernel routine,
- idle when nothing is happening (Figure 8.4), and
- one event indicator in each interrupt handler.

Once the lower level measurements were finished, all probes at lower levels in the object hierarchy were removed. Thus, the cost of permanently instrumenting this system at the process level is low - for example 198 microseconds in the case of the character handling task (Table 8.2), where each stimulus probe takes 11 microseconds. Notice that no probes have to be inserted into a user process in order to monitor it at the process level (Figure 8.4).

To instrument the system at the **task level**, we require additional stimulus probes to indicate which interrupt occurred (one handler can handle several interrupts) and, in the case of a program like the terminal administrator, which terminal it is handling. This additional stimulus information indicates which task is being performed by each process. As we only measured a single task, we did not insert this extra stimulus information. Measurement of a single task was sufficient to optimize the kernel (Section 8.4.2).

The cost of task level probes is small (Table 8.2), yet they provide all the information needed for **system level** measurements, and for **CPU usage accounting** by task. By adding customer information and disk usage data to these task level measurements, the system manager has enough information for customer billing. If desired, additional stimulus probes (for example queue lengths) can be added to provide engineering data for system modelling, and for performance studies.

In order to understand the operation of the system, all the above probes, plus some additional stimulus probes, are combined to produce a totally instrumented system. Thus we have:

- module entry and exit probes in every procedure,
- process number probes in the enter kernel, dispatch, and idle (nothing) procedures,
- stimulus probes in the interrupt handlers, and in some processes, to indicate which task is being executed, and
- appropriate stimulus probes in various modules to explain why the system is doing what it is doing.

The selection of appropriate stimulus information, to help in understanding the operation of a system, has not been dealt with in a practical way in the previous chapters, except to state that it is dependent on the function of the object under study. During the design and development of a system, the variables which help in understanding the operation of the system become fairly obvious, particularly if monitoring tools are used to debug and measure the software as it is developed. The experiments we conducted on this system have revealed which stimulus data is useful for understanding the operation of the kernel and the terminal handling processes. Much of this information can be gained intuitively by studying execution paths, but instrumentation gives a greater guarantee of correct answers.

The purpose of stimulus probes is understanding: that is, to answer the questions: 'Who requested this operation?', 'Why was it requested?', and 'Of the operations which an object can perform, which one is it performing?' We will illustrate how to answer these questions with specific examples. When we looked at the identification of processes and tasks, we saw the use of stimulus probes for answering the question: 'Who requested this operation?' As the kernel spends its time executing primitives to service requests from users, a stimulus probe to indicate which primitive is being called will answer the question: 'Which operation is the kernel performing?' As this is a message passing system, the message passing primitives are central to the operation of the system. We can study the sequence of interprocess communication by inserting probes into these primitives to answer the question: 'Which process is at the other end of the communications channel?' Many of these primitives have to wait for a response, which they do by calling the block procedure. We can obtain a record of which processes are blocked and why by inserting stimulus probes into the block procedure.

For re-entrant interrupt handlers, we use stimulus information to answer the question: 'Which event is being serviced (i.e. which terminal, and was it receive or transmit)?' Interrupt handlers which handle several events of the same type may do so during one invocation of the handler; thus the stimulus probe may occur several times. When studying the terminal administration process (Figure 2.4), we should output the character being handled as stimulus information, because different characters result in different execution paths.

All the measurements recorded in this chapter, and in Chapter 2, were made on this message passing system with the instrumentation described in this section. These measurements include probe times, because the probe time is short; but the times in the measurements recorded in Chapter 7 do not include probe times, because of the high cost of the probes on that system. The cost of instrumenting the character handling task at various levels in the object hierarchy can be found in Table 8.2. The instrumentation installed in this task took 1798 microseconds to execute, or 8.18% of task execution time. After modifications to improve the performance of the task, the time cost dropped to 1354 microseconds, but, because of the saving in execution time which resulted from the modifications, the percentage cost rose to 18.35%.

During these measurement experiments, we found a number of limitations with our hybrid performance monitor. The object generation algorithm (A6.4) simply states: find the next object and record the modules in it. Our initial implementation of this algorithm (Figure 6.13) searched for a start module number and an end module number to delimit the object. We had to modify this routine to allow for minor variations in path execution time, which caused one path to be recorded as two different paths. The execution time of a path can vary between two values, because of rounding errors caused by the limited resolution of the analyser. A second problem with our initial routine was that it could not measure a single module, so we modified it to allow us to measure a single module by specifying identical start and end module identifiers. We found measurement of a single module to be the easiest way to obtain a module spectrum (Figure 2.5 was done this way).

The measurement of a single module would be enhanced with a logic state analyser which could record a specific module identifier and the next n event records without having to specify what those events are, where n records include stimulus probes and module identifier probes. When performing spectral analysis, we are often interested in modules which perform a variety of functions, and consequently the subsequent modules may vary. As our logic state analyser does not have this feature, the complete event trace had to be recorded and searched for invocations of the module. Also, the depth of this analyser (64 words) is far too small, and continuous recording (circular list or double buffering) is desirable.

Some limitations of our implementation of a hybrid performance measurement tool were highlighted when we tried to measure infinite loops. For example, the input handling process (Figure 2.3) is normally blocked waiting for an event to occur. When the event occurs, it sends a message to the terminal administrator, waits for a reply, and, after it gets the reply, waits for an event again. Consequently, the module probes for this process always indicate continuation, and thus we are unable to define unique object start and end points in terms of module numbers.

The way to delimit this object is to record the modules which occur while its process number is in the second monitor register. For completeness, and to distinguish between object invocations in our trace, we should also record the module immediately before the process starts, and the module immediately after it terminates. The concept is: measure at one level while the probe for a higher level in the object hierarchy has a value which identifies the object of interest. This is more satisfactory than counting the number of module invocations, because this number may vary from one invocation of the process to the next, and it conforms to the hierarchical basis of the performance measurement formulation.

8.4.2 Performance measurement

From the measured data, we pinpointed several processes with poor performance. We decomposed these processes to find which modules were taking the longest time to execute. Interestingly, the modules with poor performance were not the ones that the programmer would have chosen to optimize. In fact, the greatest saving was made in a module that he would never have considered. As most of the improvements were made in kernel modules, the performance of all tasks improved. After each modification, the task was measured again to ascertain the performance improvement, to see if any bugs had been introduced (one was), and to verify that the programmer had done what he said he had done (he forgot to modify one procedure).

Table 8.3 Execution times of the character handling task (Figure 2.3) before and after modifications.

Task	*Execution time in microseconds*	*Savings*	
		Time	*% of original*
Original	21993		
After ready waiters modified	14347	7646	34.8
After swap message, block and valid id modified	13027	1320	6.0
After cooked modified	12196	831	3.8
Total savings		9797	44.6

We made a number of performance improvements to the character handling task (Figure 2.3). The execution time of the character handling task (Table 8.3) was almost 22 milliseconds, including probe costs. From the event trace graph of this task (Figure 2.3), we can see that the process which takes the longest time is the kernel immediately after an interrupt. When we looked at this process (Figures 6.14 and 8.10), we found the largest amount of execution time was consumed by the ready waiters module.

When an interrupt occurs, a flag is set in an event happened vector, which is 64 flags long. Ready waiters searches this vector looking for events which have happened, and when it finds one adds the processes waiting for that event to the ready queue. The code consisted of a for loop, a test, and a call if the test returned true. Because it scanned all vectors, a lot of time was used testing for non-existent events. We modified the loop to search between minimum and maximum values, a change which saved 4016 microseconds every time a transmit interrupt occurred (Figure 8.10). We had to modify interrupt handlers to set the minimum and maximum event variables, which added 40 microseconds to the execution time of the transmit interrupt handler. The total saving (Table 8.3) for the character handling task was 7.646 milliseconds, or 34.8% of the original execution time. As this routine is in the kernel, and is executed in response to every interrupt, this saving represents a considerable optimization of the kernel. The process execution times after this modification are shown in Figure 2.3 in square brackets.

Having started to optimize the kernel, we then looked at the second largest process: the process which sent messages. By rewriting the swap message, block, and valid-id modules in assembler, we reduced the execution time of the send message kernel process by 330 microseconds (curly brackets in Figure 2.3 show the reduced execution times). Of this time, 111 microseconds were saved by the removal of module probes from these processes, and some time was saved by speeding up procedure calls, because there is no need to save all the registers on the stack, which 'C' does. The add to ready queue procedure (Figure 8.5) was not modified because it is complex, and thus difficult to implement correctly in assembler. These modifications affected other primitives also, resulting in a total saving of 1320 microseconds, or 6% of the execution time of the character handling task.

The user process with the largest execution time was the terminal administrator (Figure 2.4). From the execution path profile for this process (Figure 2.6), we saw that the most frequently used path was the handling of simple characters. This path is one of the fastest paths through the process (Figure 2.8), but it had the highest utilization (Figure 2.10). The modules in this process with the longest execution times are cooked, delete, and tab, but only one of these modules (cooked) is used when handling simple characters (Figure 2.9). By investigating the execution times for various paths through this module (Figure 2.4), we found that handling a simple character took longer than handling either a backspace or a return character. We added a few lines of code to this module to give priority to handling simple characters, which resulted in saving a further 3.8% of execution time (angle brackets in Figure 2.3 give the new execution times).

While studying this task, we noticed that the transmit interrupt appeared to occur in the enter kernel procedure as soon as interrupts were re-enabled. This observation prompted the question: 'Were the interrupts enabled when they should be?' Investigation of the code raised our suspicion even further, but measurement proved inconclusive. The time between sending a character and the transmit complete interrupt was 1161 microseconds. At 9600 baud, a character is transmitted in 1047.6 microseconds. This time delay resulted in the transmit interrupt occurring during the enter kernel procedure when interrupts were disabled. A different experiment has to be devised to answer the question.

The *total saving from these modifications was 44.6% of the original execution time* of the character handling task (Table 8.3). At this stage, we decided that no further optimization should be done to either the kernel or the character handling task. One problem for the analyst was that the availability of accurate measurements made the task of optimization so easy that system changes rapidly made the measurements obsolete.

The *cost of the software probes was 8.18% of the original execution time* (Table 8.3), but more significantly *18.35% of the execution time saved* by modifying the programs. Thus, the inclusion of measurement facilities at design time was paid for many times over. Once system optimization was complete, we removed the module identifier probes, leaving only the process number stimulus-probes, reducing the artifact to 1.7% of the execution time. The process probes were left so that we can study the operation of the system if problems arise.

The hybrid monitoring tool was connected to the system during the development period, and we used it regularly for fault finding. When the system hung, an event trace at module level was recorded. From this trace, we could determine which modules were being executed. If this measurement indicated a tight loop within a module, we recorded an event trace at machine-code level to pinpoint the area of code included in the loop. The probe registers are at physical addresses 0, 1, and 2. A number of invalid pointers (value 0) were found by observing rubbish in the module identifier event stream, caused by spurious writes to address zero. At system start up, all memory is cleared to zero, increasing the chance of invalid pointers being zero. When a memory location was corrupted, all writes to that location were monitored to determine which code module was causing the corruption. Because instrumentation was available, a significant amount of time was saved during debugging, but, as it became second nature to use these tools, estimating how much is impossible.

In addition to finding the cause of software faults, we used the hybrid monitor to investigate faults which could have been either software or hardware. Traditionally, this is the most difficult area of fault finding. We used the hybrid monitor to measure what the software was doing when the fault occurred, and then, if it appeared to be a hardware problem, we connected hardware signals to the logic state analyser and monitored the operation of the hardware.

Using the above techniques, we found two separate faults, one hardware and one software, both of which corrupted the data in registers in the interrupt controller. Both these faults resulted from the design of the hardware. First, the priority levels in the interrupt controller were not latched in on a data write because of a 5 nanosecond delay in a timing signal. Second, because the input-output address space was not completely decoded, the interrupt controller was selected by addresses at two different locations. The initialization routine set up the controller at one address, and then, as part of a zero memory phase, cleared the contents out at the other address.

In conclusion, instrumentation of the system at design time proved its worth in performance optimization, proved invaluable for finding hardware and software faults, saved time both in fault finding and optimization, and helped us to understand the system. These experiments have contributed to the validation of the performance measurement formulation, and have shown the practicality of a performance measurement methodology based upon that formulation.

Chapter 9
Measurement of Multiprocessor Systems

Measuring the performance of multiple processor systems is a relatively new field. Most work to date has been done by research organizations on processor systems they have built. Array processors are now available commercially, heightening the need for performance measurement. Parkinson and Liddell (1983) defined the major questions asked by potential users of a multiple processor system:

- What class of problems are highly suitable for a given multiple processor system?
- What class of problems are highly unsuitable for a given multiple processor system?
- What type of performance is it reasonable to expect from a given multiple processor system?

These questions are very difficult to answer in an unambiguous fashion. A significant contribution to the complexity of the measurement problem is the multitude of ways in which processors can be interconnected. Multiprocessor architectures range from highly parallel structures, where processing elements are tightly coupled and used to solve only one problem at a time, to loosely coupled systems where each processor is working on a different problem. Highly parallel machines (Haynes *et al.*, 1982) can be divided into the following categories: multiple special-purpose functional units, associative processors, array processors, data flow processors, functional programming language processors, and multiple CPUs. Data communication is seen to be the key to the successful exploitation of parallelism, but there are a number of ways of interconnecting processors (cross-point switches, ring networks, systolic arrays, banyan networks, cube networks, tree structures), each with its own advantages and problems.

In addition to the variety of processing methods and the variety of ways of interconnecting processing elements, there is a variety of ways in which the resultant machines can be used. Illiac IV (Barnes, 1968) processed many data sets under the control of a single program, using many identical processing elements. At the other end of the spectrum, we see parallel execution of independent jobs using either monoprogrammed processors or multiprogrammed processors. In the middle, we find different parts of the one job distributed among several processors, each passing data to the other.

Many performance evaluation studies of multiprocessor computers have been concerned with measurements at a high level, for example measuring the execution time of algorithms, partly because of the difficulty of measurement and partly because of the newness of the field. Questions of interest to researchers include:

- What is the best way to configure the processing elements to solve a particular problem?
- How much overhead is generated by managing parallelism?
- What effect does varying the number of processing elements have on performance?
- What effect does changing the communication path configuration have on performance?
- How do you control and measure the synchronization of parallel processes?
- How do you instrument a parallel system for performance evaluation?

In the sections that follow, we discuss the performance measures, measurement tools, and measurement techniques that have been reported by a number of researchers. Also, we will compare their measures to the measures defined in extensions of the formulation of performance measurement.

9.1 Performance measurement of SIMD machines

Based upon the work of Kuck (1977), Siegel *et al.* (1982) have proposed a set of nine measures for evaluating the performance of algorithms on SIMD machines (single instruction stream - multiple data stream). A typical SIMD machine consists of a control unit, a set of N processing elements (each with its own memory), and an interconnection network. The control unit broadcasts instructions to all processing elements, and each active processing element executes these instructions on the data in its own memory. Each instruction is executed simultaneously in all processing elements. The interconnection network allows data to be transferred among processing elements. The processor can be configured so that all processors work on the one data set, or so that each processor works on separate data sets.

In applications where the same operation is repeated thousands of times, or where computationally intensive matrix and vector operations are frequently used, SIMD machines promise to reduce the computation time. The complexity of SIMD algorithms is a function of the size of the data set, the number of processing elements used, and the structure of the interconnection network. Performance measurements are used to select between alternative algorithms, to study the effect of varying the number of processing elements on performance, and to study the effect of varying the size of the data set on performance.

9.1.1 SIMD object hierarchy

Before discussing Siegel *et al.*'s set of performance measures, we will extend the formulation of measurement to cover SIMD machines. Extensions are required to the formulation to take into account the parallel operation of several processors. The conceptual model of an object during execution is the same: a sequence of modules. However, the hierarchical decomposition of a SIMD machine is slightly different to the decomposition of a monoprocessor.

The highest three levels, system, task, and program execution, are the same. Below this a number of decompositions are possible. The one which seems the most logical is based on the fact that one instruction stream is executed by all processors in parallel. The decomposition is: block-structure level, fixed-machine size level, high-level language level, and finally machine-code level.

At the fixed-machine size level, a new module is commenced every time the number of processors in use changes. Thus, a module at this level is defined as a sequence of one or more instructions that use a fixed number of processors. As some algorithms execute, the number of active processors is reduced until, at termination, only one processor is active. It seems appropriate to place the fixed-machine size level below the block-structure level because the number of processors in use is normally changed during the execution of a block.

At the program-execution level, and at the task level, the execution of an algorithm represents one possible path through the object. In some studies a path is divided into two modules: one is the module that solves the problem and the other is the module that manages parallelism. In practice the execution of these modules will be interleaved, requiring a mechanism for detecting pausing and resumption of modules, before measurements can be made.

At the machine-code level, a situation similar to that at the microcode level in a monoprocessor exists. In a single processor machine a single microcode instruction (object) is decoded into a number of parallel operations (parallel modules?); in a SIMD multiprocessor machine a single multiprocessor instruction (object) can be decomposed into a number of parallel processor instructions (parallel modules?). In both cases, if we go below the level of a single machine instruction we have to introduce the idea of parallel objects.

At all levels in the hierarchy, an essential piece of stimulus information is the number of currently active processors. Thus, one additional measure is the trace of changes in the number of active processors: a sequence of triples, with each triple containing a module identifier, the number of active processors, and the time since the start of measurement period.

Two other decompositions have been used in measurement studies. The first involves decomposing the task level into processes running on separate processors, then decomposing the process level as for a monoprocessor. We will discuss this method of object decomposition when we study MIMD processors (multiple instruction path - multiple data path) in Section 9.2.1. The second decomposition reflects the data flow concept of program execution, and the data intensity of the problems to which parallel computers are applied. The processing of one data point is a module (i.e. one level below a task), assuming that at least one instruction is needed to process a data point. Thus, a path is a sequence of operations on data. Again, the number of active processors is an important piece of stimulus information. One way of handling this within the proposed hierarchy is to equate the processing of one data point to the execution of a block at the block-structure level.

The measures we described in Chapter 2 for objects on a monoprocessor system all apply to SIMD machines, if the number of active processors is included in some equations. The equations where this is done are identified in the following discussion of the measures proposed by Siegel *et al.* Those measures not mentioned apply as they are.

9.1.2 Proposed SIMD measures

The measures proposed by Siegel *et al.* (1982) are as follows:

- **Execution time** ($T_N(M)$) is a measure of the time to perform an algorithm of size M using N processing elements. It is the sum of the time spent executing the problem and the time spent managing parallelism. The two main management operations (overheads) are enabling processing elements and transferring data over the interconnection network. The definition and measurement of throughput is the same as for single processor machines; however having to consider the sharing of the load across several processors can cause confusion.

- **Speed** ($V_N(M)$) is the number of data points processed per unit time. If the algorithm uses all processors to process one data point then speed is the same as module throughput (N_t) for a monoprocessor at the block-structure level. However, if each processor processes a separate data point then N data points are processed together. The throughput equation (Equation 2.30) remains the same, but the number of module executions is the number of module executions per processor multiplied by the number of active processors.

- **Speed-up** ($S_N(M)$) of an N processor algorithm over a one processor algorithm is the ratio of the execution time of the one processor algorithm $T_1(M)$ to the execution time of the N processor algorithm. This is a performance comparison which requires the measurement of the execution time and the number of active processors. The measurement of the number of active processors is a natural extension of the formulation to cover parallelism, although whether the number of active processors is considered to be event or stimulus information depends on the method of object decomposition and the level in the object hierarchy. Parkinson and Liddell (1983) question the usability of this measure in a distributed array processor (DAP) environment. The processing elements in the ICL 4096 DAP operate at the bit level, and words are handled by paralleling processing elements, and hence single processor algorithms do not exist. Speed-up calculations can only be done by comparison with algorithms executing on conventional mainframes, which introduces errors into the measure due to the dissimilarity of the processing elements.
- **Efficiency** of an N processor algorithm is the ratio of speed-up to the number of processors. Efficiency is a performance comparison, based on previous measures, which gives a feel for how the achieved speed-up compares to the ideal speed-up (N). Again, Parkinson and Liddell (1983) question the validity of this measure in a DAP environment and they propose another way of calculating efficiency: the ratio of the number of processors usefully active to the total number of processors. This measure can give a feeling for the quality of an algorithm, but it must be used carefully, because in some associative algorithms (the DAP can be configured as an associative processor as well as an array processor) each step reduces the number of active processors.
- **Overhead ratio** is the ratio of the overhead time to the total execution time. It is the module to path execution time ratio of the overhead module.
- **Utilization** ($U_N(M)$) is the fraction of time during which the processors are busy executing computations of the algorithm. Assume that for a problem of size M, there are x modules in the N processor computation. Each module uses p_x processors and takes t_x time units to execute.

$$U_N(M) = \frac{\sum_{x=1}^{x} t_x p_x}{(N * T_N(M))} \tag{9.1}$$

The information to do this calculation can be obtained directly from the event trace and stimulus information. In this equation, we have extended the formulation of performance measurement. If the alternative decomposition is used, that of decomposing to separate processors, as it is in the MIMD case, utilization becomes the summation of the set of module utilizations (U_{mn}, Equation 2.43), where the measurement period is the product of the execution time and the number of processors.

- **Redundancy** is the actual computation time (summed over all processors) divided by the execution time of a single-processor algorithm to solve the same problem. Redundancy is a performance comparison which gives a measure of redundant computations that are performed.
- **Cost effectiveness** is the ratio of the speed to the cost of the system.
- **Price of the computation** is the cost of implementing and using a parallel processor to perform a desired computation. These last two measures are performance evaluation calculations based upon measured values.

Parkinson and Liddell (1983) look at two other measures:

- Estimates of **MIPS** (millions of instructions per second), **LOPS** (logical operations per second), and **FLOPS** (floating point operations per second). Commercial estimates of these are usually based on the reciprocal of the floating point multiplication time, and hence are misleading, because they assume a totally calculation bound program, and they do not take into account word size or the number of memory accesses. As with conventional machines, these measurements produce numbers which are valid only for the program being studied. In terms of the formulation of performance measurement, they are measures of module throughput at the machine-code level, where the modules are instructions, logical operations, or floating point operations.
- **Benchmarks** of running programs, which are the same as measuring the execution time.

9.2 Performance measurement of MIMD machines

Siegel *et al.* (1982) claim that the measures for SIMD machines will also apply to MIMD (multiple instruction path – multiple data path) machines; however they leave the proof of this assertion to future research. In MIMD machines, each processor has its own instruction stream as well as its own data stream.

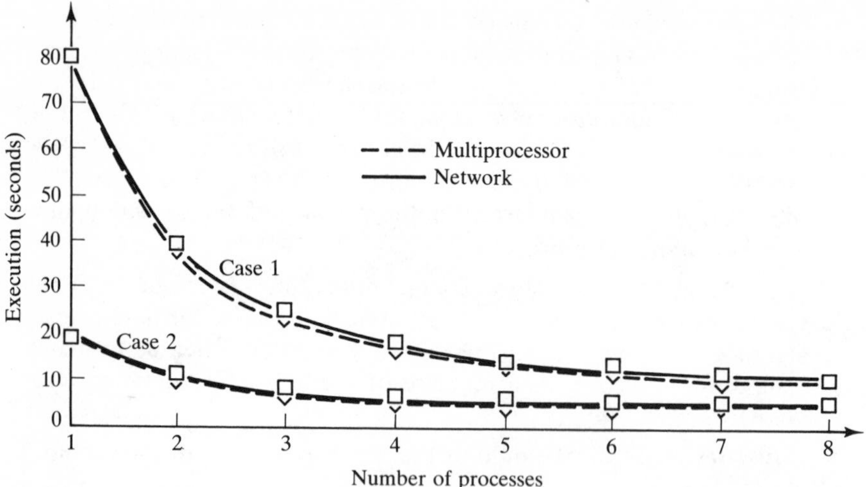

Figure 9.1 Comparison of integer programming on network and multiprocessor configurations of Cm*, with two data sets (Gehringer *et al.*, 1982; copyright © 1982 IEEE).

9.2.1 MIMD object hierarchy

The hierarchical decomposition proposed for a SIMD machine is not possible on a MIMD machine, because of the multiple instruction streams. The hierarchical decomposition to be applied to a MIMD object depends on the way in which the machine is configured. Two configurations will be discussed here, parallel processors and distributed processors, as these represent the ends of the spectrum of possible configurations. The terms parallel processor, multiprocessor, network of processors, and distributed processors are often used to mean the same thing by different authors. To reduce confusion, the following definitions are used in this chapter. In a distributed processor, the multiple instruction streams are separate tasks; in a parallel processor, the multiple instruction streams are all part of the one task. Parallel processors will be discussed in this section and distributed processors in Section 9.4.

Our conceptual model of an object during execution is still a sequence of modules. The highest level, the system level, decomposes into tasks as in a monoprocessor. However, a parallel task is spread over several interacting processors. Hence, a task is decomposed into a set of programs running in parallel on a set of processors. Thus, a new level is introduced into the hierarchy: the processor level. The hierarchy for a parallel machine is: system, task, processor. Below the processor level, the hierarchy is the same as for a monoprocessor, but it applies to several machines in parallel.

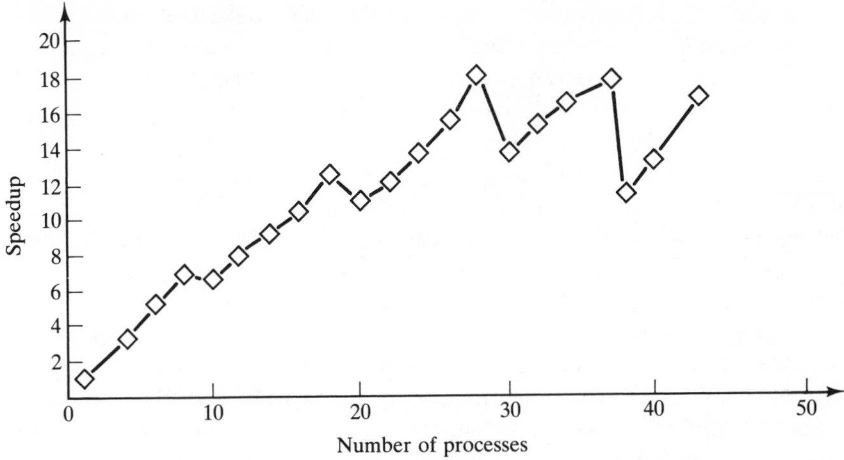

Figure 9.2 Speed-up for the quicksort algorithm on Cm* (Gehringer *et al.*, 1982; copyright © 1982 IEEE).

In a parallel processor, process interaction is of major importance. Below the task level, we measure programs on individual machines, and we can describe the interaction with other machines in terms of external events. This is analogous to the interaction between processor and peripherals on a monoprocessor. These external events will cause changes in either the execution path or the stimulus information. Thus, they can be detected in the standard measures. The number of active processors is an important piece of stimulus information at the task level, particularly as we will be recording an event stream for each processor. Parallel event streams, and their interactions, can be displayed with an event trace graph.

An alternative way of looking at a SIMD machine is to see it as a MIMD machine where the parallel instruction streams are identical. Thus, the SIMD could be considered as a special case of the MIMD. In the next section, we discuss measurements reported on MIMD machines within the context of the extended measurement formulation.

9.2.2 Measurement of parallel processors

The Cm* machine (Gehringer *et al.*, 1982) is a network of clusters of processing elements which can be configured as a parallel processor (called a multiprocessor by Gehringer *et al.*), or as a distributed processor (called a network of processors by Gehringer *et al.*), where each processing element can only access its own portion of memory. They performed some experiments to compare the execution time of algorithms on both processor configurations using a variable number of processors and different data sets (Figure 9.1). The measures they made are in accordance with the formulation of performance measurement, with an extension to allow for the number of processors.

To study whether parallel processors can perform a substantial amount of computing more efficiently than alternative architectures, they measured speed-up during a variety of experiments, and plotted it against the number of active processors (Figure 9.2). During this research, they ran experiments to evaluate: optimum processor configurations for solving different problems, the overhead penalty, the cost of synchronization, and the trade-off between locality of reference and memory contention. A railway network simulation algorithm was studied using execution time because it could only run on a parallel processor configuration larger than three processors, and hence speed-up could not be calculated due to the lack of a uniprocessor solution.

The Erlangen General Purpose Array processor (EGPA) is a three dimensional processor array which has the structure of a pyramid (Fromm *et al.*, 1983). An elementary cell consists of a processor with memory, and an elementary structure is a pyramid having one top and four bottom cells. The machine can be configured so that either each processor can execute a separate job or a large job can be distributed over several processors. The latter mode leads to a flow of control involving dynamic processor to processor interaction that is not easy to understand.

Fromm and his colleagues wanted to gain insight into the dynamic flow of activities in the pyramid, and how this was distributed among the different processes. They decomposed the executing task (object) into processes (modules) and recorded the stream of processes (module trace). Normally, only software measurements can recognize which process is active at a given time, but the operating system assigns a unique number to each process, a number which is stored in a hardware register by the scheduler. Every time this register is updated, these numbers are recorded by the hardware probe, eliminating the need for a special software probe. This highlights the gains which can be made by integrating measurement tools into the system at design time.

Fromm *et al.* used the measurements made with these tools to validate a queuing network model, to study memory contention problems when several processors access the memory attached to one processor, to study the synchronization of communicating processes, to investigate why synchronization took a long time, and to test methods of reducing synchronization time.

Franta *et al.* (1982) extend their model of a sequential program (Section 3.6) to model a concurrent program. They define an execution history for each processor as if it were a single processing unit. These histories are then composed into a set of histories (a hierarchical composition) of the multiprocessor. At this point the model does not cover interactions. Individual program histories are interleaved to make a single event history, on the basis of the ordering of data transfers between processes, via four communication primitives. This results in a single history of the changes to the data in the system. The model entertains no notions of a global clock, but one has to be introduced to make instrumentation possible, almost as an afterthought. This model is usable if you are only interested in what happens to the data, and the ordering of data transfers between processes, but it has no concept of program flow. Thus, it may be suitable for describing a data flow machine, but it is incapable of providing the measures we discussed for a SIMD machine.

9.3 Instrumentation of parallel processors

Performance measurement instrumentation has been included in the initial design of several research machines. The trend is to integrated instrumentation environments (Segall *et al.*, 1983), also called distributed system test beds (Franta *et al.*, 1982), which support: measurement of performance; execution and control of experiments; specification of synthetic workloads; control of the interprocessor communications network; and, in some cases, control of the master system clock, to the point where an experiment can be stopped in mid flight for examination of machine state.

Control of integrated instrumentation is usually centralized in an experiment managing program, running on a separate processor. The experiment management processor can be one of the processors in the parallel machine which is not used in the experiment, or a processor independent of, but connected to, the parallel processor. Hardware and software tools added to the processing elements detect events, record the state of the processing element (and its processes) at the time of the event, and transfer the state information to the experiment manager.

Information recorded by hardware tools is often transferred over a separate instrumentation bus to the experiment manager. The interface between the instrumentation bus and the processor may include event filtering and sequencing circuitry. Event filtering circuits can be similar to the plug board front ends of traditional hardware tools, but are normally closer in concept to the front end of a logic state analyser. The event sequencing circuitry ensures that the correct time sequence of the events occurring in the concurrent processes is maintained when the data is read from the parallel event streams and recorded.

Information recorded by software tools can either be written to the instrumentation bus via hardware probes (hence forming a hybrid tool) or be transferred to the experiment manager over the interconnection network of the parallel processor. As with conventional monoprocessors, software tools cause some interference to the system, and hence some degradation in accuracy. We will illustrate these techniques in the following description of the instrumentation used in two research processors. In each case, the instruments, the measurement methodology, and the parameters measured correlate closely with our formulation of performance measurement.

9.3.1 Instrumentation of the EGPA pyramid

The EGPA pyramid is instrumented with two integrated measurement tools (Fromm *et al.*, 1983):

- a hardware monitor, which is connected by electronic probes to every processor (Figure 9.4), and
- a software monitor which is an integral part of the EGPA environment.

These tools were designed on the basis of the following principles of measurement, principles which are consistent with the formulation of performance measurement. Processes are assigned process numbers, which can be used as priority numbers. When a process is active, its process number is stored in a hardware priority register. A hardware tool records the sequence of process numbers in the priority register to produce an exhaustive and precise description of all activities at the process level. An ordered set S of sequence steps s_i

$$s_i = (p_i, t_{pi}) \quad \text{where } i = 1 .. n \tag{9.2}$$

is the result of the measurement, where p_i is the number of the process which has been active in the ith sequence step, and t_{pi} is the time the process spends in the ith sequence step. Thus, the resulting trace is an event stream which contains the sequence in which objects are executed and their execution times.

Software instrumentation is used to record user oriented event traces, in contrast to the system oriented event traces recorded by the hardware instrumentation. Software probes (marks) store event descriptors (markers) in a marker buffer, the markers consist of an identification of the place in the program (mark) from which the probe was called, real time, and process CPU time (both in multiples of 50 microseconds). System marks, usually pairs of entrance and exit markers which are permanently inserted at strategic points of the programming environment, inform the applications programmer of essential events in a

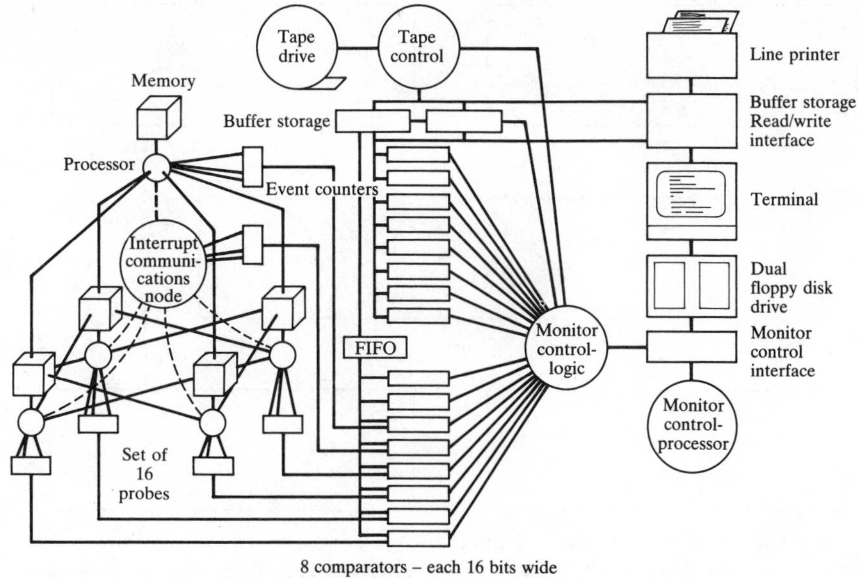

Figure 9.3 Block diagram of the hardware monitor of the EGPA pyramid (Fromm *et al.*, 1983; copyright © 1983 IEEE).

symbolic form. User marks, placed in the applications program by the programmer, can be selectively activated prior to program execution.

When studying the execution of a job distributed over several processors, Fromm and his colleagues wanted to determine the concurrency of the processes in different processors. They did this by correlating the arrival times of sequence steps in the independent event streams, one for each processor, i.e. each sequence step is effectively time stamped relative to a master clock.

To combine the event traces from asynchronous processors into a single correctly ordered trace of events, two techniques were used: one for software measurements and one for hardware measurements. Software measurements were based on periodically enforced clock synchronization in all processors. Thus, time stamps could be used by the evaluation program to determine the ordering of results which were originally independent. Hardware measurements were fed to a set of simultaneously operating comparators whose results were joined by a hardware FIFO unit (Figure 9.3).

Both types of event traces can be walked through on a graphical display (Figure 9.4), which shows the interaction and correlation, between parallel event streams. Also, an interactive program can be used to plot the distribution of the duration of interesting events (an execution time profiler).

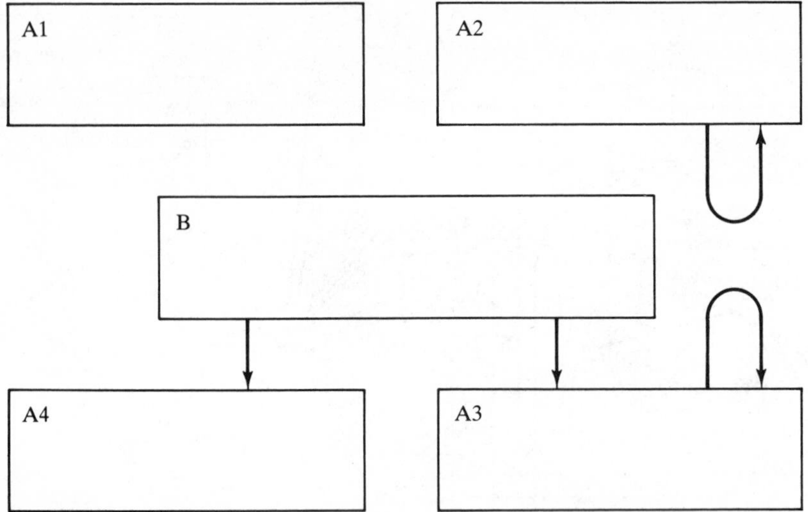

Figure 9.4 Graphical display of simultaneous events on five EGPA processors (Fromm, 1983; copyright © 1983 IEEE). Each box represents a processor and internal events; arrows returning to a box represent I/O operations; events concerning two processors are indicated by arrows between boxes.

9.3.2 Instrumentation of Cm*

The Cm* integrated instrumentation environment (Segall *et al.*, 1983) contains a set of tools (Figure 9.5) which enables the generation and measurement of experiments, where an experiment is the execution of an instrumented program in a controlled environment. This environment contains several components: a schema manager, a run time environment, an instrumented stimulus, an instrumented operating system, a database, and a monitor. A schema is a complete experiment description consisting of an application program (or synthetic workload) to be measured, monitoring directives, system configuration information, and experiment directives. The results of an execution of a schema are captured in a schema instance, containing measurements, values of schema parameters, and environmental information.

Events are generated by software sensors, which reside in the operating system and resident monitor, and may reside in the stimulus. An event record contains an indication of the operation being monitored, the name of the component performing the operation, and the name of the object the operation is being performed on. The event record may also contain a time stamp and other information about the event. Some sensors are automatically built in; for example, sensors to record timing information are inserted at the start and end of sub-tasks. When a sensor detects an event, it stores an event record in a data structure called a receptacle. There is one receptacle for each instrumented object.

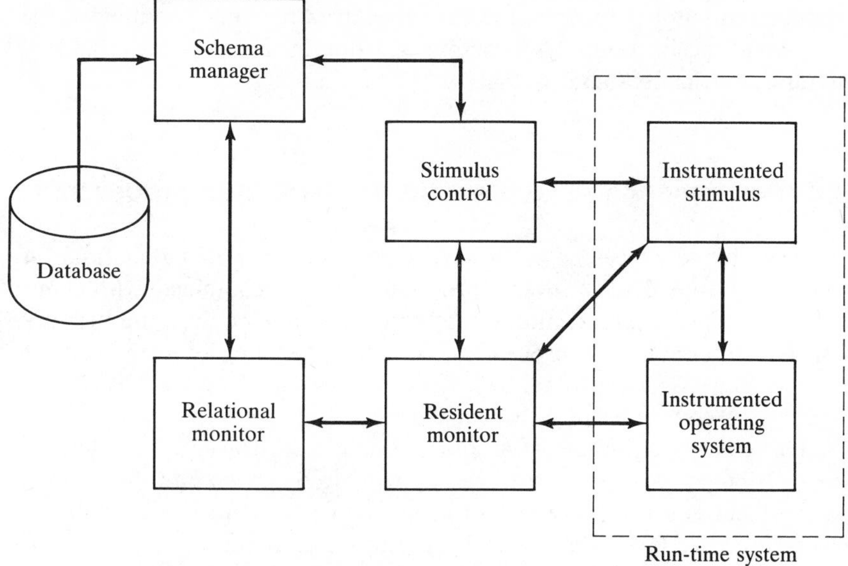

Figure 9.5 Cm* integrated instrumentation environment (Segall *et al.*, 1983; copyright © 1983 IEEE).

An event flag in the receptacle is used to control event filtering. If it is set, the resident monitor extracts the event record from the receptacle and sends it to the relational monitor.

Several tools were developed to enable rapid development of experiments. A workload generator was used to specify the behaviour of the parallel program and the placement of sensors. This generator produced a high-level language output which had to be translated before the experiment could be run. During this translation, sensor descriptions and data structures were generated. These data structures were used by the stimulus controller to control the experiment. Another program took the sensor description and generated optimized code for each software implemented sensor.

The relational monitor collected the event records passed to it by the resident monitor and built a schema instance, which was stored in a relational database. In this database, information was recorded in tables of tuples, called relations. By using a standard database management system, the tool designer avoided having to describe the organization of the data in detail, and had a ready made query language for data analysis. Because of these advantages, we can expect to see greater use of database management systems for data collection in the future.

Primitive relations contain information that is a direct translation of a set of recorded events. New relations called derived relations were defined by operations on existing relations. Derived relations were specified using a query language, and could be calculated by the relational monitor if requested in the schema. After the experiments, the user could perform analyses across schema instances using standard enquiries on the database.

9.4 Performance measurement of distributed processors

In a distributed processor, each processor works on a different task. A task is not spread over several processors, but is contained within one processor. Tasks may communicate with one another over the network which interconnects the processors. Often, scheduling of tasks is done by one supervisory processor. Thus, at system level, a distributed processor is considered to be one machine.

Our conceptual model of an object is still a sequence of modules. In the distributed processor case, the system decomposes into processors. So the hierarchy for a distributed processor is: system, processor, task. Below the task level, the hierarchy is the same as for monoprocessors. The amount of coupling between tasks depends upon the job being executed by the system and the scheduling algorithm. Tasks may be completely separate; different user, different job class, different data; or they may be loosely coupled. To perform a user's request, a task running on one processor may be pipelined with a task on another processor; e.g. compile on one, execute on the other.

Below the processor level we again have parallel event streams, but their interaction, if any, may be of no interest to the analyst. The number of active processors is an important piece of stimulus information at the system level. The instrumentation of PRIME and C.mmp is discussed in the following sections.

9.4.1 Instrumentation of PRIME

PRIME was designed to provide an interactive service to a number of terminals with very high degrees of availability and privacy (Ferrari, 1973). It consisted of five processors which were linked together, and to peripherals, with an interconnection network. Each processor could access roughly 80% of the available memory, with each 8K memory module accessible to three processors. To obtain a high level of interactive performance, resources were dynamically allocated to the processes competing for them, but to obtain a high level of privacy, different processes were not allowed to share the same memory module. The hardware was partitioned into five physical subsystems, one to carry out centralized operating system functions, and four to handle user processes. No resource sharing was allowed between the four user subsystems, forcing them to communicate over the interconnection network. Message buffering was done by the central system.

Instrumentation design was impacted by the distributed architecture and the privacy requirement. Some variables, for example traffic rates on the interconnection network, could not be measured in the central system. As a result, the instrumentation had to be distributed, but the measured data could not be sent over the network to a central point, because this would degrade the performance of the system. To overcome this problem, a separate network was added to carry data to the hardware monitor from the distributed probes. Because of the privacy requirement, one subsystem could not be used to measure another. The system manager could measure system activities, but not user activities. User activities could only be measured in the virtual subsystem created for the user.

Both general purpose and special purpose tools were included in PRIME (Ferrari, 1973). The general purpose tools were a powerful set of firmware tools, and an extensive facility for general purpose software measurement. Users were allowed to use the software tool within the privacy of their own virtual subsystem, but only the system manager was allowed access to the hardware and firmware tools.

The firmware tool consisted of two probes: one periodically sampled the contents of the microcode program counter; the other detected the execution of conditional branch instructions and generated a flag to indicate whether the branch condition was satisfied. From the information collected by the first probe, a program derived utilization factors for microcoded operating system modules. From the information collected by the second probe, a program reconstructed the flow of control of the microprogram. The data produced by these probes was collected by a hardware tool, which had access to a register in each processor. The address sample and branch trace were multiplexed and recorded in a memory module.

The software tool (Ferrari and Liu, 1975) supported three measurement techniques: checkpoints, sampling, and tracing. Event counting checkpoints, event tracing checkpoints, and measurement routines were provided as part of the tool. In addition, checkpoints could be inserted into user programs to call measurement routines written by the user. These routines were checked by the software tool for correctness, before they were used. At regular intervals, the software tool interrupted the user process to execute sampling routines. An event stream produced by event detection checkpoints was recorded by a tracing tool. Prior to program execution, all of these tools could be added, removed, enabled, and disabled using interactive commands. During program execution, instrumentation could not be changed. Data collected by the measurement routines was saved on a file for later analysis.

Checkpoints were inserted into a program by replacing a program instruction with a checkpoint call instruction – a patching technique similar to the breakpoint insertion techniques of assembler debuggers.

After execution of the measurement routine, the replaced instruction had to be executed before flow of control was returned to the program. Two ways of connecting checkpoints to measurement routines were available. In the first, a software switch called a routine to save the machine state, which then called the measurement routine. In the second, a user defined operation code called a measurement routine. When a user programmed operation code was executed, the program counter was saved and flow of control branched to a pre-defined location. The operand field of this instruction could be encoded to specify which measurement routine was required. Switches cause less time interference, but user programmed operation codes cause less space interference.

The special purpose tools included in PRIME were hardware, firmware, and software meters and logs. These are ad-hoc tools, i.e. tools designed to detect a pre-defined event or a small class of events. Ad-hoc tools were included where measurement parameters could be specified accurately at design time.

9.4.2 Instrumentation of C.mmp

A hardware monitor (Fuller *et al.*, 1973) was used to measure the C.mmp multi-miniprocessor, developed at Carnegie-Mellon University (Wulf and Bell, 1972). Each PDP-11 processor in C.mmp was a complete computer with its own primary memory, controllers, and peripherals. A cross-bar switch connected the processors to the shared memory on a per reference basis, and resolved conflicts between such requests. The researchers who built C.mmp wanted to measure:

- the interference in the switch connecting the processors to memory,
- which configuration – parallel, pipelined, network, distributed – suited which class of problems, and
- the efficiency of the decomposition of an algorithm into separate processes.

A hardware probe was connected between the two Unibuses, one bus in the monitoring processor, and the other in the target processor. As all communication between processor, memory, and peripherals occurred over the Unibus, most of the signals of interest could be found there. Also, a few signals internal to the processor were connected to the hardware monitor.

Four event detectors sensed events at the Unibus cycle level. When an event was detected, it could be counted, it could be time stamped, or it could initiate some sensing action. An event record was produced by sampling all signals after a specified number of events. The execution time of subroutines was measured by detecting start and termination events. Also, the number of instructions executed during the execution of the subroutine could be counted. Finally, memory contention was sensed by measuring the increase in memory access time.

Chapter 10
Other Measurement Applications

In this chapter, we will examine measurement for models, measurement of man-machine interaction, and measurement of networks. As the measurement requirements differ in each of these applications, we must tailor our tools, methods, and experiments to suit each case. In each application, we will use the concepts of objects, object hierarchy, sequence of modules, event trace, and stimulus information.

The first step in designing a measurement procedure for a specific application is to understand the application. From this understanding, we can clarify the purpose of measurement in the context of that application, and we can specify what we want to measure. Then we can define the object to be measured, decompose it into a sequence of modules, instrument it to produce the desired event trace, and determine what stimulus information to record. Selecting the set of stimulus information is often the most important, and most difficult, part of measurement, as it requires a thorough understanding of the application.

Tailoring our general measurement tool to a specific application may involve modifying the object data structure, and hence the data reduction and analysis algorithms. For example, we may want to record several distinct sets of stimulus information, or to count the number of occurrences of a specific stimulus variable.

10.1 Performance models

Much scientific research consists of developing models of the systems we want to study, and carrying out experiments upon those models. Models are simplified abstractions of the systems we are observing, where unnecessary detail is removed, and only important parameters are left for analysis. Models are used to reduce a complex problem to a simpler problem, a problem which is more easily understood and is mathematically tractable. Thus, modelling is a way of simplifying a system, and at the same time highlighting the important elements of that system. Detailed models give more accurate results than simple models, but can be more difficult to understand and impossible to describe mathematically.

Models have some advantages relative to direct measurement: parameters and inputs can be changed at will to study system behaviour without the problems this would cause on a real system, and models can be used to predict the impact of system changes on performance without having to make the changes. However, models are not as accurate as measurement (as they are an abstraction and simplification of the system), and measurements must be made on an actual system to calibrate the model and to validate its results (Spirn, 1977).

A number of models are in common use in performance evaluation, some of which are highly detailed and some more abstract. Models of objects tend to become more abstract as you move up the object hierarchy. At low levels in the hierarchy, detailed models are intellectually manageable because of the limited number of details. At higher levels in the object hierarchy, the level of abstraction is increased in order to keep the model intellectually manageable.

The current state of performance modelling is that we have a collection of modelling techniques, each suitable for modelling at a different level (or range of levels) within the object hierarchy. At a particular level in the object hierarchy, the model you choose to use depends on the accuracy you require, and the cost you are willing to pay. At higher levels in the hierarchy the cost of accuracy increases. Kumar and Davidson (1980) suggest that

> '... judicious use of a hierarchy [of models] can simultaneously satisfy the conflicting needs of low complexity and high accuracy ... By using a performance model hierarchy, the system analyst enjoys the tractability of analytical studies while achieving the accuracy of empirical studies'.

Current modelling techniques are clearly defined, well understood, and lend themselves to mathematical analysis, but if they are to co-exist in a hierarchy of models further work must be done on the interrelations between them. What we need is an underlying formulation of performance modelling which we can use to codify the models into a unified body of knowledge, in a similar manner to that in which performance measurement has been codified in this volume. Much work has already been done in this area (Courtois, 1977), and as we shall see, the conceptual model upon which the formulation of performance measurement is based fits into such a model hierarchy.

An interesting area of research is the study of whether one type of model can be used at all levels in the computer system. As we have seen, the conceptual model of an executing object can be applied at all levels of the hierarchy, and hence the one set of measures applies at all levels. Is this also true of other models? The concept of near complete decomposability provides a theoretical basis for a hierarchical modelling approach, and has been applied to queuing network models with encouraging results (Courtois, 1977). For a hierarchical decomposition to work well, the degree of interaction among components within a module should be high with respect to the degree of interaction between the module and other modules in the object. Also, can our models be transported from one system to another dissimilar system, or are more theoretical advances required before this can happen?

10.1.1 Types of models

Svobodova (1976a) divides system models into three general classes: structural models, functional models, and performance models. A **structural model** describes the characteristics of individual system components and their interactions. A **functional model** describes how the system operates such that the model can be analysed mathematically or studied empirically. A **performance model** is derived by the analysis of a functional model, or a structural model, for a specific model of system workload.

Examples of structural models include block diagrams, some modelling language descriptions, and some detailed simulation models. These models show the paths of data flow and control flow, but do not specify why particular paths are followed. Thus, they are more useful for understanding how a system fits together than for understanding how it works.

A number of functional models are in use. They reflect different conceptual models of object execution, and are used to study different system characteristics. A **flow chart model** is a directed graph where the nodes represent computational tasks and the arcs show the possible flow of control between tasks. Flow chart models are used for studying program efficiency and program execution time. The object flow graph, defined in Chapter 2, is a flow chart model based upon actual measurements. Thus, the formulation of performance measurement takes a flow chart model and applies it to all levels of the object hierarchy. If we obtain a flow chart model by measurement, we can use it to evaluate performance by predicting the extent of the object when it is executing synthetic workloads.

A **finite state model** is also a directed graph, but the nodes represent the state of the system and the arcs represent transitions between those states. These models can be used to represent concurrent operation, and to analyse the utilization of resources. A model of this type can be developed from a system object record if appropriate stimulus information is recorded. Stimulus information is used to calculate the probability of a certain state transition given a certain workload.

In a **queuing model**, a computer system is a set of resources and queues for those resources. These models emphasize the flow of jobs through a system in terms of the time taken by the resource to service the job, and the time the job waits in the queue for the resource. As queuing models are very widely used, measurement for queuing models will be looked at in a later section.

Two classes of performance models in common use are analytical models and empirical models. An **analytical model** is a set of mathematical equations which express the relations which exist between the basic system variables and performance parameters. Analytical models are limited to simple system models, for example queuing models, or detailed models of one resource, by the requirement of mathematical tractability. Thus, the underlying functional model must meet the conflicting goals of capturing the basic structure of the system, having the characteristics of a real workload, and being simple enough to be mathematically tractable.

An **empirical model** is developed by analysis of empirical data, often by statistical methods - for example a regression model. A regression model is calibrated to match one set of observations, and thus may only be valid for a limited range of workloads on one system. Unless the model captures the basic elements of the system, possibly due to having an analytical basis, it is not transportable. A second type of empirical model is the system, or resource, or object profile. A number of these are shown in Chapter 2 as graphical methods of data analysis.

10.1.2 Measurement for models

Measurement plays an important part in modelling system performance. To comprehend the applications of measurement in modelling, we will now look at a typical modelling methodology. A performance analyst first defines the goals of the modelling study: 'What problem is to be studied?', 'Is there a suspected performance bug?', 'Is there a need to upgrade the system to handle a larger workload?', etc. From these goals, he can decide at which level in the object hierarchy to model the system, and can select an appropriate modelling technique. Also, he should delineate the assumptions upon which that modelling technique is based, for example certain time distributions are assumed in queuing models. As with measurement, understanding the system to be modelled is important.

The analyst develops a model of the system within the constraints of accuracy and cost. Having developed the model as a set of equations (or graphs), the model must be calibrated and verified. Before he can obtain the data needed to do this, he has to define: 'What to measure?' and 'How to measure it?' A model is calibrated by calculating model constants from the measured data. This data must be collected from the system when it is operating under conditions similar to those being modelled.

Once a model is calibrated, it must be verified. A model is verified by stimulating both the model and the system with the same inputs, and then comparing the outputs to see if they agree. If they differ significantly, then the model has to be corrected. The processes of model calibration, model verification, system understanding, and system debugging often interleave and interact. A disagreement between model output and system output may well be due to a system bug. In this situation, studying the system to correct the model will lead to understanding what is wrong with the system.

Once the model has been calibrated and verified, it can be used to study the impact of varying stimuli on system performance, and to predict the impact of an upgrade on system performance. Once the upgrade is done, the system is again measured to check the validity of the predictions. Model predictions will be inaccurate if a significant parameter has been left out. This parameter may not have been significant in the initial system model, but new stimuli, or a change in system configuration, may produce a situation where it becomes significant. Such situations are detected by comparing the measured outputs to the modelled outputs. Thus, measurement plays a significant role in performance modelling. In fact, modelling is a very poor science if it is not based upon accurate measurement.

10.1.3 Measurement for queuing models

Most books on performance modelling include an overview of measurement (for example Sauer and Chandy, 1981), but rarely give a detailed description of how to obtain the data for the models discussed within the text. Many models have been developed for IBM systems, and the data is usually obtained from the files produced by accounting programs, for example the System Management Facility (SMF) (Hellerman and Conroy, 1975), the Resource Measurement Facility (RMF), and the generalized trace facility (GTF). Unfortunately, these programs do not record all the desired data, and some data has to be estimated from the recorded data (Graham, 1981). The most comprehensive study of measurement procedures for queuing network models, including a survey of tools on a variety of systems, is found in Clifford Rose's 1978 paper. Also, Tolopka (1981) discusses an event trace monitor used on a VAX 11/780 to collect data for use in a queuing model.

The XRAY monitor (Blake, 1980) monitors the performance of a network of TANDEM/16 computers to detect bottlenecks: the overuse of hardware components and the software cause of that overuse. He used a simple model founded on operational analysis (Buzen, 1976) to determine where to place software meters in the GUARDIAN operating system. The model had the following general form: system throughput in transactions per second is equal to the ratio of the utilization of a device to the demand for that device per transaction. By analysing the model,

Blake concluded that measurement of device utilization and visit rates would provide all the data needed to identify bottlenecks. He instrumented the system accordingly, and then he used the model to analyse the collected data.

Queuing network models (Figure 10.1) are based upon the following conceptual model of a computer system: a number of jobs of various workload classes competing for a limited set of resources. The system is decomposed into a set of resources for which jobs must queue if they want service from a resource. Even though this conceptual model differs from that used in the formulation of performance measurement, instrumentation based upon the formulation can be used to measure the model parameters. The data collected by the instrumentation will be more detailed than that normally used in models, in the sense that it is possible to measure the parameters for an individual job. However, measurements for a set of individual jobs can then be averaged to get the data for the model. Alternatively, modelling can be extended from looking at the average job to looking at individual jobs.

When making measurements for a queuing model, a system is decomposed into a set of jobs, and each job is decomposed into a set of modules. This set of modules is the union of four subsets:

1. modules that add jobs to resource queues,
2. modules that wait on resources,
3. modules that remove a job from a resource queue so that it can use the resource, and
4. modules that use resources.

Thus, the events we wish to detect are:

- the addition of jobs to a resource queue,
- the removal of jobs from a resource queue,
- the acquisition of a resource by a job, and
- the termination of resource use by a job.

We can detect these events by placing probes into the routines which handle the queues, and into the routines which dispatch jobs to a particular resource. These probes will generate an event trace of resource usage. In addition, stimulus probes must accompany all event probes. When a job is initiated by adding it to the scheduler queue, the job number, the job class, and the current length of the queue must be written to stimulus probes. During the lifetime of the job, and at termination, the job number, and the length of the queue, must be output as stimulus information whenever the job is added to, or removed from, a queue. Also, the job number must be output as stimulus information whenever it acquires or releases a resource.

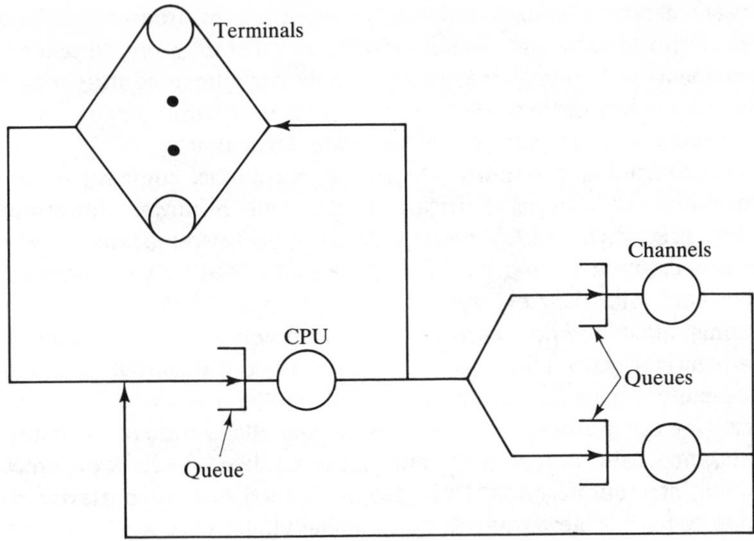

Figure 10.1 Typical queuing network model – parameters given in Table 10.1.

When measuring interactive systems, additional probes are placed in terminal handlers to measure the number of active terminals and the think time. Think time (Figure 1.1) is the time between when the computer completes the execution of a user command and when the user completes the entry of a new command. Normally, measuring think time will require the instrumentation of the particular interactive program because only the program knows when it has completed the command.

From the event trace generated by the above probes, all the information needed to calculate the parameters for a typical model (Table 10.1) by job class can be derived. Many of them have direct mappings into values in the object record; for example, CPU service time maps to module execution time, and visit counts maps to module execution counts. A modified object record, and hence a modified collection algorithm, will make measurement for queuing network models easier. The object record must be modified to store the additional stimulus information. The data collection algorithm should be modified to calculate the actual parameters, and to give the modeller the option of collecting data for only one job class, or even for only one job.

10.2 Man-machine interaction

As a general rule, measurement of human performance during interaction with computer systems is not viewed as a normal part of the software development process (Dunham and Kruesi, 1983). Yet how well the users accept a system ultimately determines its success. With the current trend toward user friendly interfaces - for example, the Smalltalk environment as implemented on the Apple Macintosh - measuring and modelling human performance during interaction with computer systems must become a significant part of software development.

The enormous variability among people makes comparison of the effectiveness of various software tools, and hardware input-output devices, very difficult. Sheppard *et al.* (1979) found that the time programmers took to find bugs introduced into FORTRAN programs did not correlate with their experience.

Some people find learning new techniques very difficult, and consequently it may take a long time for their productivity on a new, user-friendly device to surpass that on an old, awkward, but familiar device. Some people think with visual models, others with verbal models, and still others with numerical models. Each will prefer a different interaction style. Our previous experience often flavours our attitude toward a new way of doing something; for example, a person who has learned to program in a procedural language will find that programming in a functional language requires a very different mental approach. Sometimes the new device requires the same steps to be done in a different order, making it confusing to use; for example, someone who has learned to use an algebraic calculator finds a reverse Polish calculator difficult to use.

When attempting to tailor a user interface to a specific task, or to a specific level of user experience, attention must be given to:

- the choice of dialogue style,
- which input-output device suits the application,
- the consistency of command syntax, and
- choosing an interaction sequence that is appropriate to the task, suitable to the user, and predictable.

To do this, a system designer must understand the characteristics of the intended users of the system. Carey (1982) has grouped the characteristics that impact upon the acceptance of a system by a user into three categories:

1. The nature of the task to be performed and the user's associated mental model.
2. The nature and extent of the user's cognitive model of the information system. Some users approach a given system already equipped with a conceptual framework within which they quickly develop a system model; others may use a system regularly without developing more than a procedural understanding of it. Also, the user's cognitive style influences the nature of his conceptual model.

Table 10.1 Parameters of a typical queuing network model.

(a) Measured parameters	
A	number of arrivals
B_i	time server i was busy
C	number of completions
C_i	number of completions from device i where $i = 0$ is the system
K	number of devices ≡ number of users who can receive simultaneous service
M	number of users ≡ number of interactive terminals
N	maximum number of jobs in the system ≡ multiprogramming level
n_{ri}	number of class r jobs at device i
S_i	mean service time at device i
T	length of the observation interval
V_i	number of visits to device i per job
W	accumulated time in the system in job seconds $= \int A - C\, dt$
Z	mean think time
(b) Calculated parameters	
λ	arrival rate = A/T
μ	service rate $= 1/S_i = C_i/B_i$
n	mean number in system = W/T = XR
R	mean time in system = W/C
S_i	mean service time $= B_i/C_i$
U	utilization = B/T = XS
V_i	visit ratio $= C_i/C_o$
X	throughput = C/T

3. The nature and extent of the user's exposure to the system.

One method of tackling the problem (Pfaff *et al.*, 1982) of designing a standard interface for a variable set of individual users is to define user interaction in terms of a model consisting of a small set of well defined logical input and output devices. All input-output to applications programs is coded in terms of these logical input-output devices. An interface program is used to map these logical input-output devices to different physical devices, different user classes, and different applications.

A complementary approach is to direct all user interaction through a common input-output program, which individual users can tailor, to some extent, to their own desires. This common input-output program presents a consistent user interface at all levels of system interaction

(Nievergelt, 1982), eliminating the annoyance caused in many systems by one command meaning different things at different places in the system.

When faced with the great variability of users, we are tempted to forget measurement and use 'gut feel', or the subjective comments of a sample of users, as a guide in determining the effectiveness of an interactive dialogue. Whether the method of interaction has improved productivity or not can only be determined by measurement.

Two things that can be measured easily (compared to the difficulty of measuring human characteristics) are system response time (Miller and Thomas, 1977) and user response time (English *et al.*, 1967). A typical user interaction sequence is shown in Figure 1.1. Most reported measurement studies have been in these two areas. The following examples are typical of this work.

Miller (1968) gives possibly the best conceptual analysis of the effect of system response time on user response time, and suggests maximum system response times for a variety of user input situations. Appropriate and timely feedback to the user of meaningful information is one of the keys to successful interactive dialogues. Miller and Thomas (1977) give an overview of the behavioural issues involved in interactive systems, and how these can affect user response time. English *et al.* (1967) report on experiments to measure and compare response time for a variety of graphics input devices. Montgomery (1982) discusses methods of improving keyboard input, particularly wiping keys as an alternative to pressing keys.

Using the concepts of the formulation of performance measurement, we have developed an interactive object (Figure 10.2), which we can use as a conceptual model of man-machine interaction. Like our conceptual model of an executing program, our conceptual model of man-machine interaction is a sequence of modules. Again, we have a hierarchical decomposition of a high-level object into lower-level modules. The user generates input module is a lower-level interactive object. As our interactive object fits the conceptual model upon which we based the formulation of performance measurement, all the measures we defined in the formulation apply to this model.

Every execution of an interactive object, at any level, involves: input by the user, feedback to the user, error detection by the user, and the generation of a new input by the user. The time taken by the user to think about a new input depends on the nature of the task, whether it is procedural or problematic. Instrumentation of the object is the same as for any other object, but user activity can only be measured indirectly through the software, as normally we do not wire the user up to the measuring tool. Evaluating the measured data involves all the behavioural issues, and hence requires a method for measuring user characteristics. This area requires a great deal more research, particularly in the area of the psychology of human-computer interaction (Card *et al.*, 1983).

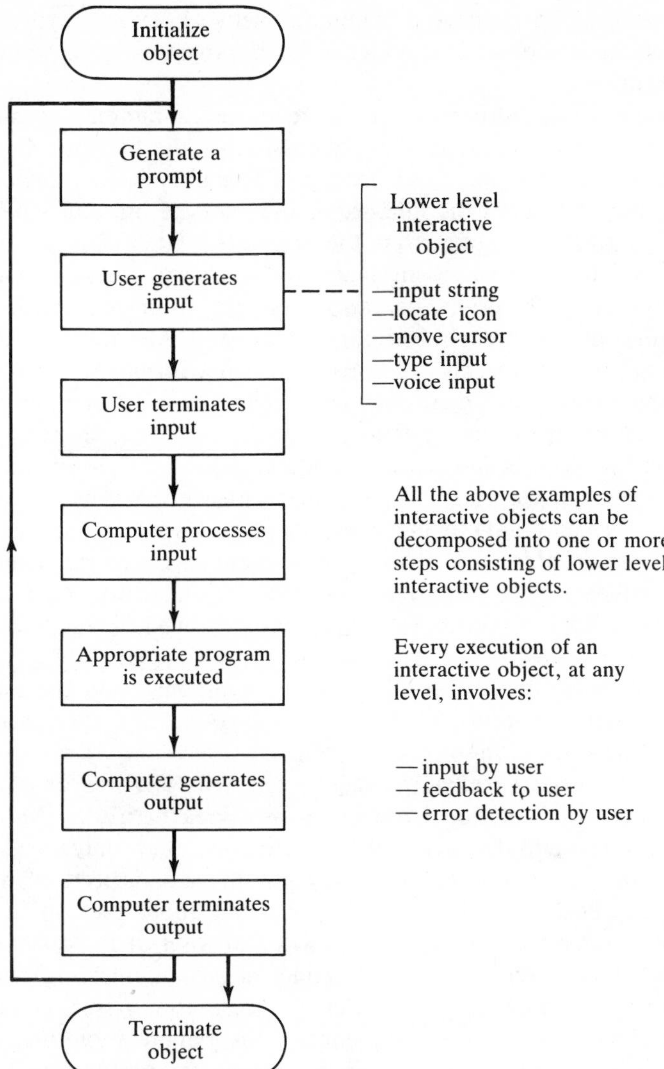

Figure 10.2 Interactive object – a conceptual model of man-machine interaction.

10.3 Computer networks

A network of computers consists of two or more computers linked together, while a computer network is either a network of computers or a set of terminals connected to one or more computers (Cole, 1971; quoted by Morgan *et al.*, 1975). Networks used to couple processors tightly together to form parallel processors have been discussed in the previous chapter. In this section, we will focus on wide-area networks and local-area networks. To manage a computer network effectively, we must monitor its behaviour as it executes a set of programs in response to its environment.

Mendicino and Sutherland (1973) identified a number of measures for networks of terminals in their discussion of the Octopus Computer Network at the Lawrence Livermore Laboratory. At regular time intervals, they measured the number of users logged on, and the volume of message traffic to and from the teletypes. They divided message traffic into four categories: messages to the system, messages from the system, messages to programs, and messages from programs. More recent work at Lawrence Livermore (Brice and Alexander, 1982) has involved an attempt to solve the problems of performance measurement on a large network of dissimilar computers (over 40 computers, five vendors, seven operating systems), by concentrating all performance evaluation functions in one network node.

In a survey of currently available performance monitors for terminal networks, Terplan (1981) included a table of performance parameters for these networks (Table 10.2). All of these parameters, except quality and possibly reliability, can be measured by carefully instrumenting the system in accordance with the methodology described in this book. The effective management of a terminal network (Terplan, 1982) requires performance measurement of all principal components in the network, preferably with the collected data being analysed and displayed by a centralized network monitor.

A computer network monitoring system (CNMS) was developed at the University of Waterloo to measure **wide-area networks** (Morgan *et al.*, 1975; Buck and Hrynyk, 1978). Although they only measured a small network, they were able to study a number of aspects of network monitoring. Their papers give far more detail about the tool than the actual measures made. Their tool consisted of a set of hybrid monitors, each located at a remote network node, all communicating with and controlled by a central network monitor. The central system could place simulated loads on the network, control the remote monitors, receive data from the remote monitors, and analyse the performance of the network.

Their hybrid monitoring tools were identical in principle to those used to monitor computers. The reasons they gave for monitoring a network are the same as the reasons other researchers give for monitoring a computer. However, a problem exists when monitoring networks which does not occur when monitoring monoprocessors. Because of the large physical distance between network nodes, it is difficult to determine the order in which nearly simultaneous events occur. In a multiprocessor, a master synchronizing clock is used; but in a network, the time delays in sending the synchronization signal from the control unit to a remote monitor may be significant.

Table 10.2 Terminal network performance parameters (Terplan, 1981).

Response Time:	Message Rate:
• network delay, and	• transmitted messages, and
• host delay.	• received messages.
Interactive throughput time.	Turnround time.
Interaction rate.	Quality of messages.
Throughput rate.	Transaction rate.
Availability.	Terminal utilization.
Reliability.	Control unit utilization.
Line utilization.	
Front end utilization.	
Error rate.	

Buck and Hrynyk used event driven monitors, where an event is a change in the system state. Two histograms were found to be useful for understanding the behaviour of the network: system state versus time in each state, and system state transitions versus the number of such transitions. A second problem when monitoring a wide area network is getting the data from the remote monitor to the central controlling unit. Data reduction mechanisms must be used to reduce the data to manageable quantities, before it is transmitted. If large quantities of data are to be transferred, a second network is required, so that the transfer of measurement data does not interfere with the operation of the network.

Silvester and Kleinrock (1983) have analysed the performance of various configurations of ALOHA networks using models. The ALOHA network is a broadcast network connecting the island campuses of the University of Hawaii, based upon a transmit when ready, collision detection and random back off technique. When they analysed this system, they found that only 18% of the channel bandwidth could be utilized. By modifying the network protocol to force transmission to commence at the beginning of slots (time divisions of length equal to a packet transmission time), the capacity can be doubled to 36% of channel bandwidth. Silvester and Kleinrock were interested in measuring:

- the number of successful transmissions per slot for any node in the network,
- the average path length, in terms of node to node transmissions, that messages traversed through the network, and
- network throughput.

Kleinrock and Opderbeck (1977) carried out a series of experiments to determine the speed at which large files transferred through the

ARPANET. They measured the time taken as a function of the number of hops (transmission from one node to the next) and calculated the throughput as a function of the number of hops. These measures gave them some feel for the delays that occur at the nodes in the network. When they investigated the occasional long network delay, they discovered extensive looping in the network. The dynamic routing algorithm could get into a situation where packets were tossed back and forth between neighbouring nodes many times, and thus were delayed until the adaptive routing procedure corrected the anomaly.

Local-area networks have a different set of characteristics to wide-area networks. The routing problem is removed because there is a common transmission medium. Local-area networks are characterized by the way they handle contention for the medium. Some use CSMA/CD (Carrier Sense Multiple Access/Collision Detect) technology similar to ALOHA net; the best known of these is Ethernet. Other networks obtain the medium before transmission; for example, token buses and token rings. With these networks, once a station acquires a token it can transmit without fear of collision. Another method is the slotted ring technique used in the Cambridge Ring, where a fixed number of slots circulate around the network and a station can acquire the next empty one. Each network topology has its own advantages and disadvantages.

Measurement of local-area networks can be divided into three areas: measurement of network performance, measurement of the response time of acknowledgements, and measurement of the cost of protocol handlers. Measuring **network performance** involves: measuring the time to acquire the network, the delay in waiting for the network, the time to send messages over the network, and the degradation of the network under heavy load - Metcalfe and Boggs (1976) discuss the performance of Ethernet under load. When we measure the **response time of acknowledgements**, we are measuring the software in the receiving computer as well. Two types of acknowledge exist in a network: a low level acknowledge to say that the message got there OK and a higher level reply to the message.

The third area is measuring the **cost of the protocol handlers** and the impact of network communications on the computers using the network. Nelson (1981) discusses the performance of programs handling a remote procedure call mechanism over an Ethernet, and looks at various ways of improving performance. Belanger *et al.* (1981) discuss the performance of two experimental protocols for ZNET (a low cost Ethernet-like network). Their measurements indicate that making higher-level software responsible for reliable message delivery greatly increases response time.

The above discussion is not intended to give a comprehensive history of network measurement, but rather to introduce the various measurement situations and to give a feel for the problems involved.

Much more effort has gone into modelling computer networks than into measuring them. Donald DuBois (1982) describes a hierarchical modelling system, consisting of both analytical and simulation models, for use in the design of networks. He used Kleinrock's open queuing model for computer networks, and derived the following performance measures: expected message delay at a node, utilization of the network, average queuing time at a node, and average number of messages at a node.

As with the other applications we have looked at in this chapter, if we can describe networks in terms of the conceptual model of an object then the measures are defined. We appear to have several network objects, one for each topology. However, some generalizations can be made.

If the network is looked at from the point of view of a program using the network, then communication over the network is just a module in our program object. The network object consists of: the network driver, which formats the message, acquires the network, and transmits the message; the destination computer which answers the message; and the network driver which receives the answer, and passes it to the program using the network. This type of network object is included in the class of normal monoprocessor objects. It can be used to measure the time taken to transmit messages over the network, the time taken to acknowledge that the message was received, and the response time of the reply. However, it gives very little feel for the behaviour of the network as a whole.

Our conceptual model of a computer involves the flow of control of the program counter. If we think of a network in terms of the flow of control of messages, then we have a conceptual model of a network very similar to our conceptual model of a multiprocessor. A network object is a set of node modules connected by a set of transmission modules. The path of a message through the network is a sequence of modules. The time taken by the message to travel through the network is the execution time of the object.

An event trace containing sufficient information to measure the network can be obtained if the arrival and departure of messages from nodes in the network are considered to be events. Stimulus information associated with each event is a message identifier, or in the case of a network where fixed path virtual links are established, the link identifier. Other stimulus information includes the number of messages queued at the node waiting for retransmission.

Measurement based on the first network object defines network parameters from the point of view of a process using the network, where measurement based on the second network object defines network parameters from the point of view of network loading and network performance. By combining these measurements, we obtain a comprehensive picture of the flow of messages through a network, and determine the impact of these messages on the sender and receiver.

Chapter 11
Conclusion

> 'When you can measure what you are speaking about, and express it in numbers, you know something about it; but when you cannot measure it, when you cannot express it in numbers, your knowledge is of a meagre and unsatisfactory kind; it may be the beginning of knowledge, but you have scarcely in your thoughts advanced to the stage of a Science.'
>
> Lord Kelvin (Dunham and Kruesi 1983)

In this book, I have sought to codify the results of the last 25 years of research in performance measurement into a unified body of knowledge. As far as I can tell, I have included all the significant advances, and credited those who made them. I have concentrated on measurement, and I have only discussed performance evaluation, performance modelling and performance improvement at the points where they are impacted by measurement. Unification of the field involved two interlocking processes: the development of a general formulation of performance measurement; and the study of measurement tools, techniques, and experiments in the context of the formulation.

Because a computer program is a mathematical object, we can not only measure its dynamic performance during execution, but we can also describe those measures mathematically. The object we measure can be as small as a single instruction or as large as a complete system. An object at one level can be decomposed into a set of objects at a lower level. We have given a full decomposition for a computer system, both for monoprocessors and multiprocessors. One consequence of this hierarchical decomposition of an object is a set of measures which applies at all levels of the object hierarchy. The conceptual model of an object during execution is a sequence of modules, and we have defined the extent of an object in terms of this conceptual model.

We can instrument an object to produce an event trace consisting of module start tuples and stimulus information triples. From this event trace, we can generate an object record, from which we can calculate values for other parameters. All these parameters can be displayed graphically for easy analysis.

The formulation of performance measurement provides an overall context in which performance measurement experiments can be conducted. We have developed a methodology for performance measurement, and have discussed the integration of performance measurement tools into a system at design time. Also, we have proposed a monitor chip for use with microprocessors, which will reduce the interference of the software probes in a hybrid tool.

A major part of this book is a historical survey of measurement tools and techniques. We have developed a philosophy of hybridization from the performance measurement formulation, designed a hybrid measurement tool, and implemented a subset of this tool. To illustrate the use of this tool, we have investigated three case studies. The tool is built from off the shelf components: a logic state analyser, a personal computer, a communications link, a simple hardware probe, and software probes. The technology is now available to build a powerful, low cost, general purpose, performance measurement tool. On the basis of the formulation of performance measurement, we have defined the characteristics of such a tool.

In the past, in the absence of a formulation of performance measurement, integration of performance measurement instruments into a system has been difficult, due to the problem of specifying what to measure on a system whose design has not been stabilized. In response, a number of approaches were taken: no instrumentation was included, a general purpose tool was added later, or a shotgun approach to instrumentation was taken. In the latter, a lot of tools were included in the hope that nothing would be missed. Instrumentation on the basis of a general formulation of performance measurement can be tailored to the needs of the system, and at the same time will be general enough to get at all variables of interest, because we understand performance measurement.

One topic in the area of performance measurement that has concerned a number of researchers is privacy and security. The tools discussed in this book are able to get past the best security system, and hence could be used to invade privacy. Access to performance measurement tools integrated into a system must be carefully controlled. Performance measurement tools in themselves are neutral. It is the people who use them who choose to use them for good or evil. We each have a moral responsibility to our fellow man, and before God, to use these tools for ethical purposes.

We proposed a number of ways of validating the formulation of performance measurement. A large part of this book is dedicated to validating the formulation and to demonstrating that it is general enough to codify the field of performance measurement into a unified body of knowledge. The research of others has been studied and compared to the performance measurement formulation. We have conducted a number of experiments based on the formulation. Corollaries to the formulation have been hypothesized and tested. Only when several researchers have carried out independent experiments will the formulation of performance measurement become generally accepted as a framework within which to do performance measurement.

A number of further research projects, following on from this research, have been mentioned. One is independent validation of the formulation of performance measurement. Another is extending the formulation to cover performance evaluation. Practical extensions of this research are the development of the general purpose tool detailed in these pages, and the integration of performance tools into new processors, via the development of monitor chips.

Bibliography

'Of making many books there is no end, and much study wearies the body.'

Ecclesiastes 12:12b

Bibliographies

Agajanian, A.H. 1975. 'A Bibliography on System Performance Evaluation', *IEEE Computer*, Vol 8, No 11, November, 63-74.

Miller, E.F. 1972. 'Bibliography on Techniques of Computer Performance Analysis', *IEEE Computer*, Vol 5, No 5, September, 39-47.

Shaw, M. 1981. 'Annotated Bibliography on Software Metrics', in Perlis A. *et al.* Eds. *Software Metrics: An Analysis and Evaluation,* MIT Press.

Tanik, M.M. 1980. 'An Annotated Bibliography on Performance Evaluation', *Performance Evaluation Review,* Vol 9, 24-30.

Journals and special journal issues

Computer Performance, Vince N.C. Ed. Butterworth Scientific Limited, Guildford, Surrey, England.

EDP Performance Review, Applied Computer Research, Phoenix, Arizona.

Performance Evaluation, Kobayashi H. Ed. North-Holland Publishing Company, The Netherlands.

Performance Evaluation Review, Highland H.J. Ed. ACM Sigmetrics, New York.

Agrawala, A.K. and Herzog, U. Eds. 1983. *IEEE Transactions on Computers*, Vol C-32, No 1, January.

Ferrari, D. Ed. 1976. 'Program Behaviour', *IEEE Computer*, Vol 9, No 11, November.

Gillette, D. Ed. 1978. 'Unix Time-Sharing System', *The Bell System Technical Journal*, Vol 57, No 6, Part 2, July.

Graham, G.S. Ed. 1978. *Computing Surveys*, Vol 10, No 3, September.

Shemmer, J.E. Ed. 1972. *IEEE Computer*, Vol 5, No 4, July.

Shively, R.R. Ed. 1972. *IEEE Computer*, Vol 5 No 5, September.

Spragins, J. Ed. 1980. *Analytical Queuing Models*, IEEE Computer, Vol 13, No 4, April.

Books, theses, conference digests, and equipment manuals

Apple Computer Inc., Cupertino, California, 1980. *Apple Pascal Operating System Reference Manual.*

Beilner, H. and Gelenda, E. 1977. *Measuring, Modeling and Evaluating Computer Systems*, North-Holland.

Borovits, I. and Neumann, S. 1979. *Computer Systems Performance Evaluation*, Lexington Books, Massachusetts.

Bunyan, C.J. Ed. 1974. *Computer Systems Measurement*, Infotech State of the Art Report 18.

Card, S.K., Moran, T.P., & Newell, A. 1983. *The Psychology of Human-Computer Interaction*, Lawrence Erlbaum, New Jersey.

Chandy, K.M. and Reiser, M. Eds. 1977. *Computer Performance*, North-Holland.

Chang, D.Y-C. and Lawrie, D. 1982. *Performance of Multiprocessor Systems with Space and Access Contention*, Report No UIUCDCS-R-82-1085, Department of Computer Science, University of Illinois at Urbana-Champaign.

Cooper, R. 1981. *Introduction to Queuing Theory*, Second Edition, North-Holland.

Courtois, P.J. 1977. *Decomposability, Queuing and Computer System Applications*, ACM Monograph Series, Academic Press.

Cutland, N.J. 1980. *Computability – An Introduction to Recursive Function Theory*, Cambridge University Press.

de Bakker, J. 1980. *Mathematical Theory of Program Correctness*, Prentice Hall.

Dijkstra, E.W. 1976. *A Discipline of Programming*, Prentice Hall.

Drummond, M.E. 1973. *Evaluation and Measurement Techniques for Digital Computer Systems*, Prentice Hall.

Dumont, D.N. 1978. *Computer Performance Measurement Tools and Techniques*, University of California, Santa Barbara, Ph.D. Thesis, University Microfilms International, No 7921039.

Ferrari, D. 1978a. *Computer Systems Performance Evaluation*, Prentice Hall.

Ferrari, D. Ed. 1978b. *Performance of Computer Installations*, North-Holland.

Ferrari, D. and Spadoni, M. Eds. 1981. *Experimental Computer Performance Evaluation*, North-Holland.

Ferrari, D., Serazzi, G. and Zeigner, A. 1983. *Measurement and Tuning of Computer Systems*, Prentice Hall.

Fosdick, L.D. Ed. 1979. *Performance Evaluation of Numerical Software*, North-Holland.

Freiberger, W. Ed. 1972. *Statistical Computer Performance Evaluation*, Academic Press.

Graham, G.S. 1981. *Computer Systems Performance Evaluation*, Lecture Notes, Advanced Management Research Symposium, Sydney.

Halstead, M.H. 1977. *Elements of Software Science*, Elsevier, New York.

Hanson, P.B. 1973. *Operating Systems Principles*, Prentice Hall.

Hartigan, J.A. 1975. *Clustering Algorithms*, Wiley.

Hellerman, H. and Conroy, T. 1975. *Computer System Performance*, McGraw-Hill.

Hewlett-Packard. 1978a. *Operating Guide for the HP 1610A Logic State Analyser*, February.

Hewlett-Packard. 1978b. *Seminar in Problem-Solving Concepts for Computer Systems, Part III: Complex Bus and Software Analysis Introduction,* October, 53-80.

Jenkins, J.H. 1975. *Assessment of the Control Structure of a Minicomputer using a Hardware Monitor*, Ph.D. Thesis, University of California, Santa Barbara.

Kayin Peripherals, Baulkham Hills, N.S.W. 1979. *Apple II - IEEE Bus Interface Model IE-01-79.*

Kobayashi, H. 1978. *Modeling and Analysis: an Introduction to Performance Evaluation Methodology*, Addison-Wesley.

Kolence, K.W. 1985. *An Introduction to Software Physics: The Meaning of Computer Measurement*, McGraw-Hill.

Knuth, D.E. 1968. *The Art of Computer Programming, Vol 1: Fundamental Algorithms*, Addison-Wesley.

Kylstra, F.J. Ed. 1981. *Performance '81*, North-Holland.

Lanciaux, D. Organizer. 1978. *Second Colloque International Sur les Systemes D'Exploitation*, IRIA - Rocquencourt, 2-4 October, Le Chesnay, France.

Lavenberg, S. Ed. 1983. *Computer Performance Modeling Handbook*, Academic Press.

Liguori, F. *Automatic Test Equipment*, IEEE Press.

Lions, J. 1977. *A Commentary on the Unix Operating System*, University of New South Wales.

McKerrow, P.J. 1978. *Control of Coating Mass on a Continuous Hot Dip Galvanizing Line*, Master of Engineering Thesis, The University of Wollongong.

Manna, Z. 1974. *Mathematical Theory of Computation*, McGraw-Hill.

Marathe, M.V. 1977. *Performance Evaluation at the Hardware Architecture Level and the Operating System Kernel Design Level,*

Ph.D. Thesis, Computer Science Department, Carnegie-Mellon University, Pittsburgh, Pa.

Nelson, B.J. 1981. *Remote Procedure Call*, Xerox Corporation, Palo Alto Research Center, Report No CSL-81-9.

Perlis, A.J., Sayward, F.G., and Shaw, M. Eds. 1981. *Software Metrics*, MIT Press.

Rafiquzzaman, M. 1984. *Microprocessors and Microcomputer Development Systems*, Harper and Row.

Sauer, C.H. and Chandy, K.M. 1981. *Computer Systems Performance Modeling*, Prentice Hall.

Scherr, A.L. 1967. *An Analysis of Time-Shared Computer Systems*, MIT Press.

Spirn, J.R. 1977. *Program Behaviour: Models and Measurements*, Elsevier.

Svobodova, L. 1976a. *Computer Performance Measurement and Evaluation Methods: Analysis and Application*, Elsevier.

Von Neumann, J. 1963. *Collected Works*, Vol 5, Taub, A.H. Ed., Pergamon.

Walpole, R.E. and Myers, R.H. 1978. *Probability and Statistics for Engineers and Scientists*, Collier MacMillan.

Wand, M. 1980. *Induction, Recursion and Programming*, Elsevier, North-Holland.

White, C.H. Ed. 1977. *Systems Tuning*, Infotech State of the Art Report.

Papers

Adrion, W.R. 1982. 'Validation, Verification, and Testing of Computer Software', *Computing Surveys*, Vol 14, No 2, June, 159-192.

Agrawala, A.K., Bryant, R.M. and Mohr, J.M. 1976. 'An Approach to the Workload Characterization Problem', *Computer*, Vol 9, 18-32.

Allan, R. 1977. 'Logic Analyzers', *IEEE Spectrum*, Vol 14, No 8, August.

Amiot, L.W. *et al.* 1972 'Evaluating a Remote Batch Processing System', *Computer*, September/October, 24-29.

Apple, C.T. 1965. 'The Program Monitor – A Device for Program Performance Measurement', *Proc. of the ACM 20th National Conference*, 65-75.

Arden, B. and Boltner, D. 1969. 'Measurement and Performance of a Multiprogramming System', *Second ACM Symposium on Operating System Principles.*

Arndt, F.R. and Oliver, G.N. 1971. 'Hardware Monitoring of Real-Time Computer System Performance', *Digest of 1971 IEEE International Computer Society Conf.*, 123-125.

Artis, H.P. 1978. 'Capacity Planning for the MVS Computer System', in Ferrari. Ed. *Performance of Computer Installations*, North-Holland, 25-35.

Aschenbrenner, R.A., Amiot, L. and Natarajan, 1971. 'The Neurotron Monitor System', *AFIPS FJCC*, Vol. 39, 31-37.

Balzer, R.M. 1969. 'Exdams - Extended Debugging and Monitoring System', *AFIPS, SJCC*, Vol 34, 567-580.

Bard, Y. 1971. 'Performance Criteria and Measurement for a Time Sharing System', *IBM Systems Journal*, Vol 10, No 3.

Barnes, G.H. *et al.* 1968. 'The Illiac IV Computer', *IEEE Transactions on Computers*, Vol C-17, August, 746-757.

Bauer, M.J. and McCredie, J.W. 1973. 'AMS: A Software Monitor for Performance Evaluation and System Control', *Proc. First Annual SICME Symposium on Measurement and Evaluation*, February, 147-160.

Belanger, P. *et al.* 1981. 'Performance Measurements of a Local Area Network', in West, A. and Janson, P. Eds. *Local Networks for Computer Communications*, North-Holland, 181-189.

Bell, T.E., Boehm, B.W., and Watson, R.A. 1972. 'Framework and Initial Phases for Computer Performance Improvement', *AFIPS*, No 41, 1141-1154.

Bemer, R.W. and Ellison, A.L. 1968. 'Software Instrumentation Systems for Optimum Performance', *Proc. IFIP Congress.*

Bergerol, C. 1981. 'Distributed Performance Monitoring System', *Computer Performance*, IPC Science and Technology Press Limited, Vol 2, No 1, 5-12.

Bisiani, R., Mauersberg, H. and Reddy, R. 1983. 'Task-Oriented Architectures', *Proc. of the IEEE*, Vol 71, No 7, 885-898.

Blake, R. 1980. 'XRAY: Instrumentation for Multiple Computers', *Performance Evaluation Review*, Vol 9, part 2, 11-25.

Blau, R. 1983. 'Paging on an Object-Oriented Personal Computer', *Proc. ACM Sigmetrics Conference*, 44-54.

Boulaye, G. *et al.* 1977. 'A Computer Measurement and Control System', *Proc. 3rd International Symposium on Measuring, Modeling and Evaluating Computer Systems*, October, North Holland.

Bourret, P. and Cros, P. 1980. 'Presentation and Correction of Errors in Operating System Measurements', *IEEE Transactions on Software Engineering*, Vol 6, No 4, July, 395-398.

Boyle, B. 1984. 'Software Performance Evaluation', *Byte*, February, 175-188.

Brampton, J. 1982. 'State Analyzers Move from Lab to Production Area', *Electronic Design*, May 13, 167-176.

Brice, R. and Alexander, W. 1982. 'A Network Performance Analyst's Workbench', *Performance Evaluation Review*, Vol 11, No 1, 138-146.

Browne, J.C. and Shaw, Mary. 1981. 'Toward a Scientific Basis for Software Evaluation', in Perlis A. *et al.* Eds. *Software Metrics: An Analysis and Evaluation*, MIT Press, 19-41.

Buck, D.L. and Hrynyk, D.M. 1978. 'Software Architecture for a Computer Network Monitoring System', in Ferrari D. Ed. *Performance of Computer Installations*, 269-287.

Bucker, I.Y. 1983. 'The Computational Speed of Super Computers', *Proc. of ACM Sigmetrics Conference*, 158-165.

Bussell, B. and Koster, R.A. 1970. 'Instrumenting Computer Systems and their Programs', *AFIPS FJCC*, Vol 37, 525-534.

Buzen, J.P. 1973. 'Computational Algorithms for Closed Queuing Networks with Exponential Servers', *Comm ACM*, Vol 16, No 9, 527-531.

Buzen, J.P. 1976. 'Fundamental Operational Laws of Computer System Performance', *Acta Informatica*, Vol 7, No 2, Springer Verlag, 167-182.

Cabrera, L.F. 1981. 'Benchmarking Unix - A Comparative Study', *Experimental Computer Performance Evaluation*, North-Holland.

Calingaert, P. 1967. 'System Performance Evaluation: Survey and Appraisal', *Comm ACM*, Vol 10, No 1, 12-18.

Campbell, D.J. and Heffner, W.J. 1968. 'Measurement and Analysis of Large Operating Systems during System Development', *AFIPS, FJCC*, Vol 33, 903-914.

Cannon, M.D., Fritz, D.H., Howard, J.H., Howell, T.D., Mitoma, M.F. and Rodriquez-Rosell, J. 1980. 'A Virtual Machine Emulator for Performance Evaluation', *Communications of the ACM*, Vol 23, 71-80.

Cantrell, H.N. and Ellison, A.L. 1968. 'Multiprogramming System Performance Measurement and Analysis', *Proc. AFIPS, SJCC*, Vol 32, 213-221.

Carey, T. 1982. 'User Differences in Interface Design', *IEEE Computer*, Vol 15, No 11, November, 14-20.

Carlson, G. 1971. 'A User's View of Hardware Performance Monitors or How to Get More Computer for Your Dollar', *IFIP Congress 1971*, 128-132.

Carlson, G. 1976. 'A Guide to the Use of Hardware Monitors - Part 2', *EDP Performance Review*, Vol 4, No 10, October.

Carlson, G. 1977. 'Hardware Monitoring for System Tuning', *Infotech Reports - System Tuning*, 255-274.

Chandy, K.M. and Sauer, C.H. 1980. 'Approximate Solution of Queuing Models', *IEEE Computer*, Vol 13, No 4, April, 25-32.

Charlton, C.C. and Mander, K.C. 1983. 'Tools and Techniques for Teaching Microprocessor Software Development', *Software Practice and Experience*, Vol 13, No 10, October, 909-920.

Cheng, P.S. 1969. 'Trace-Driven System Modeling', *IBM System Journal*, Vol 8, No 4, 280.

Cheriton, D.R. *et al.* 1979. 'Thoth, a Portable Real-Time Operating System', *Communications of the ACM*, Vol 22, No 2, 105-115.

Christensen, K., Fitsos, G.P. and Smith, C.P. 1981. 'A Perspective on Software Science', *IBM Systems Journal*, Vol 20, No 4, 372-387.

Clark, D.W. 1983. 'Cache Performance in the VAX-11/780', *ACM Transactions on Computer Systems*, Vol 3, 24-37.

Cole, G.D. 1971. 'Computer Network Measurements - Techniques and Experiments', University of California, Los Angeles, NTIS, Report AD-739-344, October.

Collins, J.P. 1976. 'Performance Improvement of the CP-V Loader through Use of the Adam Hardware Monitor', *Performance Evaluation Review*, Vol 5, No 2, April, 63-68.

Comerford, R.W. 1981. 'Measurement-Computer Era Arrives', *Electronics*, September, 8, 96-100.

Constantine, L.L. 1968. 'Integral Hardware/Software Design - Part 7: Formalization of Computer Power', *Modern Data*, November, 58-66.

Corson, D. 1983. 'Logic Tool Analyses Software Performance', *Electronic Design*, January 20, 117-126.

Coulter, N.S. 1983. 'Software Science and Cognitive Psychology', *IEEE Transactions on Software Engineering*, Vol SE9, No 2, March, 166-171.

Coutant, C.A., Griswold, R.E. and Hanson, D.R. 1983. 'Measuring the Performance and Behaviour of Icon Programs', *IEEE Transactions on Software Engineering*, Vol SE9, No 1, January, 93-103.

Cureton, H.O. 1972. 'A Philosophy to System Measurement', *AFIPS FJCC*, Vol 41, part II, 965-969.

Curtis, B. 1980. 'Measurement and Experimentation in Software Engineering', *Proc. of the IEEE*, Vol 68, No 9, September, Special Issue on Software Engineering, 1144-1157.

Deese, D.R. 1974. 'A Computer Design for Measurement - The monitor register concept', *Computer Performance Evaluation*, U.S. Department of Commerce, N.B.S. Special publication 401, 63-72.

Deniston, W.R. 1969. 'SIPE: A TSS/360 Software Measurement Technique', *Proc. 24th ACM National Conference*, 229-245.

Denning, P.J. 1978. 'Working Sets Then and Now', *Proc. of the 2nd Colloque International sur les Systemes D'Exploitation*, IRIA, Rocquencourt, October.

Denning, P.J. 1981. 'Performance Analysis: Experimental Computer Science at Its Best', *Communications of the ACM*, Vol 24, No 11, November, 725-727.

Denning, P.J. and Buzen, J.P. 1978. 'The Operational Analysis of Queuing Network Models', *Computing Surveys*, Volume 10, Number 3, September, 255-261.

Denny, W.M. 1977. 'The Burroughs B1800 Microprogrammed

Measurement System: A Hybrid Hardware/Software Approach', *Proc. of the 10th Annual Microprogramming Workshop*, 'MICRO 10', ACM, New York.

De Prycker, M. 1982a. 'A Performance Analysis of the Implementation of Addressing Methods in Block-Structured Languages', *IEEE Transactions on Computers*, Vol C-31, No 2, February, 155-163.

De Prycker, M. 1982b. 'On the Development of a Measurement System for High Level Language Program Statistics', *IEEE Transactions on Computers*, Vol C-31, No 9, September, 883-891

Deutch, P. and Grant, C.A. 1971. 'A Flexible Measurement Tool for Software Systems', *Information Processing 71*, Proc. IFIP Congress 71, North-Holland.

Ditzel, D.R. 1980. 'Program Measurements on a High-Level Language Computer', *Computer*, Vol 13, No 8, 62-72.

DuBois, D.F. 1982. 'A Hierarchical Modeling System for Computer Networks', *Performance Evaluation Review*, Vol 1, No 1, 147-155.

Dunham, J.R. and Kruesi, E. 1983. 'The Measurement Task Area', *IEEE Computer*, Special Issue on the DoD STARS Program, Vol 16, No 11, 47-54.

English, W.R., Engelbart, D.C. and Berman, M.L. 1967. 'Display-Selection Techniques for Text Manipulation', *IEEE Transactions on Human Factors in Electronics*, Vol 8 No 1, 5-20.

Estrin, G. 1974. 'Measurable Computer Systems', *Infotech Reports*, Vol 18, 285-299.

Estrin, G., Hopkins, D., Coggan B. and Crocker S.D. 1967. 'SNUPER COMPUTER - A Computer in Instrumentation Automation', *AFIPS, SJCC*, Vol 30, 645-656.

Estrin, G., Muntz, R.R. and Uzgalis, R.C., 1972. 'Modeling, Measurement and Computer Power', *AFIPS, SJCC*, Vol 40, 725-738.

Fairclough, D.A. 1982. 'A Unique Microprocessor Instruction Set', *IEEE Micro*, Vol 2, No 2, 8-18.

Febish, G.J. 1981. 'Experimental Software Physics', in Ferrari, D. Ed. *Experimental Computer Performance Evaluation*, North-Holland, 33-56.

Ferrari, D. 1972. 'Workload characterization and selection in computer performance measurement', *IEEE Computer*, Vol 5, No 4, July, 18-24.

Ferrari, D. 1973. 'Architecture and instrumentation in a modular interactive system', *IEEE Computer*, Vol 6, No 11, 25-29.

Ferrari, D. 1981a. 'Characterization and Reproduction of the Referencing Dynamics of Programs', *Performance 81*, North-Holland, 363-372.

Ferrari, D. and Liu, M. 1975. 'A General-Purpose Software Measurement Tool', *Software - Practice and Experience*, Vol 5, No 2, 181-182.

Ferrari, D. and Minetti, V. 1981b. 'A Hybrid Measurement Tool for Minicomputers', *Experimental Computer Performance Evaluation*, North-Holland, 217-233.

Fitzsimmons, A. and Love, T. 1978. 'A Review and Evaluation of Software Science', *Computing Surveys*, Vol 10, No 1, March 78, 3-18.

Flynn, M. 1972. 'Some Computer Organizations and their Effectiveness', *IEEE Transactions on Computers*, C-21, Vol 9, September, 948-960.

Ford, P. 1981. 'Simulation in Computer Performance Evaluation', *Computer Performance*, IPC Business Press, Vol 2, No 4, 186-191.

Foster, C.C. *et al.* 1971. 'Measures of Op-Code Utilization', *IEEE Transactions on Computers*, Vol C-20, No 5, May, 582-584.

Franta, W.R. *et al.* 1982. 'Issues and Approaches to Distributed Testbed Instrumentation', *IEEE Computer*, Vol 15, No 10, October, 71-81.

Freibergs, I.F. 1968. 'The Dynamic Behaviour of Programs', *AFIPS FJCC*, Vol 33, 1163-1167.

Fromm, H., Hercksen, U., Herzog, U., John, K.H., Klar, R. and Kleinder, W. 1983. 'Experiences with Performance Measurement and Modeling of a Processor Array', *IEEE Transactions on Computers*, Vol C32, No 1, January, 15-31.

Fryer, R.E. 1973. 'The Memory Bus Monitor - A New Device for Developing Real-Time Systems', *AFIPS, NCC*, Vol 42, 75-79.

Fuller, S.H. *et al.* 1973. 'The Instrumentation of C.mmp - A Multi-Mini-Processor', *Proc. COMPCON 73*, Seventh Annual IEEE Computer Society International Conference, 173-176.

Geck, A. 1979. 'Performance Improvements by Feedback Control of the Operating System', *Performance of Computer Systems*, North-Holland, 459-471.

Gehringer, E.F., Jones, A.K. and Segall, Z.Z. 1982. 'The CM* Testbed', *IEEE Computer*, Vol 15, No 10, October, 40-53.

Gerla, M. and Kleinrock, L. 1977. 'On the Topological Design of Distributed Computer Networks', *IEEE Transactions on Communications*, Vol COM-25, No 1, January, 48-60.

Gibson, J.C. 1970. 'The Gibson mix', *IBM Tech Report*, TR00 2043, June.

Glass, R.L. 1980. 'Real Time: The "Lost World" of Software Debugging and Testing', *Communications of the ACM*, Vol 23, No 5, May, 264-271.

Goodman, A.F. 1972. 'Measurement of Computer Systems - An Introduction', *AFIPS, FJCC*, No 41, 669-680.

Goodman, C.D. 1963. 'Getting Multichannel Analyser Data in and out of the IBM 7090 for processing', *Oakridge National Laboratory Tech. report*.

Gotlieb, C.C. 1973. 'Performance Measurement', in Bauer, F.L., Ed. *Advanced Course on Software Engineering*, Lecture Notes in Economics and Mathematical Systems, Springer-Verlag, 464-491.

Graham, R.M. 1973. 'Performance Prediction', in Bauer, F.L. Ed. *Advanced Course on Software Engineering*, Lecture Notes in Economics and Mathematical Systems, Springer-Verlag, 395-463.

Graham, S.L. *et al.* 1983. 'An Execution Profiler for Modular Programs', *Software - Practice and Experience*, Vol 13, 671-685.

Grenander, U. and Tsao, R.F. 1972. 'Quantitative Methods for Evaluating Computer System Performance: a Review and Proposals', in Freiberger, W. Ed. *Statistical Computer Performance Evaluation*, Academic, 3-24.

Grishman, R. 1971. 'Criteria for a Debugging Language', in Rustin, R. Ed. *Debugging Techniques in Large Systems*, 1st Courant Computer Science Symposium, Prentice Hall, 57-76.

Grochow, J.M. 1969. 'Real-time Graphic Display of Time-Sharing System Operating Characteristics', *AFIPS, JFCC*, Vol 35, 379-386.

Grosch, H.R.J. 1953. 'High Speed Arithmetic - The Digital Computer as a Research Tool', *Journal of the Optical Society of America*, Vol 43, No 4, 306-310.

Gupta, A. and Toong, H.D. 1983. 'An Architectural Comparison of 32-bit Microprocessors', *IEEE Micro*, Vol 3, No 1, 9-22.

Guteri, F. 1982. 'Design Case History: Biomation's Logic Analyser', *IEEE Spectrum*, Vol 19 No 5, May.

Hamming, R.W. 1980. 'Error Detecting and Error Correcting Codes', *Bell System Technical Journal*, Vol 26, No 2, 147-160.

Haynes, L.S. *et al.* 1982. 'A Survey of Highly Parallel Computing', *IEEE Computer*, Vol 15, No 1, January, 9-24.

Heidelberger, P. and Lavenberg, S.S. 1984. 'Computer Performance Evaluation Methodology', *IEEE Transactions on Computers*, Vol C-33, No 12, p 1195-1219.

Hellerman, L. 1972. 'A Measure for Computational Work', *IEEE Transactions on Computers*, Vol C-21, No 5, May 1972, 439-446.

Hellerman, H. and Ron, Y. 1970. 'A Time-Sharing Simulation and its Validation', *IBM Tech Report 320-2984*.

Hempy, H. 1977. 'IBM 3850 Mass Storage System, Performance Evaluation Using a Channel Monitor', in Chandy, K.M. and Reiser, M. Eds. *Computer Performance*, North-Holland, 177-196.

Herbst, E.H., Metropolis, N., and Wells K.B. 1955. 'Analysis of problem codes on the Maniac', *Maths Tables and Other Aids to Computation*, Vol 9, No 49, 14-20.

Hercksen, U., Klar, R., Kleinoder, W., Kneibl, F. 1982. 'Measuring

Simultaneous Events in a Multiprocessor System', *Performance Evaluation Review*, Vol 11, No 4, 77-88.

Hill, C.J. 1974. 'The State of Logic Analysers', *IEEE Spectrum*, Vol 11, No 12, December, 63-70.

Hoare, C.A.R. 1969. 'An Axiomatic Basis for Computer Programming', *Communications of the ACM*, Vol 12, No 10, 576-583.

Holdsworth, D. 1983. 'A System for Analysing Ada Programs at Run-Time', *Software - Practice and Experience*, Vol 13, No 5, 407-421.

Holtwick, G.W. 1971. 'Designing a Commercial Performance Measurement System', *ACM Sigops Workshop on System Performance Evaluation*, Cambridge, Massachusetts, 29-58.

Howard, P.C. 1974. 'Update on Hardware Monitors', *EDP Performance Review*, Vol 2, No 10, October.

Huang, J.C. 1980. 'Instrumenting Programs for Symbolic-Trace Generation', *IEEE Computer*, Vol 13, No 12, December, 17-23.

Hughes, J.H. 1980. 'Diamond - A Digital Analyser and Monitoring Device', *Performance Evaluation Review*, 27-34.

Hughes, J.H. and Cronshaw, D. 1973. 'On Using a Hardware Monitor as an Intelligent Peripheral', *Performance Evaluation Review*, 2, 4, 3-19, December.

Hughes, P.H. and Moe, G. 1973. 'A Structural Approach to Computer Performance Analysis', *AFIPS*, Vol 42, 109-119.

Ingalls, D. 1972. 'The Execution Time Profile as a Measurement Tool', in Rustin, R. Ed. *Design and Optimization of Compilers*, Prentice Hall, 129-136.

Johnston, S. 1980. 'Development of a Software Monitor', *Computer Performance*, Vol 1, No 2, 61-80.

Johnson, S.C. and Ritchie, D.M. 1978. 'UNIX Time-Sharing: Portability of C Programs and the UNIX System', *Bell System Tech. Journal*, Vol 57, No 6, 2021-2048.

Kashtan, D.L. 1980. 'UNIX and VMS: Some Performance Comparisons', *SRI International*.

Kearns, J.P., Meier, C.J. and Soffa, M.L. 1982. 'The Performance Evaluation of Control Implementations', *IEEE Transactions on Software Engineering*, Vol SE8, No 2, March, 89-96.

Keefe, D.D. 1968. 'Hierarchical Control Programs for Systems Evaluations', *IBM Systems Journal*, Vol 7, No 2, 123-133.

Kernighan, B.W. and Mashey, J.R. 1981. 'The UNIX Programming Environment', *IEEE Computer*, Vol 24, No 4, 12-24.

King, P.J.B. and Mitrani, I. 1982. 'Modelling the Cambridge Ring', *Performance Evaluation Review*, Vol 11, No 4, 250-258.

Klar, R. 1981. 'Hardware Measurements and their Applications on Performance Evaluations in a Processor-array', *Computing*, Suppl. 3, Springer Verlag, 65-88.

Kleinrock, L. 1966. 'Sequential Processing Machines (SPM) Analyzed

With a Queuing Theory Model', *Journal of the Association of Computing Machinery*, Vol 13, No 2, 179-193.

Kleinrock, L. and Opderbeck, H. 1977. 'Throughput in the ARPANET – Protocols and Measurement', *IEEE Transactions on Communications*, Vol COM25, No 1, January, 95-104.

Knuth, D.E. 1971. 'An Empirical Study of Fortran Programs', *Software - Practice and Experience,* Vol 1, 105-133.

Knuth, D.E. 1977. 'Algorithms', *Scientific American*, Vol 236, No 4, 63-80, April.

Kolence, K.W. 1971. 'A Software View of Measurement Tools', *Datamation*, Vol 17, No 1, January, 32-38.

Kolence, K.W. 1972. 'Software Physics and Computer Performance Measurements', *Proc. ACM National Conference*, 1024-1040.

Kolence, K.W. 1975. 'Software Physics', *Datamation*, June, 48-51.

Kolence, K.W. and Kiviat, P.J. 1973. 'Software Unit Profiles and Kiviat Figures', *Performance Evaluation Review*, Vol 2, No 3, September, 2-12.

Kuck, D.J. 1973. *Complexity of Sequential and Parallel Numerical Algorithms*, Traub, J.F. Ed., Academic Press, New York.

Kuck, D.J. 1977. 'A Survey of Parallel Machine Organization and Programming', *ACM Computing Surveys*, Vol 9, March, 29-59.

Kumar, B. and Davidson, E.S. 1980. 'Computer System Design Using a Hierarchical Approach to Performance Evaluation', *Communications of the ACM*, Vol 25, No 9, 511-521.

Larsen, R.L., Agre, J.R., and Agrawala, A.K. 1981. 'A Comparative Evaluation of Local Area Communication Technology', *Performance Evaluation Review*, Vol 10, No 2, 37-47.

Lazos, C. and Yandle, J.R. 1979. 'Improving CPU Utilization in a Multiprogramming System', *The Computer Journal*, Vol 22, No 3, 203-205.

Lee, K.F. and Smith, A.J. 1984. 'Branch Prediction Strategies and Branch Target Buffer Design', *IEEE Computer*, Vol 17, No 1, 6-22.

Lerner, E.J. 1982. 'Instrumentation', *IEEE Spectrum*, Vol 19, No 1, January.

Levy, H. and Clark, D. 1982. 'On the Use of Benchmarks for Measuring System Performance', *Computer Architecture News*, Vol 10, No 6.

Lonergan, R. and Androxiani, V. 1970. 'SUPERMON: A Software Monitor for Performance Evaluation', *Technical Memo No 30*, Stanford Computation Centre, California, January.

Lorentzen, R. 1979. 'Troubleshooting Microprocessors with a Logic-Analyzer System', *Computer Design*, March 1979.

Lucas, H.C. 1971. 'Performance Evaluation and Monitoring', *Computing Surveys*, Vol 3, No 3, September, 79-91.

Lynch, W.C. 1972. 'Operating System Performance', *Communications of the ACM*, Vol 15, No 7, July 1972, 579-585.

McCarthy, J. 1960. 'Recursive Functions of Symbolic Expressions and Their Computation by Machine, Part 1', *Communications of the ACM*, 184-204.

McCarthy, J. 1962. 'Towards a mathematical science of computation', *Proc. IFIP*, North-Holland, 21-28.

McDaniel, G. 1982. 'The Mesa Spy: An Interactive Tool for Performance Debugging', *Performance Evaluation Review*, Vol 11, No 4, 68-76.

MacEwen, G. 1974. 'On Instrumentation Facilities in Programming Languages', *IFIP Congress*, North-Holland, 198-203.

MacGregor, D. and Rubinstein, J. 1985. 'A Performance Analysis of MC6800-based Systems', *IEEE Micro*, Vol 5, No 6.

McKerrow, P.J. 1983. 'Evaluation of Interrupt-Handling Routines with a Logic-State Analyser', *Performance Evaluation*, Vol 3, 277-288.

McKerrow, P.J. 1984. 'Monitoring Program Execution with a Hybrid Measurement-Tool', *Australian Computer Science Communications*, Vol 6, No 1, 22.1-22.10.

McLeod, J. 1986. 'Special Report: How the PC is Changing Testing', *Electronics*, March 24, 31-38.

McQuillan, J.M. *et al.* 1978. 'A Review of the Development and Performance of the ARPANET Routing Algorithm', *IEEE Transactions on Communications*, Vol COM-26, No 12, December, 1802-1811.

Mahjoub, A. and Ekanadham, K. 1980. 'A Compile Time Approach to Response Time Computation', *Computer Science Department*, SUNY at Stony Brook, N.Y.

Mendicino, S.F. and Sutherland, G.F. 1973. 'Performance Measurements in LLL Octopus Computer Networks', *IEEE Compcon 73*, Digest of Papers, 109-112.

Metcalfe, R.M. and Boggs, D.R. 1976. 'Ethernet: Distributed Packet Switching for Local Computer Networks', *Communications of the ACM*, Vol 19, No 7, July, 395-404.

Miller, L.A. and Thomas, J.C. 1977. 'Behavioural Issues in the Use of Interactive Systems', *International Journal of Man-Machine Studies*, Vol 9, 509-536.

Miller, R. 1978. 'UNIX - A Portable Operating System?', *Operating Systems Review*, Vol 12, No 3, 32-37.

Miller, R.B. 1968. 'Response Times in Computer Conversation Transactions', *AFIPS FJCC*, Vol 33, 267-277.

Montgomery, E.B. 1982. 'Bringing Manual Input into the 20th Century: New Keyboard Concepts', *IEEE Computer*, Vol 15, No 3, 11-18.

Morgan, D.E. *et al.* 1974. 'A Performance Measurement System for Computer Networks', *Information Processing 74*, North-Holland.

Morgan, D.E., Banks, W., Goodspeed, D.P. and Kolanko, R. 1975. 'A

Computer Network Monitoring System', *IEEE Transactions on Software Engineering*, Vol SE-1, No 3, September, 299-311.

Morris, M.F. 1976. 'Kolence: True or False?', *Computerworld*, October 18, page 1.

Mosher, D.A. 1980. 'UNIX Performance: An Introspection', *Ampex Corporation*, Redwood City, California.

Murphy, R.W. 1969. 'The System Logic and Usage Recorder', *AFIPS FJCC*, Vol 35, 219-229.

Nemeth, A.G. and Rovner, P.D. 1971. 'User Program Measurement in a Time-Shared Environment', *Communications of the ACM*, Vol 14, No 10, 661-666, October.

Nievergelt, J. 1982. 'Errors in Dialog Design and How to Avoid Them', in Nievergelt, J. *et al.* Eds. *Document Preparation Systems - A Collection of Survey Articles*, North-Holland, 1-10.

Nutt, G.J. 1975. 'Tutorial: Computer System Monitors', *IEEE Computer*, Vol 8, No 11, November, 51-61.

Nygaard, K. 1982. 'Seminar at University of Wollongong, NSW', verbal communication, November.

Parkinson, D. and Liddell, H.M. 1983. 'The Measurement of Performance on a Highly Parallel System', *IEEE Transactions on Computers*, Vol C32, No 1, January, 32-37.

Patrick R.L. 1964. 'Measuring Performance', *Datamation*, Vol 10, No 7, 24-27.

Patterson, D.A. and Piepho, R.S. 1982. 'Assessing RISCs in High-Level Language Support', *IEEE Micro*, Vol 2, No 4, 9-19.

Patterson, D.A. and Sequin, C.H. 1982. 'A VLSI RISC', *IEEE Computer*, Vol 15, No 9, 8-18.

Pearson, S.W. and Bailey, J.E. 1980. 'Measurement of Computer User Satisfaction', *Performance Evaluation Review*, 59-68.

Penny, J.P. and Sheedy, C.R. 1980. 'Measurement of Response Time Performance in Small Time-Sharing Systems', *The Australian Computer Journal*, Vol 12, No 1, February.

Peterson, T.G. 1974. 'A Comparison of Software and Hardware Monitors', *Performance Evaluation Review*, Vol 3, No 2, June, 2-5.

Pfaff, G., Kuhlmann, H. and Hanusa, H. 1982. 'Constructing User Interfaces Based on Logical Input Devices', *IEEE Computer*, Vol 15, No 11, November, 62-68.

Plattner, B. and Nievergelt, J. 1981. 'Monitoring Program Execution: A Survey', *IEEE Computer*, November, Vol 14, No 11, 76-93.

Pomeroy, J.W. 1972. 'A Guide to Programming Tools and Techniques', *IBM Systems Journal*, Vol 11, No 3, 234-254.

Price, T.G. 1976. 'A Comparison of Queuing Network Models and Measurements of a Multiprogrammed Computer System', *Performance Evaluation Review*, Vol 5, No 4, 39-62.

Prichard, E.L. 1976. 'Logic of Software Physics Gives Guide to Change', *Computerworld*, October 18, 19-20.

Rafii, A. 1981. 'Structure and Application of a Measurement Tool – Sampler/3000', *Performance Evaluation Review*, Vol 10, No 3, 110-120.

Rajulu, R.G. and Rajaraman, 1982. 'Execution-Time Analysis of Process Control Algorithms on Microprocessors', *IEEE Transactions on Industrial Electronics*, Vol IE-29, No 4, November 312-319.

Rhodes, F.H.T. 1965. 'Christianity in a Mechanistic Universe', in MacKay D.M. Ed. *Christianity in a Mechanistic Universe and other Essays*, Inter-Varsity Press, London, 11-48.

Rodriguez-Rosell, J. 1976. 'Empirical Data Reference Behaviour in Data Base Systems', *IEEE Computer*, Vol 9, No 11, November, 9-13.

Roek, D.J. and Emerson, W.C. 1969. 'A Hardware Instrumentation Approach to Evaluation of a Large Scale System', *ACM National Conference Proc.*

Rose, C.A. 1977. 'A Calibration-Prediction Technique for Estimating Computer Performance', *AFIPS, NCC*, Vol 46, 813-818.

Rose, C.A. 1978. 'A Measurement Procedure for Queuing Network Models of Computer Systems', *Computing Surveys*, Vol 10, No 3, September.

Rosen, S. 1968. 'Hardware Design Reflecting Software Requirements', *AFIPS FJCC*, Vol 33, Part 2.

Rozwadowski, R.T. 1973. 'A Measure for the Quantity of Computation', *Proc. First ACM/SIGME Symposium on Measurement and Evaluation*, ACM, New York, 100-111.

Ruud, R.J. 1972. 'The CPM-X, A Systems Approach to Performance Measurement', *Proc. FJCC*, Vol 41, Part II, 949-957.

Saal, H.J. and Shustek, L.J. 1972. 'Microprogrammed Implementation of Computer Measurement Techniques', *Proc. ACM 5th Annual Workshop on Microprogramming*, September, 42-50.

Sakman, H., Erikson, W.J. and Grant, E.E. 1968. 'Exploratory Experimental Studies Comparing On-line and Off-line Programming performance', *Comm. ACM*, Vol 11, January.

Saltzer, J.H. and Gintell, J.W. 1970. 'The Instrumentation of Multics', *Comm. ACM*, Vol 13, No 8, 495-500.

Saunders, R.S.J. 1981. 'The PDSP – A Performance Measurement Tool for a Packet-Switching Network', *Performance 81*, North-Holland, 531-545.

Schach, S.R. 1982. 'A Unified Theory for Software Production', *Software – Practice and Experience*, Vol 12, 683-689.

Schulman, F.D. 1967. 'Hardware Measurement Device for IBM System/360 Time Sharing Evaluation', *Proc. of the ACM National Meeting*.

Schwetman, H.D. and Browne, J.C. 1972. 'An Experimental Study of Computer System Performance', *Proc. ACM National Conference*, 693-703.

Sebastian, P.R. 1974. 'HEMI - Hybrid Events Monitoring Instrument', *Proc. 2nd Sigmetrics Symposium on Measurement and Evaluation*, Montreal, 127-139.

Sedgewick, R. *et al.* 1970. 'SPY – A Program to Monitor OS/360', *Proc. AFIPS FJCC*, Vol 37, 119-128.

Segall, Z. *et al.* 1983. 'An Integrated Instrumentation Environment for Multiprocessors', *IEEE Transactions on Computers*, Vol C32, No 1, January, 4-14.

Serazzi, G. 1981. 'The Dynamic Behaviour of Computer Systems', in Ferrari, D. Ed. *Experimental Computer Performance Evaluation*, North-Holland, 127-163.

Shannon, C.E. 1948. 'A Mathematical Theory of Communication', *Bell System Technical Journal*, Vol 27, page 379.

Shemer, J.E. and Heying, D.W. 1969. 'Performance Modeling and Empirical Measurements in a System Designed for Batch and Time-Sharing Users', *AFIPS*, Vol 35, 17-26.

Shemer, J.E. and Robertson, J.B. 1972. 'Instrumentation of Time-Shared Systems', *IEEE Computer*, July/August 1972, 39-48.

Shen, V.Y. *et al.* 1983. 'Software Science Revisited: A Critical Analysis of the Theory and its Empirical Support', *IEEE Transactions on Software Engineering*, Vol SE9, No 2, March, 155-165.

Sheppard, S.B. *et al.* 1979. 'Modern Coding Practices and Programmer Performance', *Computer*, Vol 12, No 12, December, 41-49.

Siegel, L.J. *et al.* 1982. 'Performance Measures for Evaluation Algorithms for SIMD Machines', *IEEE Transactions on Software Engineering*, Vol SE8, No 4, July, 319-331.

Silvester, J.A. and Kleinrock, L. 1983a. 'On the Capacity of Multihop Slotted ALOHA Networks with Regular Structure', *IEEE Transactions on Communications*, Vol COM-31, No 8, August, 974-982.

Silvester, J.A. and Kleinrock, L. 1983b. 'On the Capacity of Single-Slotted ALOHA Networks for Various Traffic Matrices and Transmission Strategies', *IEEE Transactions on Communications*, Vol COM-31, No 8, August, 983-991.

Smith, A. 1982. 'Cache Memories', *Computing Surveys*, Vol 14, No 3.

Spiegel, M.G. 1980. 'Measuring and Evaluating Performance', *Performance Evaluation Review*, Vol 9, 33-34.

Stanley, W.I. 1969. 'Measurement of System Operational Statistics', *IBM Systems Journal*, Vol 8, No 4, 299-308.

Stevens, D.F. 1968. 'System Evaluation of the Control Data 6600', *Proc. of the IFIP Congress*, 34-38.

Stonebraker, M., Woodfill, J., Ranstrom, J., Murphy, M., Meyer, M. and Allman, E. 1983. 'Performance Enhancements to a Relational Database System', *ACM Transactions on Database Systems*, Vol 8, 167-185.

Stucki, L.G. 1972. 'A Prototype Automatic Program Testing Tool', *AFIPS FJCC*, 129-136.

Sumner, F.H. 1974. 'Measurement Techniques in Computer Hardware Design', *Infotech Reports*, Vol 18, 367-390.

Svobodova, L. 1973a. 'On-line System Performance Measurements with Software and Hybrid Monitors', *Operating Systems Review*, Vol 7, No 4, October, 45-53.

Svobodova, L. 1973b. 'Measuring Computer System Utilization with a Hardware and a Hybrid Monitor', *Performance Evaluation Review*, Vol 2, No 4, December.

Svobodova, L. 1974. 'Monitoring and Controlling Performance of a large Computer System', *COMPCON Fall*, 79-82.

Svobodova, L. 1976b. 'Computer System Measurability', *IEEE Computer*, June, 9-17.

Terplan, K. 1981. 'Network Monitor Survey', *Computer Performance*, Vol 2, No 4, IPC Business Press, 158-173.

Terplan, K. 1982. 'Network Performance Reporting', *Performance Evaluation Review*, Vol 11, No 1, 156-170.

Tolopka, S. 1981. 'An Event Trace Monitor for the VAX 11/780', *Performance Evaluation Review*, Vol 10, No 3, 121-128.

Toong, H.D. and Gupta, A. 1982. 'Evaluation Kernels for Microprocessor Performance Analyses', *Performance Evaluation*, Vol 2, No 1, 1-8.

'Update on Hardware Monitors'. 1974. *EDP Performance Review*, Vol 2, No 10, October, 8 pages.

Von Neumann, J. 1946. 'On the Principles of Large Scale Computing Machines', in Taub A.H. Ed. *Von Neumann's Collected Works*, Vol 5, Pergamon, Oxford, 1-32.

Wang, R.T. and Browne, J.C. 1981. 'Virtual Machine-Based Simulation of Distributed Computing and Networking', *Proc. ACM Sigmetrics Conference*, 154-156.

Warner, C.D. 1974. 'Hardware Monitors: The State of the Art', *Infotech Reports*, Vol 18, 623-631.

Wilner, W.T. 1972. 'Design of the Burroughs B1700', *AFIPS FJCC*, Vol 41, 489-497.

Wirth, N. 1971. 'Program Development by Stepwise Refinement', *Comm. ACM*, Vol 14, No 4, April, 221-227.

Witschorik, C.A. 1983. 'The Real-Time Debugging Monitor for the Bell System 1A Processor', *Software - Practice and Experience*, Vol 13, 727-743.

Wulf, W.A. and Bell, C.G. 1972. 'C.mmp - A Multi-mini-processor', *AFIPS FJCC*, Vol 41, Part II, 765-777.

Yannacopoulos, N.A., Ibbett, R.N. and Holgate, R.W. 1977. 'Performance Measurements of the MU5 Primary Instruction Pipeline', *Information Processing 77*, North-Holland, 471-476.

Yuval, G. 1975. 'Gathering Run-Time Statistics Without Black Magic', *Software - Practice and Experience*, Vol 5, 105-108.

Index